THE POLTERGEIST PHENOMENON

John and Anne Spencer have been active researchers of the paranormal for over twenty years. They are members of the Ghost Club, the Society for Psychical Research (SPR) and the Association of the Scientific Study of Anomalous Phenomena (ASSAP).

John and Anne are at the forefront of experimental work and research into poltergeists. They are team leaders and participants in many current poltergeist investigations. They have organised group meetings (head-to-heads) of poltergeist victims and researchers; the first of such exchanges of information.

The Poltergeist Phenomenon

An Investigation into Psychic Disturbance

John and Anne Spencer

HEADLINE

First published in 1996
by HEADLINE BOOK PUBLISHING

First published in paperback in 1997
by HEADLINE BOOK PUBLISHING

10 9 8 7 6 5 4 3 2 1

ISBN 0 7472 5492 3

Typeset by
Letterpart Limited, Reigate, Surrey

Printed and bound in Great Britain by
Cox & Wyman Ltd, Reading, Berks

HEADLINE BOOK PUBLISHING
A division of Hodder Headline PLC
338 Euston Road
London NW1 3BH

Acknowledgements

We are very grateful for the assistance and efforts of everybody who has helped our research in many different ways. Without wishing to underplay the contributions of these people, some of whom are mentioned in the text, we would like to pay particular thanks to Manfred Cassirer, Canon Carl Garner, Maurice Grosse, Mike Lewis, Canon Dominic Walker, Chris Walton, and Philip Walton. Thanks also to David Fontana, for introducing us to the Cardiff case witnesses and for background to the case, and to the many ASSAP (Association for the Scientific Study of Anomalous Phenomena) vigil team members.

Our thanks are also due to those individuals and families affected by the poltergeist, who are mentioned in the text either by their real names or pseudonyms, or in passing. A special acknowledgement must go to Jerry and Elizabeth, for inviting us so warmly into their home over a number of years. Thanks also to those who have not been named but have been willing to share their experiences with us during our years of study of the phenomenon.

The authors and publishers are grateful to the following for permission to reproduce photographs:

Fortean Picture Library: 3, 5, 6, 15
Manfred Cassirer: 4
Mary Evans Picture Library: 1, 2

All other photographs © John and Anne Spencer

Contents

Introduction

The children were floating model boats in a large tub of water. Suddenly, a stone fell into the tub, making an unusual amount of noise for so small an object. Then another, larger stone fell, followed by more. The children went to the garden to tell the adults, and a stone fell among them there. Later, larger stones began falling at shorter intervals. The following evening, stones were falling *inside* the house. The commanding officer of the military station where the family lived posted troops on the roof. Stones began falling around them as they stood guard.

One evening, the table was set for dinner when the plates disappeared. A loud crash in another room heralded their reappearance – in pieces all over the floor.

The children's uncle took a crucifix from the wall and stated, 'I defy anything to touch this cross.' As he was walking to the door, the crucifix flew across the room and hit him in the back.

Father Lee came to bless the house. During the ceremony his vestments were pulled and the Book of the Rituale he was using flew up and stuck to the ceiling, its pages flapping as if blown by the wind.

Later, the family discovered that they could no longer open the doors of the house. They called to passers-by for help. Through the window, the passers-by explained the problem, which from their perspective was very simple: stacked against the doors were large boulders, 'which could not be carried by any man'. It took a team of people to come and remove them to release the family.

The stone-throwing poltergeist was getting ambitious . . .

This is an abridged version of an extraordinary tale of manifestations which occurred at a military station in Madras in the 1870s. It is tempting to regard it as the product of a far-off place in a far-off time, or the product of a fevered imagination; but as you read this book you will find that your astonishment has not yet even begun to be challenged. For these manifestations – and hundreds of other strange, frightening and awesome experiences – have not only been occurring for over two thousand years, but are still happening to people in Britain, America and all over the world today. They are witnessed – sometimes by many people together – by police officers, priests, respected figures of authority, and by researchers such as ourselves. They are happening in the workplaces, schools and homes of ordinary families. These are not the gloomy mansions of the horror movies; they are factories with high-tech equipment, modern and well-lit homes in leafy suburbs. While conducting our research, we have sat in a newly built house in the 'stockbroker belt' where thousands of such manifestations have persisted for over three years – and they continued while we were there. In one school in Scotland, the teacher told us how her heavy oak desk had lifted into the air and slowly turned ninety degrees before lowering itself to the floor – in front of a classroom full of astonished children.

The word *poltergeist* is commonly translated from the German as meaning 'noisy ghost', but this is a poor translation. *Geist* means 'ghost' – arguably an imprecise word for these experiences – but *polter* comes from the noun *polterer*, meaning a blusterer, bully, or rowdy person. The verb *poltern* means 'to make a rumbling noise'.

Polterabend is a German word for a party on the eve of a wedding (i.e. a stag or hen night), and refers to boozy partying accompanied by lewdness and practical joking. *Polter*, therefore, is less about noise alone; rather it describes frolicking, unruliness and rumbustiousness. This truer definition corresponds with what we know about these extraordinary experiences: they are invariably noisy, destructive and disruptive.

Poltergeists are a reality. But they are also a mystery as complex as any you will encounter. To unravel that mystery is as exciting and challenging a quest as one could wish for.

This book is divided into progressive sections. We introduce the poltergeist in the first section using a range of cases, from past history to the modern day. In Section Two we examine the characteristics of the poltergeist in some detail. Section Three provides some theories that attempt to explain the phenomenon; and in the final section we look at the families and individuals who seem to attract the poltergeist, to discover what we can learn from their experiences.

SECTION ONE

INTRODUCING
THE POLTERGEIST

Chapter 1

A Historical Overview

The poltergeist throughout time has been varied and ingenious. The following is a small selection from many hundreds of diverse cases recorded over the centuries. Later we will see how these events are being mirrored even today.

North Aston

Twenty-one-year-old George Lee had become concerned by events at his family home in North Aston, Oxfordshire. The Lee family – father Edward and his children George and Anne – were notable figures of the local community, and employed several workmen and servants on their farm. On 29 November, George had seen several stones that appeared to fall from or through the roof of the house. The stones varied in weight, from a pound or two to twenty-two pounds. George was moved to investigate events, and had men climbing ladders inside and outside the building in an attempt to locate the origin of these stones, but the team could not locate their source. The roof tiling and slates were apparently intact, and the floors and ceilings inside had no obvious holes through which the stones could have passed.

Apart from the family, the stones were witnessed by neighbours and staff, and by Edward Giles, the local vicar. Eventually, the events became too much for the family, who temporarily moved out of the house, staying with the vicar for a short time. But Edward Lee wanted to understand the phenomenon that had driven his family to such action. He sent his daughter Anne and a maid, Joan Measey, to spend the night in the house. This they refused to do, after approaching the gates and hearing stones hitting and rattling about in the empty building.

They returned, together with three of the workmen – John Yeomans, John Wright and George Wright. Again, even before stepping over the threshold, they could hear the stones striking within, but this time they entered. John Yeomans spoke to the 'force' that he presumed was causing the falling stones they could now plainly see, first calling, 'In the name of God,' and then pointing out that they meant no harm and would be grateful if no harm came to them. They then walked upstairs to a bedroom where two stones struck, one knocking a curtain rod off its hooks.

On 17 December the house was visited by two others: William Whing and Richard Hickes. At first these two saw and heard nothing, and their attitude quickly became mocking. Whing named the alleged force 'Jack', and asked if 'Jack' would be good enough to throw them down a quoit so they could play a game. They shortly heard a stone drop, and on locating it found it to be the shape and size of a quoit. Whing got bolder still: could he have another one for his companion so they could both play? A second, identical stone fell. They asked for two more, and received them both. They noted that one of them seemed to have been used; it had grass stains on it, as though it had just been picked up from the garden.

The following night Edward Lee stayed at the house, together with four others – William King, Thomas Churchill, and two maids, Mary Alder and Joan Measey (who had been on earlier visits). In the early hours of the morning, King and Churchill left and Mary was sent on an errand. Shortly afterwards, Joan woke Lee and told him she had been assailed with stones, and had heard footsteps in the room above. On investigation they found a previously closed window open, and a sword (which had been lying on the bed) hanging out of the window. In another room they found bolsters thrown off the bed, which they both agreed had been in place earlier. Lee asked Joan to fetch some chalk, and with it he marked the position of the bolsters before replacing them on the bed. Shortly afterwards they found the chalk lines had gone, although the two of them – the only people in the house – had stayed together all the time. Lee replaced the chalk lines and secured the door. Half an hour later, on their return, the chalk lines had again disappeared. Further tests were carried out: on one investigation they found, near where the bolsters had fallen, 'the print or forme of a paw, resembling the paw of a yong Bear,' and (what we think was described as) a hawk's claw.

The stones continued to rain into the New Year, these and other events stopping for a time on 6 January. But on 15 February the 'force' was back with a vengeance, and stronger than ever. The events were attributed to George (although stones had been known to fall when he was not in the house) because sometimes they 'followed him', presumably falling on or near him. The events were examined even by the local High Sheriff.

In the period of disturbances new and varied events arose. Blood was found on the hall table; the house seemed at one point to be filled with fire though it was not burning; and apparitions of animals were seen.

In May, George 'ended his life' (whether it was suicide or not is not made clear, but he was only twenty-two years old) and the events stopped, apparently forever.

The Lee family's disturbances clearly fit into the poltergeist category. The throwing and spontaneous appearance of stones is commonly reported in such cases; and the willingness of the poltergeist to respond to requests (in this case for quoits) is also a feature. What makes this case a worthy beginning to our study is that it took place in the years 1591 and 1592. As suggested by Alan Gauld, the researcher who unearthed the case, it is probably the first detailed account of a poltergeist in England. Although it has certain uncommon features, it is a report that could easily have been made today. Research of any great detail is impossible over four hundred years after the events, but Gauld was satisfied that it was a responsible account. He found the names of the persons involved listed in the records of the time; and that the pamphlet setting out the details was published within the lifetime of Edward Lee, who died two years after the occurrences stopped. Indeed, the publication was brought out within months of the events, suggesting an accurate account of eye-witness testimony.

We can find reports of poltergeist-type phenomenon as far back as we have written records. Sixteen hundred years ago the philosopher Porphyry was writing about unusual events that correspond with poltergeist activity, and the first Latin writer whose works of fiction have survived in any quantity – Titus Maccius Plautus (251–184 BC) – wrote of similar occurrences in *Mostellaria*. Titus Livius, or Livy (59 BC–AD 17), whose *History of Rome* is one of the main sources of information on the Roman Empire, refers to showers of stones that alarmed the Romans during the Second Punic Wars. Many writers, however, have pointed out that these could just as easily be meteorites – equally alarming at that time, presumably. (In any case, it is generally agreed that Livy was indiscriminate in his selection of reference material, and he is known more for style than accuracy.)

Flavius Josephus (AD 37–101), a Jewish historian, included in his twenty-volume work *Jewish Antiquities* an account of events that at the time were regarded more in the nature of possession, but certainly take the form of poltergeist disturbance. Spontaneous stone throwing was reported in the home of Helpidius, the physician to Theodoric the Great (AD 454–526). In AD 700 (760 in other accounts), Alcuin, in his biography of Willibrord, the first bishop of Utrecht, described food and clothing being pulled away, fires lighted, a baby thrown into a fire and, ultimately, the house destroyed.

Jacob Grimm, of the brothers Grimm, was a student of philology and folklore. In his book *Deutsche Mythologie* he noted several poltergeist cases. In AD 355 and 856, at Bingen-am-Rhein, two cases were reported where stones were thrown, walls vibrated, spontaneous fires broke out, people were pulled out of bed, and blows and other noises were heard, along with voices accusing people of crimes. One of these voices accused a farmer of a sexual relationship with the daughter of one of his foremen. The poltergeist followed the farmer, embarrassing him and causing him to be ostracised by the community. Grimm also refers to a poltergeist that communicated with Rudolph of Fulda (858 BC). These cases may be the first reports suggesting that the poltergeist can acquire 'special knowledge', or can read the minds of those present. As a writer of folklore, it may be supposed that Grimm would include superstitions and legends, yet the accounts are consistent with modern claims.

There are many other reports dating from before AD 1000. From China, for example (where objects were moved, clothing was damaged and written messages were received), from Turkey, the Netherlands, and so on. After so many years they can add nothing to ongoing research, but they remain important simply because they are, again, consistent with modern claims.

In 1170 St Godric, in his hermitage, was bombarded with stones and had wine poured over him. Events escalated until almost every movable object in his room had been thrown at him. Giraldus Cambrensis, a Welsh writer, wrote of poltergeist phenomena in Pembrokeshire in 1190. At the home of Stephen Wiriet, 'foul spirits' threw dirt and other objects. The voice of the spirit spoke to the people and told them of their secrets. It taunted them with things they had done in their lives which they would never want to be known or spoken about. Shortly afterwards, the home of William Not, also in Pembrokeshire, suffered similar disturbances resulting in some injury to himself and his guests and damage to clothing.

In the same year, at Dagworth in Suffolk, at the home of Sir Osborne of Bradaewelle, objects were thrown about and a voice was heard, which also revealed 'the secret doing of other people'.

In these early cases there is little recognition of a 'focus': one person around whom the poltergeist is active. Perhaps the first such implication comes in the case of Anthoinette de Grollee.

St Pierre de Lyon

In 1526 (1528 according to Harry Price), Anthoinette de Grollee, a young sister at the nunnery of St Pierre de Lyon, was alone in her room when she sensed someone lift her veil, make a sign on her forehead and gently kiss her. Opening her eyes and finding herself alone, Anthoinette dismissed the experience as a dream. Within a few days she heard a rapping sound, coming, it seemed, from below the floor where she stood. The noise was heard by other nuns and seemed to follow Anthoinette; it was never heard when she was not present. Adrian de Montalembert, asked by the bishop to investigate, wrote of the noise: 'I have often heard it,' and, 'It would rap as many blows as I demanded.'

Anthoinette suggested that it might be communication from a former nun, Alis. Alis de Telieux had left the nunnery some years before after stealing items of value. She had died destitute and diseased. Anthoinette and Alis had been close, and Anthoinette claimed to have often dreamed of her friend. By communication through rapping it was confirmed that the spirit was indeed Alis, who wished to be buried in the abbey. The Abbess agreed and, after a search, the body was dug up and brought to the abbey. During the service for the deliverance of Alis from purgatory, Anthoinette apparently took on the personality of the deceased and asked for absolution. (In the present day we might regard this as a mediumistic phenomenon.)

Some days after the service, Montalembert returned to the abbey, and Alis, through the rappings, reported herself free of purgatory. It is also reported that, at this time, Anthoinette was levitated into the air!

After this the activity died down, although, as a final act, thirty-three loud blows were heard, followed by an 'unendurable' bright light which lasted for eight minutes. This occurred on the feast of St Benedict, the patron saint of the convent.

Portsmouth, New England

Increase Mather, who in 1685 became president of Harvard, wrote of various disturbances in *An Essay for the Recording of Illustriousa Providences*. One case was corroborated by another writer, Richard Chamberlain, the Secretary of the Province of New Hampshire, who was staying at the house where the manifestations occurred. (The events, from 1682, compare well with the 1937 case from Mauritius [see p. 94].) They began on 11 June 1682, at the house of George Walton in Portsmouth, New England, when stones started bombarding the walls of the roof. The people of the house went outside to investigate, where they found a gate some distance away had been pulled off its hinges. All this time the stones were still falling around them. Although some people felt the stones' contact, they were not injured or hurt by them. The description given (one that is often mirrored in modern claims) was: 'though they seemed to come with great force, yet did no more than softly touch them . . .'

Stones were also reported still flying about inside the house, and breaking windows. The lead casement windows were found to have been broken and bent outwards, suggesting the windows were smashed by stones from inside. A hammer and candlestick were also reported thrown, the former just missing Secretary Chamberlain. Nine of the stones were collected and put on the table, only to be found later, flying about again. The stones were described as being hot, 'as if they had come out of the fire'.

That night the door to one of the bedrooms was broken by a stone, which Chamberlain locked in his chamber, 'but it was fetched out, and carried with great noise into the next chamber'. The spit from the fire was 'carried up the chimney', and after it had been retrieved it was 'by an unseen hand thrown out at [the] window'.

George Walton seems to have been something of a focus to these disturbances, as the happenings seemed to follow him. It was reported: 'The stones were most frequent where the master of the house was, whether in the field, or barn etc.' The problems followed him to a farm, where he was disturbed by stones and certain objects which moved about while he was there, and on his boat.

Chamberlain, at least on the first night, felt he may have been a target: 'Then as if I had been the designed object for that time, most of the stones that came (the smaller I mean) hit me (sometimes pretty hard) to the number of about twenty.'

Noises of a horse trotting and snorting and a dismal whistling were also heard. Of the stranger occurrences: 'A cheese had been taken out of the press and crumbled all over the floor. A piece of iron . . . stuck into the wall and a kettle hung thereon. Several clumps of English hay, mowed near the house, were taken and hung upon the trees; and some . . . put all up and down the kitchen, *cum multis aliis*, etc.' Chamberlain collected the signatures of eight witnesses, who attested to being present when at least ten stones were thrown by an invisible force.

We are not sure how long the disturbances lasted. Mather reports that 'the Demon' was quiet all winter, but in the spring he (the demon) 'moved axes'.

Mather recorded several other poltergeist happenings in the same area. Describing one, in Hartford, Connecticut (also in 1682), he wrote of a molestation of stones, earth and corn, both inside and outside buildings. Several people were hit by the flying objects; again none were hurt.

In England, more so than in America, poltergeist disturbances in these earlier years were generally associated with witchcraft and sorcery. One such case arose in England in 1661. Once the legends and interpretations of witchcraft are stripped away from the case, it can be shown to be a classic poltergeist disturbance. It is the case of the Tedworth Poltergeist, often referred to as the Tedworth Drummer.

Tedworth

In 1661, while her husband was away, a Mrs Mompesson, together with her children, were disturbed by noises in their house. She complained of this to her husband on his return. Soon he, too, could hear the noises. The sound was described by the Reverend Joseph Glanvill, who wrote a contemporary account, as 'a very great knocking at his doors, and the outsides of his house'. Although Mr Mompesson searched the house and opened all the doors he could find no cause for the banging, which continued as if coming from the roof.

These thumping and drumming noises were heard most nights for approximately one month, as if coming from outside the house. After that they seemed to be emanating from within the house. The noises would start soon after the family had gone to bed. (In several cases poltergeist noises begin outside the house, or at least seem to come from the outside walls, roof or attic.)

This particular poltergeist, it seems, could be considerate. While Mrs Mompesson was confined to bed while having a baby the poltergeist kept quiet. (This is not the only case; in the Bell Witch case there are also signs of consideration; actual gifts to the mother of the house while she was unwell, for example.) When it returned, though, the poltergeist took to beating the bedsteads of the younger children quite violently, and for periods of one hour it would drum out military tunes. After this, scratching noises could be heard from below the children's beds, and 'it would lift the children up in their beds'.

The poltergeist was now focusing on the children, and would frequently disturb the room where they were, even 'following' them when they moved into rooms previously unoccupied and unaffected.

On 5 November 1662, over a year after the manifestations started, the poltergeist was creating a lot of noise when a servant in the children's room witnessed two boards moving. He asked to be given one, and the board moved to a point near him. The servant continued, 'Nay let me have it in my hand,' and the board was thrust upon him. He then pushed it back, and a sort of reverse tug-of-war ensued, the board being pushed invisibly towards the servant and the servant pushing it back. (This responsiveness is another classic factor of poltergeists that shall be examined further.) This amazing scene took place in daylight and was witnessed by 'a whole room full of people'.

Word of the phenomenon spread, and Mr Cragg, the minister, among others, came to the house. Mr Cragg led prayers in the children's room, during which the poltergeist was quiet. But as soon as the prayers were over – and in view of everyone – 'the chairs walked about the room of themselves, the children's shoes were hurled over their heads, and every loose thing moved about the chamber . . .' A bed staff was thrown at the minister, which hit him on the leg (but importantly did not hurt him – another factor that arises time and again in poltergeist cases). The Reverend Glanvill visited the house, and even spent the night there. He was able to interview many of the witnesses and himself experienced some of the phenomena, including the banging noises. The poltergeist was by now imitating noises, and Glanvill found it responded several times to his scratching. Although he searched, he could find no 'trick, contrivance, or common cause of it . . . we could discover nothing. So that I was then verily persuaded, and am so still, that the noise was made by some demon or spirit.'

Glanvill went on to report sensing an animal in the bedroom, and then witnessing the linen bag hanging on a bed move as if an animal (he suggested a rat or mouse) was struggling within. Glanvill quickly grabbed the bag by its top, but found no creature – in fact, he found nothing at all. As he said, 'I stepped and caught it by the upper end with one hand, with which I held it, and drew it through the other, but found nothing at all in it. There was no body near to shake the bag . . . no one could have made such a motion, which seemed to be from within, as if a living creature had moved in it'.

Finding that his children were suffering from these events, Mr Mompesson arranged for them to stay with a neighbour. His eldest daughter, aged ten, remained with him. The younger children were not affected while away, but were disturbed again after they returned three weeks later. The noises had continued at the house throughout this period, suggesting that the elder daughter was the focus.

Many other classic poltergeist effects were reported: covers were pulled from the bed; a bible was moved and found open at St Mark's discourse on unclean spirits (which compares to the Phelps case, described in Chapter Four); an apparitional shape with 'red and glaring eyes' was seen; a horse was found with its foot in its mouth; there was an offensive, sulphurous smell reported; and Mompesson alone, at one time, heard a voice calling, 'A witch, a witch!'

It seems word of the case finally reached the King and Queen. They sent investigators to the house, but it seems they failed to witness any of the happenings.

During the seventeenth and eighteenth centuries, it seems, there was an increase in the overall number of reports. This apparent rise may simply be a result of better records being kept, or, with the invention of the printing press, a new medium with which to report events. By this time, any fear of witchcraft was becoming a thing of the past. However, by the nineteenth century, there was definitely a growing public fascination with spiritualism, and the search for confirmation of life after death.

Bristol, England

This poltergeist was active in Bristol from November 1761 to December 1762, in the house of Mr and Mrs Giles, who lived with

17

their two daughters, Dobby (aged eight) and Molly (aged thirteen). There are believed to have been other children, but they may have lived away from home. An account by Henry Durbin, who visited the family, was published in 1800.

Very typically, the phenomena started with rapping and scratching noises, occurring mostly at night, in the girls' bedroom. The disturbances progressed to the movement of objects, including china, utensils and furniture. Durbin described an event he witnessed, when a glass was lifted from a chest of drawers: 'It rose gradually about a foot, perpendicularly from the drawers; then the glass seemed to stand, and thereupon incline backwards, as if a hand had held it; it was then flung with violence about five feet, and struck the nurse on the hip a hard blow . . . There was no person near the drawers when it rose . . . I was so amazed at it, that I said, do I see what I see?'

In January it was found that communication with the poltergeist was possible, with the use of a code. Durbin found that answers were given to questions asked in Greek or Latin – languages the girls did not know – and also to questions asked mentally. On some occasions a voice could be heard, sometimes by the girls alone although others claimed to have heard it whispering. The voice claimed that the disturbances were caused by a witch employed by a rival of Mr Giles.

X The two girls were assaulted by the poltergeist. They were bitten and pins were stuck into them. They were also cut, as if with a knife; on one occasion, one girl was seen to have more than forty cuts on her arms, face and neck. The children claimed to see a hand making the attacks.

X Durbin witnessed some of the attacks. On one such occasion Dobby claimed a hand was around her sister's throat. Durbin watched and later wrote, 'I saw the flesh at the side of her throat pushed in, whitish, as if done with fingers, though I saw none. Her face grew red and blackish presently, as if she was strangled but without any convulsion or contraction of the muscles.'

18

Dobby was bitten on her arms, neck, shoulders and back. She was often bitten in the company of others, who would see white marks, still wet with spittle, on her body. Of one attack witnessed by Durbin, he wrote: 'I was talking to her, she cried out she was bitten in the neck. I looked and saw the mark of teeth, about eighteen, and wet with spittle. It was in the top part of the shoulders, close by the neck; therefore it was impossible for her to do it herself, as I was looking on all the time, and nobody was near her but myself.'

Durbin tested the poltergeist in front of witnesses. In one experiment he marked pins and, sitting Molly in a chair, asked her not to move. He jabbed a marked pin into a cushion and almost immediately Molly was pricked in the neck. Durbin wrote, 'The identical pin that I marked, was run through the neck of her shift, and stuck in her skin, crooked very curiously. It was not a minute from the time I put the pin in, to her being pricked in the neck.' This test was repeated with four more pins, which were all subsequently found in Molly's neck.

The younger daughter and Mr Giles became very ill and died. The 'witch' they had communicated with claimed responsibility for this (another clear similarity to the Bell Witch case). The witch also claimed she would have power over the children for a further forty weeks.

Mrs Giles sought the help of another witch from Bedminster who, we are told, was able to stop the phenomena.

It is worth noting that forty weeks is also the period of gestation in humans. Similarly, other studies of the poltergeist have indicated a connection to the menstrual cycle.

Despite the apparently harmful potential of poltergeists they rarely inflict considerable injuries, and even more rarely cause death. However, one famous case resulted in the prediction of, and death of, the victim. The case started in 1817, and is known as the Bell Witch case.

Tennessee (The Bell Witch)

The story related here is based on the writings of Richard Williams Bell, the younger brother of the girl suspected of being the poltergeist focus, Elizabeth Bell (known as Betsy). Richard Bell wrote his account in 1846, around twenty-five years after the cessation of the hauntings. There is inevitably some inaccuracy in the story, through verbal retelling, differing perspectives and so on, but two factors stand greatly in its favour: the first is that there appear to have been some occurrences about which there is a fair consensus, and it is therefore reasonable to presume some accuracy in the accounts; the second is that many of the phenomena described are consistent with poltergeist reports still being received today.

The case arose at a time when terminology was in a state of flux. The true witch-hunts of former years were over; the term poltergeist on the other hand was still considerably in the future; and the official birth of spiritualism – following the Hydesville case of the Fox sisters – was still thirty years away. However, the case became commonly known as the Bell Witch when the entity involved actually described itself as a 'witch', communicating as a human voice.

The Bell family lived in a wooden dwelling in the timber country of North Central Tennessee. The happenings started, like so many others, with light knockings and scrapings outside, around, and eventually within, the house. The sounds would cease if a lamp was lit. They sounded like (and were perhaps at first attributed to) small animals such as rats or dogs gnawing or pawing their way around. No animals were found. Similarly, flapping sounds like a bird beating against the ceiling were also heard. These continued for many months, building greatly in intensity but not changing in nature. After about a year the poltergeist developed a different character. Covers were pulled off beds, and the noises of what seemed to be a human in distress were heard; gulping sounds, choking and strangling sounds and the smacking of lips. Great thumps could be heard, as if stones or furniture were being

20

dropped. Richard Williams awoke in fright one night, feeling that something was pulling at his hair; his brother Joel yelled out simultaneously, and shortly afterwards Betsy was screaming, having experienced the exact same sensation.

The family – perhaps for practical reasons relating to their social standing, or religious reasons – had kept the hauntings a secret. But when Betsy continued to be attacked, the family decided to discuss the hauntings with a close friend and neighbour, James Johnson, in the hope that he could help them to explain or stop the activities. By confronting the force 'in the name of the Lord', Johnson believed that the response – a lessening of the activities – indicated that there was intelligence at work. However, when the activities recommenced it was with greater vigour, decidedly persecuting Betsy. Witnesses saw her cheeks reddening from visible handslaps and watched her hair pulled painfully.

Johnson, John Bell, and the family and other friends created some kind of 'committee of investigation' which, Richard Williams believed, was designed to keep a watch on all members of the family – but they were able only to watch helplessly as Betsy continued to be attacked.

For a time Betsy was sent to live with neighbours, but the activity did not cease around her and she was attacked there as vigorously as at home – with the added embarrassment of the disturbances affecting the neighbours themselves. Eventually Betsy went home.

Word had got around the neighbourhood. Despite, no doubt, the best intentions of those involved, secrecy among small communities is almost impossible. By now many people were visiting the house just to see 'the Witch'. They sought communication, calling on it to rap or make its other noises. Richard Williams' account tellingly states, 'In this way the phenomena were gradually developed'. First the poltergeist made a whistling noise, which gradually developed into a faltering whisper, then apparently gained strength, confidence and volume. 'Soon the utterances became distinct in a low whisper, so as to be understood in the absence of any other noise.' The poltergeist had developed a voice.

During this period of intense attention, anomalous lights were seen outside the house, 'like a candle or lamp flitting across the yard, and through the field'.

When the father, boys and workers were returning to the house, 'chunks of wood and stone would fall along the way, as if tossed by someone, but we could never discover from whence, or what direction they came'. As is common in poltergeist cases, the missiles did no harm. Indeed a friend, William Porter, described as 'a gentleman of high integrity', commented that the missiles were thrown 'never with much force, and we soon learned not to fear any harm from this pastime'. In a quote that could almost be from the Cardiff poltergeist case (see next chapter), Porter continued that they 'frequently cut notches on the sticks, casting them back into the thickets from whence they came, and invariably the same sticks would be hurled back at us'.

The Witch chose to prove its presence in these excursions away from the house by each evening recounting with great accuracy events that had happened during the walks. On other occasions, the Witch showed itself to be a gossip, denouncing the acts of drunkards, child abusers and others of less than good character, and revealing unpleasant secrets between members of the small community.

Despite its original reluctance to make any sound with the lamp lit, the poltergeist was now quite happy to perform at any time of day. In a forerunner of tests that would be attempted by poltergeist researcher Maurice Grosse in Enfield in the 1970s, a visiting doctor 'placed his hand over Betsy's mouth at the time when the voice was heard, and soon satisfied himself that she was in no way connected with these sounds'.

Betsy was by now widely considered to be the focus of the Witch. It was observed that she had several fainting spells, exhibiting shortness of breath before becoming unconscious for short periods, after which she would be fully recovered almost immediately. The voice of the Witch was always heard shortly after these spells. (It has been suggested that these were manifestations of Betsy entering a trance state, and she was therefore acting as a medium, 'channelling' the voice.)

The Witch soon identified itself: 'I am a spirit; who was once very happy, but has been disturbed, and made unhappy.' It went on to say that the target of its anger was 'Old Jack Bell' (the father), and threatened to torment him to the end of his life.

The Witch then embarked on a series of practical jokes. First it announced to the family that it was the spirit of a native American Indian whose grave had been disturbed and his bones scattered; it claimed that one of his teeth was under the Bells' house. This had the family running round looking for the tooth, which they never found. It also claimed to be the spirit of a person who had died leaving a fortune, the location of which it revealed to Betsy. The Bell family dug fruitlessly for hours at the location given. Again, the Witch laughed at them that night for falling for the joke. It then stated, 'I am nothing more nor less than old Kate Batts' witch and I am determined to haunt and torment Old Jack Bell as long as he lives.' Kate Batts, according to Bell's account, was a local woman believed by some to be a witch. At the time of these events she was still alive.

The Witch, it is claimed, used a variety of voices, two sounding male and two female. All used obscene language and spoke like drunken thugs, indeed 'fuming the house with the scent of whisky'.

The Witch made predictions, some of which seem to have been accurate. It is said to have predicted the American Civil War (which arose forty years later), the First and Second World Wars, the emancipation of the black race, the prominence of the United States as a world power, and even the ultimate end of the world – undated! The prophecy suggested destruction by rapidly increasing heat followed by a mighty explosion. (Hereward Carrington and Nandor Fodor, writing in 1953 – at a time when the Western world in particular was obsessed with fear of the atomic bomb – suggest that this is a prediction related to destruction of the planet by nuclear warfare. But it is a vague description, and could as easily be outlining what may happen several million years in the future if our own sun explodes – leaving a wide range of time for that prediction to come true!)

The Witch was also very clear on one surprising aspect. John Bell Jr sought evidence of life after death. The poltergeist hinted that any such evidence would be fraudulent, saying that, following the death of John Bell, no contact with him would be possible. The Witch even gave a physical demonstration of how effective fraud could be, by mimicking John Bell's footprints in the snow as if he was approaching the house. (Carrington and Fodor point out that the Witch refers to John Bell after his death as being 'not of this world', implying that the Witch regarded itself as belonging to this world.)

The poltergeist activity was not always to the negative. The Witch seemed to enjoy giving gifts, once presenting a large basket of oranges, bananas, grapes and nuts at Betsy's birthday party, stating, 'Those came from the West Indies. I bought them myself.' When Betsy's mother, Lucy Bell, was ill, the Witch dropped hazel nuts into her hands. When Lucy pointed out she could not crack them, cracked hazel nuts appeared on her bed, followed by grapes (which the Witch was certain were for her good health). Examination of the ceiling above the bed revealed no obvious way in which the nuts and fruits could have been deposited. On another occasion a bunch of grapes was presented to Betsy in much the same way. But this generous attitude alternated with malice; occasionally, pins were found in bedding and chairs, pointing outwards.

In an attempt to rid herself of the haunting, Betsy sought a 'witch doctor', who gave her medicine which he believed would rid her of the spirit. She took the medicine and became extremely sick. On examination, her vomit was found to be full of pins and needles. Immediately, the Witch roared with laughter, stating that if it happened again she would have enough to set up a shop. All witnesses to this event, including Betsy's mother, agreed that either the Witch had somehow produced the pins and needles in Betsy's stomach at the moment of evacuation, or it had secreted them in the vomit prior to inspection.

In what could be regarded as a most extraordinary attempt at exorcism, William Porter awoke and found the Witch in his bed, rolled up in the bedcovers. He attempted to grab the covers and throw them, and the Witch, into the fire. But the poltergeist put into use what might be regarded as some sort of bizarre defence mechanism: Porter discovered that the bundle became incredibly heavy and increasingly foul-smelling, causing him to drop it on the floor and rush out for fresh air. He stated, 'The odour emitted from the roll was the most offensive stench I ever smelled. It was absolutely stifling, and I could not have endured another second.' On returning, the bed clothing was 'empty'. Whether or not the increase in weight or the smell were caused by the Witch, or subjective impressions created by Porter, or subjective impressions created in Porter by the Witch, is of course open to speculation.

When Betsy fell for, and looked likely to become engaged to, a Mr Joshua Gardner, the Witch pleaded with her to give up the relationship. 'Please, Betsy Bell, don't have Joshua Gardner, please Betsy Bell, don't marry Joshua Gardner.' It resorted in the end to revealing the most personal and embarrassing aspects of their relationship until eventually they did split up. A local friend of the family, Frank Miles, took up cudgels on Betsy's behalf, apparently incensed at the break-up of Betsy and Joshua's relationship. He came to the house and addressed the Witch: 'Take any shape you desire, just so that I can get my hands on you.' The Witch apparently hit him viciously in the face and then the stomach, so that Frank, unsurprisingly, backed off.

It is pointed out that the Witch appeared to match the likes and dislikes of Betsy, attacking her father and protecting and helping her mother and John Jr, though there is no firm evidence of Betsy's feelings either way. However, its extreme hatred of John Bell led to the most famous aspect of the case: Bell's 'murder'.

Bell had already exhibited some illnesses, and had developed a twitch and a swollen tongue. He suffered attacks which confined him to bed for several days. The arrival of these symptoms had coincided with the first manifestations of the Witch. He was later physically attacked, knocked off his feet and his shoes pulled off. Richard Williams Bell witnessed some of these attacks, stating, 'I was terrified by the spectacle of the contortions that seized Father, as if to convert him into a very demon to swallow me up.' Eventually John Bell took to bed, and the Witch crowed, 'It's useless for you to try to relieve Old Jack – I have got in this time; he will never get up from that bed again.' He never did, dying the following morning, on 20 December 1820. When a very strong poison was found in a nearby cupboard, the Witch said, 'I put it there, and gave Old Jack a big dose of it last night while he was fast asleep, which fixed him.' On testing the substance on a cat the animal died instantly. No analysis of the substance was ever undertaken, as the contents were thrown on to a fire.

At John Bell's funeral, the Witch sang 'Row Me Up Some Brandy, Oh' in joyful voice.

Shortly afterwards the Witch announced it was leaving in dramatic form. Something like a huge ball of smoke flew out of the chimney and exploded, and a voice said, 'I am going, and will be gone for seven years. Goodbye to all.' The infestation had lasted for approximately four years.

The return of the Witch in 1827 amounted only to a few scratching noises and bedclothes pulled off. It is possible that these events occurred quite naturally, and the remaining members of the household misguidedly associated them with the poltergeist. (No doubt the Witch had preyed heavily on their minds in the intervening years, and would have increasingly done so towards the promised return period.) In any case, the disruption lasted only two weeks.

The Witch promised to return in 107 years (1934), but there is no evidence that it did so.

The Bell Witch has, perhaps inevitably, become the subject of American legend, and questionable details have crept into the story over the years.

Possible explanations for the Bell Witch are varied. Probably the most common claim is that it was the unconscious mind of Betsy acting out her desires, fears, and so on. Claimants to this have suggested that the likeliest scenario is that she had suffered sexual abuse at the hands of her father and, in an extraordinarily elaborate way, murdered him in revenge. However, this is circular logic; there is no evidence to substantiate the allegation that he had abused her in the first place. The main exponents of this claim, Carrington and Fodor, take a clearly psychoanalytical line towards the phenomenon of poltergeists. (Fodor was a psychoanalyst who strongly supported Freud's theories.)

Colin Wilson, in his analysis of the case, points out that since the Witch was not in the slightest bit reticent about revealing secrets of all manner to all members of the community, it would surely have revealed any incest in the family, had it been occurring. Wilson believes that mischievous spirits, 'the other-worldly equivalent of a cage full of monkeys', are behind the Bell Witch case, and makes the assumption, 'We must suppose that the Bell household was not a particularly happy one – this deduction arises from the fact that there is no record of a poltergeist haunting taking place in a happy family.' This again would seem to be circular logic. There is no evidence that the Bell family was an unhappy one; indeed, they seem to have largely stuck together through quite a trying time.

Even the most famous aspect of the Bell Witch – that it is the one poltergeist which killed its victim – may itself be poor attribution. Certainly the poltergeist appears to have centred around Betsy –

described as a healthy and robust girl entering puberty – a typical aspect of poltergeist cases. Much of the poltergeist activity is very common and similar to that reported throughout history. John Bell appears to have been ill prior to the utterances of the poltergeist; thus it is possible that the poltergeist did not kill Bell but simply attributed his death to its own action. Poltergeists are not notorious killers, but they can be notorious liars and this one certainly exhibited a predilection for mischief and lying. The actual reason for Bell's death is unknown; neither is it certain that he actually took any poison.

Amherst

This most famous – and controversial – case arose in 1878. Eighteen-year-old Esther Cox lived in a small two-storey cottage in Amherst in Nova Scotia. The house was occupied by Daniel and Olive Teed, their two sons George and Willie, Olive's sisters Jennie (Jane in some accounts) and Esther herself, and their brother William; also Daniel's brother John. The family were all Methodists.

On one night in August 1878 (September in some accounts), Esther jumped from her bed, screaming, and claimed that there was a mouse under the covers. She and Jennie, who shared the bed, searched but found nothing. The following night they heard a scratching noise coming from a box under the bed, and they assumed that the mouse had been caught in it. To their horror the box started leaping about, apparently under its own force.

The following night Esther seemed ill-at-ease when going to bed. During the day, little had been discussed of the 'mouse' by the girl's disbelieving family, probably because they wanted to play it down for fear of alarming her. That night Esther nudged Jennie awake in an obvious state of alarm. Jennie was shocked by what she saw: Esther was bloated, blood red, and her eyes were bulging. She cried out that she thought she was dying. Her body continued to swell, and she screamed in obvious pain. Then there was a huge

28

sound (Daniel Teed thought a thunderbolt had struck the house) and Esther returned to normal.

Four nights later, Esther and Jennie had their bedclothes ripped away from them, then thrown through the air. Esther's body was bloated again. When Teed replaced the bedcovers, they were ripped off again. Loud raps could be heard. The covers flew at John Teed, hitting him on the head, and he fled, never to return to the house again.

A doctor, Carritte, was called. He was concerned for Esther but unimpressed by claims of ghostly manifestation. However, his opinion changed while he examined Esther. Her pillow was moving in and out from under her head, despite his best efforts to hold it down. He could hear knocking and scratching noises, so bad that the plaster was coming off the walls. It seems that the family considered these noises to be a form of crude communication. As if in response, words slowly etched themselves into the bedroom wall: 'Esther Cox, you are mine to kill.' Carritte observed these manifestations over two hours.

The doctor revisited the next day and found the poltergeist activity still virulent. Esther complained she had just been hit from behind, as if by a chunk of wood. Together in the cellar, Esther and Carritte experienced potatoes 'thrown' at them without obvious cause. Carritte left the house, shaken.

The banging sounds became locally famous, and people would stand outside just to hear the sounds from within the house. The crowds grew so large that the police were called in to assist.

Teed had realised by now that, whatever the origin of the disturbances, they were centred on Esther. He was probably somewhat relieved when, during a period of illness, the activity ceased. Esther also spent some time convalescing away from the house, living with another sister in New Brunswick. When she returned, so did the poltergeist.

This time the manifestations came in the form of voices threatening to set fire to the house. Teed laughed it off; a pity, since his next action was to have to extinguish a lighted match that fell on to the bedcovers next to him from somewhere above. For ten minutes he was extinguishing falling lighted matches. The poltergeist then continued with a new set of banging and thumping sounds.

Jennie, who had found that she could achieve rudimentary communication with the poltergeist through its rapping noises, asked it to confirm its intention to burn the house down, which it did. For three days the family found fires breaking out spontaneously. On one occasion Olive's skirts were set alight, as was a bucket of cedar shavings in the cellar.

Teed, now presumably at his wits' end, asked Esther to leave. She went to live locally with her employer, John White, who owned a restaurant, but he was forced to 'let her go' when the poltergeist proved as virulent around Esther there as at her former home. The oven door in his kitchen removed itself from its hinges, and metal objects attached themselves to Esther as if she were generating a strong electromagnetic force.

Some time later she was taken in by Captain James Beck. Interestingly, he wanted the poltergeist because he was of a mind to investigate it. However, little of significance happened while she stayed with him. (This awkwardness on the part of poltergeists is a matter we shall examine more fully in later chapters.)

Confident that the poltergeist was gone, Teed invited Esther back, but the poltergeist returned with her.

The writer Walter Hubbell became involved with the family, unashamedly seeing commercial potential in the interest people were showing in Esther's poltergeist. Hubbell lived with the family for a time, witnessing events such as the movement of objects, and even persuaded Teed to let Esther 'perform' on stage. On stage, nothing happened. Modern investigators of poltergeists would be less surprised at this than Hubbell apparently was.

As far as is known, Esther's life was pretty much ruined by the poltergeist; she even received a jail sentence for burning down an employer's barn (though whether or not this can be attributed to the poltergeist is unclear).

The case is a dramatic one, yet it appears to be genuine. Walter Hubbell documented the case in *The Great Amherst Mystery*. This work was subsequently investigated by respected psychic investigator Hereward Carrington, who confirmed from his own enquiries that the account was basically correct, if somewhat dramatised in later parts.

To look for an explanation to the Amherst poltergeist we must inevitably look at Esther. The activity was so obviously focused around her that it seems she must be a part of the mechanism of its manifestation. One point to consider is that she had apparently suffered attempted rape just prior to the disturbances starting. Her boyfriend, Bob MacNeal, seems to have tried to rape her at gunpoint in the woods, but was interrupted by a passing vehicle. He ran away from her and left Amherst, perhaps fearing the family's reprisals. The suggestion is therefore that the poltergeist was generated by Esther's own mind. Colin Wilson considered this as a possible explanation for the activity, but in more recent years has come to view the poltergeist as an 'external' entity. He asks of this case: 'How did Esther's mind know the number of Hubbell's watch and the dates of the coins in [his] pocket – which no doubt he did not know himself?' (These were some of the tests that Hubbell had conducted on Esther.) Wilson suggests: '. . . the unconscious mind theory needs to be stretched so much that it loses the chief virtue of a good theory – simplicity.'

Walter Hubbell, however, makes a point which brings Esther's state of mind and body back into question. He indicates in his examinations that the intensity of poltergeist activity (which lasted almost exactly a year) was highest every twenty-eight days – the period of the menstrual cycle.

In the final analysis, what we learn from the Amherst story – and the reason it is highly likely to be a genuine case – is that it is not unique. We shall be revisiting such experiences time and again during our study.

Quebec

We have seen that poltergeists, when vocal, can be obscene, embarrassing and violent. Their physical manifestations can also be very unpleasant.

The Dagg family lived on a farm in Quebec, Canada, and consisted of George and Susan Dagg, their children (Mary, aged four, and Johnny, aged two), and an eleven-year-old adopted Scottish child, Dinah.

The first curious event took place on 15 September 1889, when Dean, a young man employed on the farm to do chores, found a five-dollar bill which he handed over to George Dagg. Dagg recognised it as one that he had placed in a bureau drawer the previous night, along with a two-dollar bill. Checking the drawer, he discovered that the other note was missing, and on looking in Dean's room discovered it in his bed. He suspected the boy of theft but said nothing at that time.

Later in the day, Mrs Dagg discovered a streak of filth, presumably excrement, on the floor of the house. She assumed it was Dean and ordered him out. Mr Dagg took the boy to a local magistrate, but while they were absent the same streaks of filth continued to appear in the house, suggesting that Dean was as innocent as he had protested.

These streaks of filth continued to appear for a week, along with other unusual activities. Milk pans were emptied and refilled with butter from butter dishes. The family transferred the food to the attic for safety, but the activities continued there. As the poltergeist progressed, windows were smashed, fires spontaneously started, and quantities of water appeared from nowhere.

Dinah soon became the target of the poltergeist. She often felt her hair pulled, and once her braid was almost cut off. Dinah appears to have been present during all the manifestations. The happenings went on for some two months before the poltergeist began to develop a voice. It was Dinah who could hear the poltergeist first, but very soon it became audible to all present.

The family was visited by a local artist called Woodcock, who stayed with them for several days. Woodcock and Dinah were together in an open shed at the rear of the farmhouse when she 'saw something'. She asked, 'Are you there, mister?' and received a reply not specified in the report but which was clearly abusive and probably obscene. The voice was described as 'deep, gruff . . . as of an old man seemingly within four or five feet from [Woodcock]'. Woodcock asked, 'Who are you?' The voice replied, 'I am the Devil. I'll have you in my clutches. Get out of this or I'll break your neck.'

For a while the voice continued to shout obscenities, but both Woodcock and George Dagg, now also a witness, pleaded with it to be more restrained. Eventually it did temper its language. After some investigation, the witnesses satisfied themselves that the voice could not have come from Dinah – whose own voice was very high pitched – and that there was no one hidden around the shed who could be playing a joke.

Woodcock decided to request a written communication, and offered the 'spirit' paper and pencil, putting them on a bench. He saw the pencil stand up and move across the surface of the paper unaided, but on examining what had been written, again he had to complain about the foul language. The voice was in no mood for complaint, and commented, 'I'll steal your pencil,' whereupon the pencil rose from the bench and was thrown violently away.

Dagg asked why the voice was bothering the family, and the 'spirit' replied, 'Just for fun.' Dagg then complained that there was no fun in throwing a stone at young Mary (who had presumably been struck earlier), and the voice explained that it was not meant to hit her, but was aimed at Dinah, before adding, 'but I did not let it hurt her'. The voice also apologised for starting the fires.

The witnesses negotiated with the voice, who agreed to leave the house for good on the following night, Sunday. Throughout the next day the farm became a local tourist attraction, with people arriving early in the morning.

At this point the 'spirit' was at its most ingenious and demonstrative. It tempered its language as promised, but started making amusing and intimate comments on various people as they entered the room, displaying a detailed personal knowledge of the private affairs of many. When asked why it had so readily agreed to temper its language, it replied, 'I am not the person who used the filthy language. I am an angel from Heaven sent by God to drive away that fellow.' However, Woodcock pointed out that the voice was exactly the same as the previous one. Indeed, during the many questions of the day the 'spirit' became contradictory, entangled in its own statements, losing its temper and generally not demonstrating the attitude of 'an angel from Heaven'.

At a later point during the questioning the voice claimed to be the spirit of a person who had died twenty years before at the age of eighty. At different times, Dinah, Mary and Johnny had reported seeing the 'spirit' take the form of 'a tall, thin man with a cow's head, horns, tail and a cloven foot', and, at another time, 'a black dog', and ultimately as 'a man with a beautiful face and long white hair dressed in white, wearing a crown with stars in it'.

Woodcock drew up a statement setting out the events, which was signed by seventeen witnesses (including members of the Dagg family), all of them responsible local people. However, it is worth noting that, although they signed their names as witness to the phenomena, there are certain events they could not have seen: for example, Mrs Dagg having water thrown in her face when alone in the house (the signature of Mrs Dagg is not appended to the document).

Woodcock left on the Sunday, but those who remained saw the 'spirit' totally change in character again. The voice altered, from gruff to more harmonious, and declared that it 'had only maintained this harsh accent because otherwise people would have believed that Dinah was doing it'. The 'spirit' then sang hymns in a 'beautiful flute-like voice'.

The 'spirit' had of course promised to leave, but by now the witnesses were asking it to stay. However, at three in the morning, the 'spirit' said goodbye, promising only to show itself to the children later in the day.

Sure enough, one of the children later confirmed that 'he took little Johnny and me in his arms, and, oh, Mama, I played on the music and he went to Heaven and all was red!' The children apparently saw the beautiful white-dressed man with the crown; Dinah saw him briefly lift Mary and Johnny up, before rising into the air and disappearing.

We have thus far examined the actions of poltergeists in the private homes of people, and it appears that this is their 'normal' domain in these early reports. Of course, in the agricultural environment before the Industrial Revolution, workplaces as such would not have been so prevalent. We must also remember that the larger, richer, homes *were* the workplaces of servants and the like. In modern times, though, we receive many reports from poltergeists active away from the home. The first such workplace incident appears to be as reported in the *Journal of the Society for Psychical Research* (SPR) in 1907.

Vienna

A smith's shop in Vienna was run by Mr Zimmerl, who employed two apprentices. In July 1906, tools and bits of iron were thrown about the shop. Mr Zimmerl and one of his apprentices were both hit, and became afraid to continue work. Mr Zimmerl was losing customers, and it was partly for that reason that he called the police for help. They were unable to find any cause for the disturbances.

Mr Warndorfer, a member of the SPR, visited the premises and witnessed many objects being thrown around. Three of these hit him on the head, and he was 'perfectly certain none of the persons present could have thrown them'. This poltergeist had a habit of attacking the people around it. On one occasion, when Mr Warndorfer was watching the apprentices working and could see that all their hands were involved with the work, one of the boys screamed that he was hurt. Mr Warndorfer saw a large pair of iron compasses ricocheting off the boy's head. The compasses had previously been lying on a bench a yard behind the boy.

Unfortunately – and as is often the case – the objects were spotted just as they were about to land or hit; they were never seen to lift off and move or fly. However, on one occasion Mr Zimmerl had his pipe pulled straight from his mouth and deposited on the lathe.

The disturbances lasted for about two months, until Mr Zimmerl dismissed the boys, one of whom was later fined in court. However, the boy denied he had caused the happenings.

These early stories of poltergeists serve to remind us that this is a real phenomenon whatever the cause. It has not evolved over time, nor as a phenomenon has it become integrated into folklore. The poltergeist, like rain and thunder and lightning, is the same now as ever. We once thought the gods made rain and thunder as they moved about in the heavens; when we found a more rational explanation the weather did not alter. Thus it is with the poltergeist; suggested explanations have varied over time, as we shall see, but the phenomenon continues.

Poltergeists, as we will discover, have found more tools to play with over time – electricity and computers, for example. Whereas they once rang servants' bells, now they ring telephones. In more modern cases, their contemporary nature allows for more reliability, and for the authors of this book, also the advantage of personal experience.

Chapter 2

Modern Cases

There are several modern cases that demonstrate that the poltergeist is as active now as it ever was. They compare favourably with the earlier cases, and combine to form the foundations on which the analysis is based. It is important to note, however, that the study of cases in modern times concentrates more on the focus – the person at the centre of the manifestations – than in the previous cases.

Dalby, Isle of Man

A most fascinating case – and one seriously underrated by researchers in our view – is that of Gef, the so-called Talking Mongoose.

Before examining the case we should point out why it has attracted little positive attention on the part of researchers. Bayless, for example, in his book *The Enigma of the Poltergeist*, dismisses the report in just ten lines as 'a very entertaining, controversial and dubious case', and comments that a number of investigators rejected the allegations as being false. It is possible that the case simply got a bad label, identifying itself with the somewhat comical idea of an intelligent, talking animal. Lionel Beer, a long-term researcher of the flying saucer phenomenon, once pointed out that the subject would never have had the same following had the objects first identified with the phrase 'flying saucer' been long and green and called 'flying cucumbers'. Another researcher within that subject has always had difficulty putting across the credibility of an otherwise plausible claim, after the press dubbed it 'The Case of the Mince Pie Martians', based on one small incident within the report. Sometimes the answer to the question 'What's in a name?' is 'Quite a lot', and the case of the 'Talking Mongoose' seems to have been rejected by those not wishing to have their credibility dented by appearing to accept such an outrageous suggestion.

The happenings started in 1931, in an isolated home near Dalby, on the Isle of Man. The family living in the house were James and Margaret Irving and their thirteen-year-old daughter, Voirrey. The first manifestations of Gef* came in September of that year, when the family heard a tapping noise that seemed to come from the attic. The following night similar, louder sounds were heard, along with 'barking, growling, hissing, spitting and blowing' noises, which Mr Irving described as 'animal sounds'. The sounds were followed by a 'crack' that shook the house and sent the pictures on the walls swinging.

Irving seems to have decided at this early stage that the cause was an animal. He states: 'It was plain that an animal had got into the house, but the crack was a mystery. I did not think that an animal could make that sound.' He might have been less inclined to the animal theory if he had been aware of poltergeist lore.

Later, an animal was apparently spotted around the house several times by members of the family. These sightings serve to reinforce the phenomenon's association with an animal, though

---

* The 'visitor' was named 'Gef' by the family, apparently to its pleasure; thus we use the name Gef to refer to it in this narrative, without meaning to infer an acceptance of 'it' as a real mongoose or any other physical animal.

there appears to be no connection between these sightings and later events. Further 'encouragement' for the infestation to take animal form came from Mr Irving; in response to him making animal noises, he heard them repeated without hesitation.

The first time a voice was heard was in November. The voice apparently developed in response to the family's 'request'. Mr Irving wrote to Harry Price, who investigated the phenomenon: 'Its first sounds were those of an animal nature, and it used to keep us awake at night . . . It occurred to me that if it could make these weird noises, why not others.' At first Mr Irving got it to repeat bird and animal noises. Then they tried nursery rhymes, which it also repeated. Irving commented: 'The voice is quite two octaves above any human voice . . . but lately it can and does come down to the range of the human voice.' In other words, the voice had developed from animal noises, to nearly human, to human – a 'normal' progression for a poltergeist.

Over the next few months the voice became abusive. It took particular exception to Voirrey, who was the victim of a stone-throwing attack. Her parents moved her bed into their bedroom with them, and from behind the bedroom panelling they could hear thumps and bangs, which they assumed were made by Gef moving within the walls, and a voice that shouted, 'I'll follow her, wherever you move her.'

Other objects were thrown around the house: crockery in the pantry; pins; bells; furniture; and, inevitably, stones, some as much as one pound in weight. Once, a workman outside threw a piece of bread and watched it carried off by 'no visible thing'. In the area around Dalby it was reported that 'stones and pieces of turf fly through the air . . . doors and windows of lonely cottages are bombarded by gravel and soil'. All this was assumed to be caused by an invisible Gef.

Gef exhibited 'special knowledge'. He would wake up the family and tell them the correct time. He told the family of gossip at the local bus station (which they interpreted as the animal going to the station and listening). He calculated arithmetic problems correctly. Gef was able to say what was in the newspaper that Mr Irving was reading. He knew when Mrs Irving had put a tin of apricots in the cupboard – something no one else in the family apparently knew.

The family received a large number of dead rabbits from Gef. Such gifts could again strengthen the belief that they were dealing with an animal, but in fact gifts from poltergeists are well known, and do not lack for variety.

Gef demanded and ate food. (This may seem unusual for a poltergeist, but there have been several instances of food being taken or apparently eaten; in one case we investigated, food was regularly removed from the fridge and teeth marks would be found, particularly in cheese. There were gifts of food in that case also.) Gef's voice was heard by a reporter. Writing in the *Daily Dispatch*, he claimed: 'The mysterious man-weasel has . . . spoken to me today . . . leaves me in a state of considerable perplexity. Had I heard a weasel speak? I do not know, but I do know that I've heard a voice which I should never have imagined could issue from a human.' Those hearing voices in poltergeist cases often comment on their unusual quality.

The reporter also considered that Gef might be a sub-personality of Voirrey. While he was listening to the voice he watched Voirrey's reflection in a mirror, but he did not have a clear view and could not see her lips. Several examinations of poltergeists have included such observations, often concluding that although the voice is 'attributed' in some way to the focus it is not through direct speech.

Gef was also not modest. He revelled in his special knowledge, and in surprising the family. He stated once: 'If you knew what I know, you'd know a hell of a lot.' He made some pretty outrageous claims: 'I am the fifth dimension'; 'I am the eighth wonder of the world'; 'I can split the atom'; 'I am the Holy Ghost'. These sorts of statements compare fairly well with the Bell Witch case outlined in the previous chapter. Gef also claimed to be 'a ghost in the form of a weasel', but at a different time said, 'thou wilt never get to know what I am'. And on one occasion Gef admitted of his actions, 'I did it for devilment.' So many poltergeists exhibit that attitude!

The phenomena in this case were attributed by the family to a mongoose, and Gef either confirmed this or at least seemed happy to play along with the image. This may seem, at first, to be preposterous. However, the design of the Irvings' house made a perfect home for a small animal to live – inner walls of boarding had been erected with a space between them and the original walls. So it is almost certain that small animals could enter or live there, also given the house's remote rural location. From time to time animals might well have been seen in and around the farmhouse – and the family were after all 'looking' for Gef as an animal. It is likely that, having started out by 'identifying' Gef as an animal, the family always 'saw' it that way and attributed animal qualities to it. Direct contact with Gef was through walls and holes; he could be felt (as when Mrs Irving was allowed to feel his paws) but he could not be seen at the same time. A typical poltergeist in any case would probably have played to their belief in him as an animal; frequently the poltergeist offers the witnesses and the investigators exactly what they want.

But if we separate the animal from the manifestations, we discover that what we have here is a relatively early, classic poltergeist claim. Rapping sounds, thumps from inside the walls, and so on, are certainly very common. Stone and other object throwing, and furniture movement, is also common enough. A voice from somewhere not identified we have seen in many cases. Special knowledge of people in the family and the locality is also reported. Gef was said to leave wet patches (from his natural functions), but water phenomenon is well reported in poltergeist cases. (In one such case, in Pontefract, the pools of water even made one family member question if an elderly lady living there had 'had an accident'.)

Fodor, who also looked at this case, suggested that Gef was different because he 'has a lovable personality', but Gef was not always friendly. On occasion Gef and Irving threatened each other, and Gef was at times unpleasant to Voirrey – the probable focus of the manifestations. Fodor, on summing up the case, asked if Gef was a poltergeist and answered that he was not. 'Poltergeists are malicious or malignant,' he said. 'Gef is not. He is amusing. He has a lovable personality.' Fodor goes on to say that, although he cannot prove it, the evidence suggests that Gef is just what he says he is: a talking animal. However, fourteen years later he included the story in detail in a book on poltergeists, noting that Gef 'has shown many characteristics observed in typical poltergeist disturbances'.

We said at the beginning that the label 'Talking Mongoose' probably gave this account a bad press; Fodor admits, having concluded that it was indeed an animal, that 'it is, perhaps, partially due to my investigation that Gef was dropped as a case for psychical research'.

The main difference between this and many other poltergeist cases is the view of the family involved. It seems that they generally enjoyed having Gef around. This is not typical. But the fact that they identified Gef as a small, furry animal might have made him easier to feel affection for.

The story of Gef makes a good bridge between the historical accounts of the previous chapter and the modern accounts to follow. Stripped of its stranger interpretations it is a good poltergeist case, though like its forerunners it is difficult to authenticate because of the distance of time. But it will be confirmed in these next cases that the poltergeist remains unchanged in today's world.

Sauchie

In 1960, Mrs Annie Campbell and her eleven-year-old daughter Virginia moved from Donegal, Ireland, to Sauchie, a small village in central Scotland. Virginia started at the local school, Sauchie

Primary School. She appeared to settle and, although a shy girl, soon make friends. But all was not well; shortly after the move, poltergeist activity became apparent in the house. The local paper in December reported: 'Just over a week ago strange things began to happen to Virginia. Heavy pieces of furniture were seen to move when she entered a room, doors opened when she approached them and then were found difficult to shut.'

Dr A. R. G. Owen, a fellow at Trinity College, Cambridge, heard of the case through the newspapers and was able to visit the girl and study the case at first hand. He was also able to interview several witnesses (whom he regarded as 'responsible') who had witnessed the phenomena and 'observed it critically'. These witnesses included: the Revd T. Lund, a minister of the Church of Scotland; Dr W. H. Nisbet, a physician; Dr Logan, also a physician; Dr Logan's wife, herself a physician; and Miss Margaret Stewart, a teacher at Sauchie Primary School.

It had been on 22 November that the first disturbances were noticed: a 'thunking' noise described as similar to the sound of a bouncing ball. The next day furniture was seen to move, including a sideboard that slid out from the wall some five inches and then back again, unaided. That night, more noises were heard coming from the head of the bed that Virginia slept in with her nine-year-old niece, Margaret.

The fact that these two shared a bed might be important. It is possible that both girls were unhappy about the situation: Virginia because she had had to leave her home and her father in Donegal, and was now forced to share a bed with her niece; and Margaret having had to relinquish the privacy of her room. It is noticeable that on the second night, when Margaret attempted to get back into bed, 'violent knocking erupted'.

Reverend Lund and Dr Nisbet visited Virginia, and both were witness to some occurrences. A service was conducted, but this did not cause the events to stop. Indeed, they continued even after Virginia had been sedated.

One of the other witnesses present told Malcolm Robinson, local investigator for Strange Phenomena Investigations and its magazine, *Enigma*, 'I was in Virginia's bedroom with a number of other individuals. I was standing close to the bed in which Virginia was lying; she had the covers up to her chin. Suddenly I observed the covers making a rippling movement, from the bottom of the bed up to Virginia's chin . . . Seconds later, I then observed the pillow next to Virginia which had been plumped up, suddenly take what appeared to be the shape of a person's head. A clear indentation of the pillow was seen by myself and others in the room. Now during this time, strange knockings, bangings, and scratchings, and what sounded like sawing noises were coming from all over the room. You couldn't really pinpoint the exact source of the noise; it was coming from everywhere! Most unusual was the sound . . . like a ping-pong ball constantly being bounced.'

Virginia's poltergeist 'followed' her when she went to stay in the nearby town of Dollar. It also went with her to school, where her teacher, Miss Stewart, was witness to several of the odd happenings.

While staying at Dollar, on Thursday 29 November, Virginia was visited by her doctor and others. The visitors heard many rapping noises that centred around the girl. Dr Owen's account states: 'Mrs Logan had previously been sceptical about the reported manifestations, but satisfied herself that the noises came from within the room, but were not caused by the activity of anyone in it.' Later that night Dr Logan was able to see Virginia in a trance, talking in a loud and unnatural voice. She was calling for Toby, her pet dog left behind in Donegal, and Annie, a friend in Ireland. Owen's account notes that 'her replies [to questions] indicated a lack of normal inhibition, as if repressed thoughts were emerging'.

At this time Virginia was 'going through a burst of . . . extremely rapid physical development and maturation. Puberty in the full sense [had] not arrived, but she [was] going through a very rapid pubescence.' Dr Owen stated that although Virginia was often upset at the times of the poltergeist activity, 'this cannot in itself be taken as evidence of basic mental ill health.'

Of the events at school, Virginia's teacher, Miss Stewart, told Malcolm Robinson in 1994, 'Virginia was a shy, withdrawn girl, but very pleasant. She wasn't really forthcoming but was normal in every other way, and she was good at her lessons. I had never really heard the word "poltergeist" before; indeed I thought it was a name for some form of medicine! That's how naive I was to the word. The first time I became aware of something strange was when I had given the class an essay to do. The class was quiet, and all the children had their heads down, bent over their jotters busily writing away. In 1960 we still had the old school desk which had a lid top. Anyway, I looked over at Virginia, and noticed she was sitting with both hands pressed firmly down on top of her desk lid. I rose from my chair and walked over to her. I was then surprised to see the desk lid rise and fall, with Virginia trying her best to keep the lid shut with her hands.' When the child sitting in front of Virginia left her desk to take a jotter to Miss Stewart's desk, as Miss Stewart described it, 'her desk rose a few inches off the floor'.

Miss Stewart told us in an interview in 1996 that at first she simply could not believe her eyes. Wary of childish pranks, she went straight to the desk and checked it for ropes or other signs of trickery. She found none.

During her talk with Robinson she claimed, 'The most unnerving thing that I experienced in the classroom was on one occasion I was sitting behind my large oak table, Virginia was standing on the other side . . . with her hands clasped firmly behind her back. Suddenly a large blackboard pointer cane, which was lying flat on my table, started to vibrate. At first it was vibrating slowly, then increased as the seconds wore on. I sat transfixed looking at this. Then the table, which was quite a heavy one, started to rise up very slowly into the air and also vibrate. I put my hands on the table and tried to push it back down but with no success. I was quite horrified, but it did not stop there. The table continued to vibrate as it hovered a few inches off the floor. Then the table rotated ninety degrees, so that, where I had moments before sat behind the long edge of the table, the table had rotated so that its narrow edge was now directly in front of my stomach. I looked up at Virginia, and saw she was quite distressed, and I remember her saying, "Please, Miss, I'm not doing that, honest I'm not." I calmed her down.'

On a later date, Miss Stewart watched a bowl of bulbs (that Virginia had looked after through the Christmas holidays) move across her desk in much the same manner as the pointer had before.

As well as the above mentioned incidents, Dr Owen reports many other phenomena that were noted but perhaps uncorroborated. These include the levitation of an apple from a fruit bowl, and the apparent movement of small objects, such as a shaving brush, a small vase, and a china dog. The girls were troubled in bed, having their pyjamas pulled off or rolled up their bodies, and had their legs pinched or poked.

After the beginning of December the events quietened down, but did not cease completely. The girls had begun to call the prankster 'Wee Hughie', a sign perhaps that they were becoming less troubled by the events.

Miss Stewart took the lead in calming down a potentially disruptive situation in her classroom. In her interview with us, she said, 'I explained to the children that sometimes people are ill and don't know what's wrong with them. That doesn't necessarily mean there is anything really odd or strange. And I explained that something like that was happening to Virginia. They had heard stories about ghosts, but I assured them, "I wouldn't be staying in a room if there was a ghost in it, but if I stay in it you are all right," and they accepted that quite happily.'

Miss Stewart became aware that the events peaked in a twenty-eight-day cycle. 'I didn't actually notice it to start with. It was only when I checked back after the event that I saw it was following a pattern. It started off fairly violently, then it levelled off, disappeared, and then came back again. And it seemed to be following almost a twenty-eight-day cycle.'

The event with the bowl of bulbs happened fifty-six days after the disturbance to Miss Stewart's desk. As recorded by Dr Owen: 'Miss Stewart took especial care to record the date, as she found it noteworthy that the time interval between this event and the earlier one was fifty-six days . . . a very suggestive figure, if the phenomena are related to physiological happenings associated with a quasi-menstrual cycle occurring as a result of exceptionally rapid pubescence.'

Dr Owen commented about one intensive period of study, 'It will be seen from the diary of the main events that the five witnesses believed themselves to have heard certain sounds and seen certain movements of objects. It is just possible in principle to suppose that one person could be the victim of illusion or hallucination. It is, however, beyond all possibility that five responsible persons should be so deceived at various occasions over a period of two weeks. Thus we must conclude that they heard actual noises and saw actual motions of real objects.' Dr Owen also pointed out: 'The happenings seem to the Revd Mr Lund as being, on balance, more consistent with the functioning of a force or forces originating in Virginia than with the operation of a discarnate entity. Dr Logan and Miss Stewart, independently of one another and of Mr Lund, both very definitely put forward the same interpretation. On the evidence, this finding is much to be preferred to any other.'

Jabuticabal

In December 1965, pieces of brick began to fall inside the house of a Catholic family living at Jabuticabal near São Paulo, in Brazil. An unsuccessful attempt was made to exorcise the building by the local priest, but – as is often the case with poltergeists – this merely seemed to exacerbate the activity. A neighbour, Volpe, recognised that eleven-year-old Maria Jose Ferreira, a girl living in the house, was somehow the centre of the activity, and took her for a while to stay at his home. After a few days the activity resumed, and Volpe was later able to count 312 stones that had fallen in his home since Maria's arrival.

Although the stones continued to fall unexpectedly, Maria seemed to be accepting the phenomena, which became responsive to her requests. If she asked for something such as a sweet or other object, one would fall at her feet. This happened one day while Maria was out walking with Volpe and a companion; she mentioned that she would like a little brooch, and immediately the desired object appeared at her feet.

The poltergeist, however, soon changed its character and began to cause havoc in the house. All the crockery was broken, some furniture was thrown about, and pictures were flung from the walls and moved into other rooms. Maria herself began to suffer. She was slapped by an invisible hand that left bruises on her body, she felt herself bitten, and it is suggested that the poltergeist attempted to kill her by suffocation when she was asleep, by placing objects over her mouth and nose. Needles were found stuck into her flesh, as many as fifty-five on one occasion. At school, Maria's clothing caught fire. Fires also occurred spontaneously in the house.

Volpe took Maria to a Spiritist centre (an offshoot of Spiritualism), where the obsessor 'came through' and told the observers, 'She was a witch. A lot of people suffered and I died because of her. Now we are making her suffer too . . .' Maria underwent a form of spiritual healing at Volpe's 'home circle', and it seems that many of the disturbances died away. The girl went back to live with her mother.

When she was fifteen or sixteen, Maria swallowed a soft drink into which had been mixed formicide, and died almost instantly. Although this may well have been a suicide, we are forced to remind ourselves of the much earlier case of the Bell Witch, in which John Bell died after apparently drinking poison. The poltergeist in that case, known as 'the Witch', rejoiced at his death and claimed to have been responsible.

Miami

On 14 January 1967, the manager of Tropication Arts Incorporated, a wholesalers of novelties and souvenirs at 54th Street in Miami, Florida, called the police for help. He told them a ghost was damaging his goods. Day after day items had been falling from the shelves; many were broken, and the manager was worried that eventually someone would be hurt. As many as fifteen people together witnessed some activities, including police officers. One officer was hit by a flying object. One report stated that a sergeant had pulled out his gun and threatened to shoot anything moving; suddenly so many objects moved or fell that he had to give up and put his gun back.

Suzy Smith, a ghost researcher, was being interviewed on radio WKAT about her research into ghosts when the station received a phone call from Bea Rambisz, an employee at Tropication, who told of beer mugs smashing and other objects moving about. Suzy commenced an investigation, asking for help from William Roll, the project director of the Psychical Research Foundation in North Carolina, who promised to arrive as soon as he could. Roll in turn later brought in his colleague, J. Gaither Pratt, to assist. Pratt was in the medical department of the University of Virginia, and had formerly been working under Dr J. B. Rhine at the Parapsychology Laboratory at Duke University.

Tropication Arts was now seething with investigators and researchers. There were also a few policemen, various newspaper reporters, television crews – even a magician who was convinced the whole thing was trickery. The *Miami Herald and News* was running the story on its front pages; United Press was calling from New York; and Associated Press sent their investigator round in person. Of course there were also present the ten people who worked there.

The magician was Howard Brooks, who seemed to think he had the answer. He explained – and even demonstrated – how it was possible to attach thin wires to objects with 'releasable' gum, then

49

distract people and pull the objects off shelves. Few were impressed; most people thought the poltergeist did it much better. Later, according to Smith, even Brooks seemed to have been less certain of his own explanation of fraud.

Most people who visited the warehouse were able to see some of the activity for themselves. It was clear to those witnesses that much of the activity could not have been produced fraudulently.

The poltergeist retained a familiar shyness with television cameras. CBS insisted on setting up their cameras, even though Smith told them nothing would happen while the cameras were turned on. Nothing did. Shortly after the cameras were packed away the beer mugs were breaking again.

The activity had begun in December 1966; the investigators had first come in on Friday 13 January 1967; and events reached their climax by 23 January. It seems that happenings were occurring nearly every day during this time, and each day had many happenings. On two days Roll noted twenty-eight separate incidents, for thirteen of which he himself was present and 'in a position to satisfy myself that no one could have caused the occurrence by simple trickery.'

Larry Wolfe, a sales rep, reported to Suzy Smith, 'Around twelve-thirty on Monday I was standing by the order desk . . . I heard a glass crash behind me and found a jigger had been broken. In rapid succession after that a Coke bottle crashed to the floor. Then another shot glass hit in the middle aisle . . . and then a shot glass fell in the third aisle. Moments later another bottle broke in aisle four and then one of those carved coconuts . . . landed in aisle two. Almost immediately after that an old cowbell they used to keep on the back door for delivery men to ring, clanged down in that last aisle that seemed to be its favourite playground.' As Smith reported, Wolfe's conclusion was: 'I knew that something was happening in which humans were not involved.'

In total, over three hundred separate incidents were recorded by

Smith, and dozens of people signed statements confirming what they had witnessed, and that they could offer no 'obvious' explanation for it.

The poltergeist at Miami would often move the same object on different occasions. Because of this habit, the investigators were able to set up targets in set positions. In one test, Smith placed a Coca-Cola bottle on a shelf and ensured no one went near it. It flew off the shelf. Roll also set up a number of target objects. He later commented, 'It was the best chance I've ever had to observe the breakages and movements of objects by some unexplained force . . . In Miami I was able to observe with my own eyes numerous instances of movement of objects and check for the possibility of fraud or accident. Neither existed.'

The investigators noticed that the phenomena seemed to centre on a Cuban refugee, Julio Vasquez – a nineteen-year-old who was apparently under a lot of stress. He had been thrown out of his home and he disliked his new boss. Interestingly, there had been some poltergeist-like activity at his own house a few days before the first manifestations at Tropication. It was noticed that the phenomena which occurred around him were not present on the days he was off work. The investigators decided that a special watch was to be kept on him, and soon confirmed that he was the centre of the activity, while also checking that he was not producing the effects by 'normal' means. Vasquez denied deliberately causing any damage, but he did admit to feeling happy when items in the warehouse fell over or smashed.

The problems forced the owners, Alvin Laubheim and Glen Lewis, to fire Vasquez. The poltergeist activity stopped at Tropication Arts after he left.

After Julio left the company, he spent some time being tested by Roll. Vasquez had got himself into some trouble; there were indications of criminal activity, theft and hold-ups – which Roll commented might have been part of Vasquez's 'rich, fantasy life', and might have reflected a need for punishment. He was jailed for six months for one robbery; and Roll comments that one hold-up could have reflected suicidal tendencies.

Roll and Smith managed to persuade Vasquez to go to Durham in North Carolina to the Psychical Research Foundation where he could be studied while he was still – in Suzy Smith's word – 'hot'. It seems some poltergeist activity arose while he was at the foundation; for example, while he was standing near a table in the hall, a bottle fell off it and broke. Roll points out that on this occasion Vasquez was under considerable scrutiny, and stated: 'There was no way in which the four young men and I [those who were watching him] could see how he could have caused the incident fraudulently.'

Guarulhos

One of the most virulent and persistent poltergeists of recent time disrupted the homes of a family living in Northern São Paulo. Marcos, Noemia and their family were troubled in different ways for over eleven years. During the time of the disturbances the family lived in different homes, and it is clear that the phenomena were apparent at all of them. From their first house in Guarulhos, they moved to a temporary home in Guaianazes, then spent a time at Noemia's parents' house in Artur Alvim, some time at Marcos' father's house in Guaianazes, before a move to a new house in Guarulhos, a period in Noemia's sister's house in Suzano, and then a third house in Guarulhos.

The original investigator of events was Hernani Guimaraes Andrade of the Brazilian Institute of Psychobiophysical Research. The analysis of the case, by Michel-Ange Amorim, as reported in the Journal of the SPR (Volume 56, Number 820), divided the case into four separate 'stages'.

Stage One: 27 April–1 May 1973
The first occurrence, at the end of April 1973, was when the family found large parallel cuts in their furniture and mattresses. This was

at first thought to have been done by a young boy in the house, but three people later witnessed similar cutting apparently performed by an invisible agent.

Marcos' father, Pedro, saw the apparitional arm 'of a wild beast . . . it was very strong and big; sharp ended claws . . . black, shiny and curved'. Noemia saw a shadowy form, and a neighbour, who had been called in to witness the cuts, fainted when she saw an enormous hand with dark brown fur and long fingers.

The appearance and disappearance of money was to be a feature throughout the case. Early on in the events some money disappeared, replaced by a piece of paper displaying a red cross.

This stage of events came to a spontaneous end on 1 May 1973.

Stage Two: April 1974–25 October 1974
This period began with stoning. Gravel and bricks fell on the house. It was said that the stones 'didn't seem to be thrown but dropped on the house'. Occasionally people were hit by the stones, which weighed between four hundred and seven hundred grammes. Marcos was hit while repairing the roof.

The people hit by the stones were not hurt. This apparent harmlessness in stone-throwing cases is common, as described in the following chapter. Objects moved, and cups and glasses were smashed, within the house. (This activity continued into Stage Three.) The movements of money continued during this second phase. Coins and notes would disappear or appear spontaneously. 'The money was thrown on the floor or on some furniture, within everyone's sight, but it wasn't seen from where nor how it came.'

The cutting that had first alerted the family to the poltergeist also continued during this stage, with many slashes in furniture, clothes, pillows and blankets; even Bibles were cut with the shape of a cross. The cutting was not confined to inanimate objects. On 2 May 1974 Marcos awoke and found his arm bleeding. Soon other people were being cut as well. Two visiting children were cut on their legs, and Noemia found her face had small cuts appearing daily.

During this time Noemia was witness to more apparitional beasts – 'something horrible with a face in fire and big teeth'. Animal apparitions were also seen by the children. In May 1974, Pedro, an amateur exorcist with – it seems – more than a touch of Don Quixote, conducted a magical struggle with an invisible entity which he then killed with an imaginary sword. This stopped the phenomena for two months. (An interesting version of the placebo effect, perhaps; researcher Jacques Vallee once described to us how he cured his son of fear of an imaginary tiger outside his bedroom by giving him an imaginary gun to shoot it with!)

The cutting that had thus far been a feature of the disturbances ceased permanently during this stage.

Spontaneous fires became a feature. Two floor-polishing machines exploded into flames as they were being used. Some of Marcos' working tools and materials caught fire. Small fires erupted behind the meat safe.

In October 1974 the family asked the Church for help, and an evangelic exorcism was performed. The phenomena ceased for a time.

Stage Three: 28 March 1975–October 1976
The stoning continued throughout this period. Marcos and a girl staying with the family, Eliza, were both struck by stones while in the house. Some church missionaries who had come to help were also hit.

In March 1975 the family were saying prayers in the kitchen with their minister, Lamartine Ribeiro, and his wife Maria, when a glass left a basin and smashed near Maria's feet. Later, as the couple were leaving, a bible 'jumped' from a table and fell to the floor. There were many other reported movements but, as is usually the case, the objects were not witnessed in flight, only noticed when breaking or landing. However, Marcos did see a shoe levitate and hit the ceiling, where it left a mark before falling.

'Gifts' were found, including branches of rosemary and plates that had disappeared some time before. They even found lighted candles in the bedroom.

The spontaneous fires continued to occur in the family homes. The wardrobe seemed to be a target, and clothes inside the wardrobe caught fire.

Two of the people in the case suffered from trances and fits which it was thought might be a sign of possession. The youngest daughter, Ruth, who was eighteen months old at the start, one day woke up in fright, saying she had seen beasts on the wardrobe. Noemia saw a 'shape' in the house, near the bedroom, and Marcos was later hit by a brick while praying there. Soon after this, Ruth began to suffer fits, but the hospital could not discover their cause. A girl staying with the family in 1976, Eliza, also showed signs of possession, but only in Marcos' house.

A second exorcism by the Church in October 1976 effectively ended the experiences.

Stage Four: Dates unspecified or uncertain

Although credited with lasting eleven years, the investigators noted that after October 1976 (three and a half years from the start) the disturbances were very rare. The final interview with the family was conducted on 21 April 1984. During this period of seven and a half years few events had arisen, chiefly some disappearance of money and movement of objects. There is little reason to doubt that these may have been poltergeist activities, given what had gone before, but it is also fair to suggest that the fear of the poltergeist returning may have forced the family to overreact to everyday events and normal misperceptions and errors that would normally have gone unnoticed.

Enfield

August 1977 brought a dramatic change to the circumstances of the Harper family of Enfield. For over a year their lives were to be disrupted almost beyond endurance. Their semi-detached house became home to one of the most virulent poltergeists of recent years.

Peggy Harper and her four children did not know what to believe when two of the children, Janet and Pete, complained that their beds were shaking. The next night, at about the same time, everyone heard unusual noises and loud knocks that they could not explain. Then, in front of Mrs Harper, a very heavy chest of drawers started sliding along the floor. To quote researcher Guy Lyon Playfair in his account of the case, *This House is Haunted*, 'As many people probably do when they suddenly realise they are in the presence of something totally strange, Mrs Harper began, literally, to shake with fear.' The Harpers left the house in a hurry, went to their neighbours who took them in, and did what anyone with an intruder would do. They called the police.

Sergeant Brian Hyams was on duty that night, and sent WPC Caroline Heeps with a colleague to investigate. The poltergeist at Enfield was not shy; on her first visit, WPC Heeps watched a chair moving some three or four feet, apparently unaided, towards the kitchen door. She knew she could not explain how it was happening – the police, of course, have no means to control a poltergeist – and so had to leave without having solved the mystery, promising instead to 'keep an eye on the house'.

The next day the family were bombarded by flying objects; marbles and other items flew across the room. A neighbour, also named Peggy, called the *Daily Mirror* newspaper and once more the police were asked to help. Both the reporters and the police were witness to the poltergeist happenings that day.

It was a newspaper reporter who suggested calling in the Society for Psychical Research (SPR), who sent Maurice Grosse to investigate the reports. He realised from the atmosphere alone that the case was genuine, almost from the moment he walked in. Maurice was to lead one of the most intense investigations ever, and brought to the house experts from many fields.

The disturbances at Enfield were typical of the poltergeist phenomenon: the movement of objects and furniture, raps and knocking sounds etc., as well as the less common occurrences such as apports (see p. 107), spontaneous fires and pools of water, assaults, apparitions and written messages. The Enfield case also involved some of the rarer phenomena, such as a voice (less common in modern cases, though more frequently reported in the past); and the levitation of the focus, Janet. Such levitation is very rare; however, one instance had been reported in London twenty years earlier. Janet is also reported to have been hauled down the stairs, first in her sleep and then when fully awake (this is similar to the Pontefract case (see Chapter Nine)).

What Maurice found to be most persuasive about the Enfield poltergeist was no single event, rather the sheer volume of activity, in circumstances where any trickery would simply not have been possible. The total number of happenings at Enfield could never accurately be counted, but after just a few months the investigators estimated over fifteen hundred instances.

It soon became clear that the events were centred around Janet – the 'epicentre', as Maurice Grosse calls the focus. It was also apparent to observers that, while some of the activity might have been the mischief of children seeking attention and playing to their audience, neither Janet nor anyone else could possibly have faked everything.

Reading through the account of the case in *This House is Haunted*, it is clear that the poltergeist was responsive not only to the desires and whims of the focus – as is often the case – but also the investigators. Grosse observed: 'Look at its timing – the moment you go out of a room, something happens. You stay in the room for hours, and nothing moves. It knows what we're up to.' The poltergeist acted, and reacted, mischievously and deliberately, often meeting challenges from the investigators about things they stated 'it could not do'.

The family learned to communicate with the poltergeist through raps and knockings, as had been done in many previous cases. It was suggested to Mrs Harper by the investigators that she ask for a message. 'Leave me a message so I can help,' she requested. Within five minutes the first written note arrived: 'I will stay in this house . . .'

The Enfield poltergeist attained a voice through Janet. Before this, however, the family had heard barks and whistles. Grosse decided it was time to challenge it to some verbal communication. 'You can whistle and you can bark so you can speak. I want you to call out my name . . . Maurice Grosse.' The poltergeist responded to this direct challenge, and after some practice got it right. Slowly, it learned other names, then it seemed to find its own identity, claiming to be a man who had died in the house before the Harpers moved in.

On 12 March 1996 we spoke to (now Inspector) Brian Hyams, who had sent WPC Caroline Heeps and a colleague to the house that first night. 'I remember Caroline talking about it,' he recalled, 'saying that she . . . saw the chair move or ripple across the floor.'

Two nights later Hyams was again on duty when, at about two o'clock in the morning, an agitated man came into the station and asked for help – his neighbours were so disturbed they were staying at his house, and talking about wanting to be rehoused. The family wanted someone in authority to be a witness to the disturbances. Hyams agreed to go along personally this time, and he took an officer with him. First he visited the neighbours' house agreeing to go next door if Mrs Harper went with him. (This caution was not the product of a fear of the paranormal, but the legal responsibility of the police 'in case of any allegations of theft or damage'.) The three people went into the house; the officer went upstairs and Hyams went into the lounge. Mrs Harper remained in the hall.

Hyams could see Mrs Harper and was in fact talking to her when 'all of a sudden I heard a thump. I thought it came from the ceiling. It quite possibly came from the wall but it was a definite thump . . . Having heard that I shouted to my colleague and he thought in all honesty it was me and I thought it was him. So I decided to go and join him upstairs and told him it wasn't me and he assured me it wasn't him.' Throughout this time Mrs Harper was in sight and Janet was not in the house.

Shortly afterwards Hyams was downstairs, when 'Lego bricks just started to levitate, or move about I should say, jump about like jumping beans.' This scared him and he ran from the house. He had no problem admitting his fear to us twenty years later, and told us he remembered the sight vividly. 'There was a bird in a cage and that started squawking. And suddenly one or two Lego bricks started to fly towards us. And . . . I'm no hero, I went straight out of the door and I think there was a rush between us who got out the swiftest.'

Hyams continued: 'Outside we were joined by a *Daily Mirror* reporter and a photographer, so the five of us . . . stood around talking and it was decided that we would go back . . . into the house. Inside, the photographer set up his camera . . . I can specifically remember him saying that this was one of the latest models, a Nikon with failsafe apparatus, and nothing ever goes wrong with it . . . While we were standing there talking . . . the Lego bricks started to vibrate again and started pinging towards us. And so we got up very, very quickly again.' The camera had malfunctioned, and they got no pictures from the event.

Hyams concluded in his interview with us, 'Well, to be honest, I didn't know what to make of it . . . in twenty-eight years in the police service, that's the only time I've consciously become aware of something like that, and I think that it is so rare and few and far between . . . when I tell the story here people still look at me as much as to say, you know, "Is he or isn't he telling the truth?" and I say, "Look, this is really what happened and what I saw." I don't think I would like to see it again. If I did I don't think I'd react any other way.'

Cardiff

The poltergeist which arose in an engineering workshop and retail shop in Cardiff was essentially a stone-throwing poltergeist, but with remarkably responsive abilities. Over the two years or so during which the poltergeist was 'present', a number of other activities, seemingly using local materials, also took place. The case arose some time around 1988 (the precise date is not clear). By the time of SPR investigator David Fontana's visit in June 1989, fifteen manifestations had been listed.

The people involved were, principally, John and Pat, who owned the business, a sister-in-law, Gerry, who worked for them, and Gerry's husband, Fred. Stones, coins and bolts bounced off the walls and the floor, and sometimes hit people without causing injury. The objects were usually seen as they landed but were sometimes witnessed in mid-flight.

There occurred also the arrival of items, seemingly in response to requests. For example, when the proprietors spoke of writing down what was happening, a pen and paper appeared from nowhere and dropped to the floor. It was the headed notepaper of the business above the shop. (This further emphasises the point that poltergeists use local materials. Certainly the stones that were found were similar to those located in a nearby churchyard.) There is some evidence that there was also poltergeist activity in the premises on the first floor.

Another of the workforce asked for a sovereign, and a Jubilee Crown appeared, dropping beside him. It seemed to be the one that was usually kept in the proprietor's house. The employee then asked for more coins, and three old pennies (dated 1912) fell to the floor.

There were a number of other disturbances in and around the workshop. Perhaps one of the most notable involved a paint scraper which went missing; when it reappeared it was too hot to touch, as if it had been heated with a blow-lamp.

Other items favoured by the poltergeist were carburettor floats, small components used in machinery, which would often be found with needle ends embedded in the polystyrene ceiling tiles, and occasionally turning up under slightly more bizarre circumstances. On one occasion a float was left in the workshop and 'challenged' to be moved by the morning. That night, on buying cigarettes in a newsagents, Fred found a carburettor float in his change. He and John returned to the workshop and found the float had gone.

In the premises upstairs, a diary disappeared and was found on the roof of a nearby building. John and Pat, at home, received several telephone calls but the line went dead when the receiver was picked up. British Telecom could not account for this. One spectacular display occurred when John said to Pat, 'All we need now are some planks of wood.' Instantly, planks were thrown violently into the workshop; they were too heavy to have been thrown by hand, even if there was someone who could have responded that quickly to the request.

When investigator David Fontana first visited the premises, a stone 'pinged' on some machinery at the moment he arrived. Fontana is certain that no one could have seen him coming, or would have known exactly the moment he was going to arrive. He states: 'Though minor in itself, the apparent incident of the stone hitting the machinery at the exact moment I arrived appeared to have some significance.' During the time of Fontana's investigation, and while he was present, several poltergeist phenomena arose similar to those already reported, with one or two additions. Telephone calls, with the line dead, would now come to the shop. Carburettor floats were appearing in the ceilings in the homes of both Fred and Gerry and John and Pat. On one occasion a float appeared inside Fred's shirt, and another time one was pushed into a parasol in the garden of his house. A heavy brass shellcase was twice thrown violently in the shop, and once, when the poltergeist was challenged to 'fire the shell', blue flames emerged from it.

One of the most remarkable features to this poltergeist was its tendency to 'return' stones thrown into a particular corner. Sometimes the stones were marked, and were the ones returned. During one test, John pretended to throw a stone but did not, yet a stone was returned. Various keys appeared mysteriously, many of an unknown origin which were never identified. Cutlery was laid out crudely in John's kitchen.

To demonstrate its 'skill' the poltergeist was challenged to hit the brass shell with a stone, which it did very successfully – although others found this accuracy quite difficult unless they were very close.

These phenomena were witnessed not just by the people working in the shop and Fontana, but also by several customers, salesmen and so on, some of whom we were able to speak to, and many of whom became convinced of the genuineness of the phenomena after personal observation. Several reported that the flight of objects was sometimes unusual and non-ballistic, for example coins might follow a slow and flat trajectory. One witness reported watching engineering bolts 'materialise' just below the ceiling and then fall to the floor. He examined the ceiling and found no hole through which the bolts could have fallen.

In his report, Fontana lists sixteen incidents which he personally witnessed, including being struck by stones and a ball bearing, watching various objects move spontaneously, watching the arrival of a pen following an invitation to 'bring a pen', watching a paper clip fall to John's feet at his request, and so on. On one occasion, a large steel strimming wheel crashed against the door as Pat was entering the workshop. Had it arrived a split second sooner it would have seriously injured her. This 'near miss' phenomenon is common in poltergeist cases; actual injury is very rare.

Fontana also experimented with the responsive return of stones, stating, 'I found that I was able to reproduce this phenomenon myself, and did so on a number of separate occasions. There was no question of my stone bouncing back and being mistaken for that thrown by Pete.' (Pete is the nickname given to the poltergeist by the people at the workshop.)

Fontana examined the case very thoroughly for any fraudulent activity, and dismisses the possibility on the counts of both motive and opportunity.

Our own impression of the investigation, having met and spoken to Fontana and the principal witnesses concerned, is that the research was thoroughly and objectively conducted and that this poltergeist was a genuine phenomenon. Fontana makes an interesting comment, however. He states: 'As a psychologist, observation of my own frame of mind during the course of the investigation was almost as interesting as the investigation itself. Each time I witnessed the phenomena, and noted not only the physical behaviour but also the emotional reactions of the other people present, I felt that normal explanations could safely be ruled out. However, on thinking things over afterwards, my rational mind would always intervene and insist that some rational explanation there *must* be. The result was that I would fix on any possibility, no matter how absurd, rather than stay with the conclusions produced by actual observation. In other words, my mind would prefer abstract post hoc speculation to direct practical observation.' Fontana goes on to say, 'Parapsychological literature is full of examples of investigators who initially have been convinced by their experiences only later to doubt the evidence of their own senses. In this way, this is as unscientific as the opposite extreme, that of gullibility.'

Fontana, a year later, followed up his investigations for the SPR with a fresh report, including one or two new 'inventions' of the poltergeist. Clouds of fertiliser fell on a customer, frightening him out of the shop without waiting to pick up his change. One Monday morning, on opening up the premises, John found the engine of a petrol lawnmower running, despite the fact that it would have taken three separate manoeuvres to start it. It was a noisy machine, and could not have been left on accidentally when the shop was closed on Friday (and had it been, it would have run out of petrol long before Monday morning).

Carburettor floats continued to appear, including one which flew through the open window of Fred's car while he was sitting in a supermarket car park. Money totalling around £70 appeared over a period of weeks. Sometimes coins and sometimes notes – and once notes were pinned to the ceiling by carburettor floats.

Several incidences seemed to point towards the theory that a young child's spirit was involved. Fred claims to have seen the apparition of a small boy sitting on a high shelf, which disappeared when a carburettor float was thrown from the 'responsive corner' of the workshop. On another occasion, Fred saw a small figure in short trousers and a peaked cap, waving as if to say goodbye. A large rubber ball and child's teddy bear which had been kept in the workshop disappeared. Only after investigating sounds coming from the ceiling cavity did they find both items secreted away up there.

When we met the witnesses on 9 March 1996, we discovered that, although the poltergeist activity at the workplace had stopped (they had moved to new premises in any case), some occurrences continued at Fred's house: for example, pound coins would regularly be found, sometimes as many as five a day. Although perhaps somewhat irritated by the disturbances, it was very clear that Fred found the whole experience very special and closely associated himself with the phenomenon.

We visited the site of the original activity. The shop is now a café, and the workshop at the rear has been demolished. Speaking to the owner of the café, he confirmed that there had been no 'activity' since he took over the building.

The poltergeist may have finished with the workplace – and with John and Pat – but activity continues at the home of Fred and Gerry. They presume it is still 'Pete'. In their previous home around twelve pairs of scissors had once appeared. 'They were stuck in the cornice, on the shelf, thrown out into the garden, and so on,' Fred told us. One pair appeared stuck upright in the curtain track. (We asked him why scissors might be involved, and he suggested, laughing, that Pete was 'cut up' about something!)

More recently, in their present home, and for a long period of time, coins have been appearing, sometimes to the value of £10 or £15 a month. While we were interviewing Fred and Gerry by telephone some months after our initial meeting, a coin apparently fell into their sink; certainly we heard the noise it made and it had recorded on the tape. Fred made the point that nothing much had happened for some time prior to our visit, but since then coins had been arriving almost daily. Pictures on the walls had moved, turning around in their frames; and, for some reason, they had found themselves unable to keep oranges in the house. If oranges were left overnight in a fruit bowl, they would be gone in the morning.

Pudsey, England

Early in 1995 we were contacted by Catherine Kirk, who was in some distress after experiencing poltergeist phenomena in her house. It was an interesting start to a case: Catherine telephoned our office in the middle of the night, and left a message on our answerphone describing mists that were surrounding her in her bedroom as she was recording the message. We knew we had to react quickly – but Catherine was calling from around two hundred miles away, and so we initially contacted Sue Mantle, a local researcher we had known for some years. Catherine and Andrew were interviewed by Sue on 21 April 1995. (We later interviewed the couple ourselves, in their house, where they confirmed the information given to Sue.)

At the time of the initial interview, the couple had been in the house for approximately two years and four months. The first activity they had noticed was that keys would go missing.

Sometimes they would turn up later; others were lost for ever. This obviously caused inconvenience and costs, as Andrew explained: 'Our keys disappeared for two days. Meanwhile we replaced the locks. And the keys then turned up.'

Shortly afterwards they found that furniture was being disturbed during the night. Andrew described it: 'The first instance that I had within this house of some other form of life, if you like, was when I came downstairs after sleeping to find that one of the armchairs had been turned upside-down in the centre of the room, allowing no access through.' They are a careful couple, and always ensured before going to bed that furniture was not left near the open fire, so finding the chair in that place was strange. On this occasion, 'it was impossible to walk through the room'. Catherine also confirmed that at other times a huge settee in the room had moved.

One New Year's Eve, Andrew gave Catherine a bunch of carnations which they put into a vase. They were sitting together on the sofa when they 'actually saw one of the carnations lift, physically lift itself up and flung [sic] itself into the middle of the room. It was as though someone had purposely gone up, picked up a flower, and just flung it.'

Around the same time, a small ornamental Christmas tree in the living room was affected. Andrew and Catherine were entertaining their friends, Debbie and Dennis. Andrew described what happened: 'We put a small Christmas tree up on the shelf. The tree was about two feet high, with the lighting wire running down the back. All of a sudden it just lifted up and fell off the shelf. There was no wind, the curtains were closed.' Andrew and Catherine confirmed that they thought the tree had levitated; it had not simply fallen but had lifted up and moved horizontally before it fell.

We spoke to Debbie and she confirmed this, saying, 'It didn't just topple over; it suddenly just went. It didn't slide or go slowly; it just seemed to . . . Oh, how can you describe it? We just heard this noise. You could not explain how it could have gone forward like that . . . it was really weird.'

Other things moved in different parts of the house. A light bulb fell on Andrew while he was sitting on the lavatory. We examined the room and found that the light fitting was several feet away from the WC. Even if the light bulb had not been inserted properly and had worked loose, to land on Andrew it would have had to travel in an unnatural trajectory. Since the light was on at the time, it seems unlikely that it was not properly fitted. Andrew described the impact. 'It actually brushed my hair . . . and hit my shoulder.' He confirmed to us that it did not hurt him: 'I just felt warmth next to me.'

The couple also experienced the malfunctioning of many electrical devices: the television, video, kettle, and so on. (As recently as 19 March 1996, Catherine telephoned us to tell us that all her light bulbs had broken and that the pictures on the walls were being removed from their places.)

Just after the light bulb incident the couple heard footsteps in the house, and the sounds of the door latches being lifted upstairs: 'We could actually hear the latch go up and drop . . . they are dead latches that fall down, they don't lift up. And that was [a] regular [happening] for about six or seven months.'

Debbie also confirmed that when she was alone in the house she would hear latches lift, and find previously closed doors open, though she could not explain how that could happen, given the nature of the drop-catches. She also described an incident in the kitchen: 'I was in the kitchen on my own . . . thinking of making myself a drink of tea. And I felt something had walked up behind me. When I turned round there was nothing there at all . . . It was a big shock. I definitely felt there was something there. I was so convinced. I even looked under the table; there was nothing there.'

On one occasion, while around fourteen friends were with Catherine and Andrew at the house, they heard an 'almighty crash' from upstairs. They all suspected that the large, heavy wardrobe had fallen over – but when they ran upstairs to investigate they found nothing out of place.

Catherine said that she feels a presence around at night, and admits that she finds it frightening. At times she is scared to leave the bedroom. A misty blue form has also been seen, and she has experienced a choking sensation. 'I just feel something, somebody trying to drag me away, drag me out of bed. And I've had this experience . . . on a lot of occasions . . . It's so real, and it's so vivid . . . and I'm thinking, I'm not asleep, and this is happening.' At other times Catherine feels something touching her and trying to get into bed with her. Sometimes, after a night-time experience like this, Catherine has found herself covered in bruises, on her arms, legs, and buttocks.

Andrew told us about something similar. He had felt something in the bed with him on a night when Catherine was away. Andrew described it to us. 'I actually felt something next to me. I'm not the kind of person to react to anything unless there is definitely something there. After about ten minutes in bed, I just felt the bed go down at the side nearest the door. And I thought one of the cats has escaped and jumped on the bed. That's exactly what it felt like except that this time it was, like, next to me – right up to me. And I felt something pushing, and I got hold of the bed clothes and threw them back and there was nothing there. So I came downstairs and checked all the cats and dogs; they were all fast asleep.'

There have been other occasions when Catherine has felt she is floating above the bed; perhaps an out-of-body sensation. On one occasion, when she was ill and lying in bed, Andrew heard her talking in a language unknown to him (that he thought might be Yiddish).

A medium who visited the house described seeing a figure in the living room. When the figure moved elsewhere in the house the medium followed it, and described a man 'playing' the piano. Andrew said of the piano: 'No noise was coming from it, not that I could hear anyway. I was then told that the man's name was Bill and I was asked whether I had a relative of that name. I said I had a great uncle Billy who lived in Barrow but I didn't know anything about him. I had heard he painted, that was all I knew.' (Andrew later told us: 'The following day I rang my mum up and said, "Did Uncle Billy used to play the piano?" And my mum said, "Yes, he was a concert pianist." Now I didn't know that.')

Andrew had not been keen on encouraging the medium, and was sure he had given her no clues when she offered the information, so the details about Billy surprised him. At one point in the meeting he could hear a child crying, but he stoically refused to react. 'Then they actually told me that I was hearing a little girl crying, and I had to admit it – I wasn't going to tell any lies. I had to admit that I could actually hear something.'

The medium brought a comforting message: 'She said we were being looked after.'

Of the more unpleasant experiences in the bedroom, she advised Catherine and Andrew to tell it to go away. Shout at it. Even swear at it. Tell it to stop invading you. 'And that's what I've been doing,' Catherine told us. 'Lord knows what next door thinks if they can hear me.'

The experiences of this case continue at the time of writing, but the couple have come to feel more comfortable with the poltergeist now that they have had time to study it, and have accepted the opinions and advice of the medium.

Hertfordshire

Jerry and Elizabeth lived in a modern house in Hertfordshire. They had moved to the house in June 1991, and over time they had both, individually, noticed that some odd things were happening. Both were critical enough to question even their own experiences, and for a while neither mentioned their concerns to the other.

In February 1992, while Elizabeth was alone in the house, she felt the whole building shake. In September of the same year, Jerry had the same experience when he was by himself in the house.

Strange phone calls were received at the house with no one on the other end; so many that the couple took to using an answer-phone to save them picking up the 'dead' calls. This also happened at Jerry's workplace. Up to the time of writing, Jerry's exchange had not been connected to the 'call back' facility (the 1471 service), so no trace was possible.

One day in the summer of 1992, Jerry and Elizabeth were riding in a field. (Jerry was keen to point out that the field is the site of an old burial ground.) They had a disagreement, and Jerry wanted to go back to the car and head home. But he was unable to find his keys, and they turned up months later, in October, in the house, much to the surprise of the couple who had by now given them up for lost.

Three weeks after Jerry had experienced the house-shaking, the couple had what both described as the worst week of their lives.

On the morning of Sunday, 4 October 1992, Jerry left the house to buy a paper. When he returned shortly afterwards he found Elizabeth in floods of tears. The house had felt as if it were shaking again, and some small objects had moved on to the floor. Moved, not fallen. Indeed, some of the items were very breakable and the couple are convinced a 'real' fall would have shattered them. But these objects (such as a fragile model coaching house) appear to have been gently placed on the floor.

Jerry stated in a written detail he presented to us in August 1993, 'From that day to this, no day has been normal.'

Both Jerry and Elizabeth were now convinced their house had a ghost, or at least that they were experiencing something strange and unnatural. But both were still too scared to utter the words that would commit themselves to their fears.

On Monday 5 October Elizabeth was starting a new job. It was an important job of some considerable responsibility, and Elizabeth was anticipating some pressures. That morning was therefore a time when they might have appreciated some peace and stability in the home. But they came downstairs to find various objects had been moved. A large ginger jar that normally sat on a window-sill was placed on the floor; the lid was off and inside was a watch that Elizabeth had lost a long time previously – before they had even moved into the house. (This incident convinced the couple that they should discuss their fears with each other.) On another occasion they found a necklace that Elizabeth had lost three years earlier, in a cake tin that was in constant use.

They decided they had 'a ghost', and asked the local church for help.

They approached the local Catholic priest who told them, 'You probably haven't got a ghost. Your only hope is to come back to the church; you have to start coming to church. I will come and see you sometime.' The couple were already on edge because of their experiences and their recent discussions with each other. Thus they could not face waiting until Sunday before they could do anything – and it seems they felt the church had been less helpful than they had hoped. The following week turned out to be everything they feared – a 'total nightmare' in their words.

They heard a 'clank' from a room upstairs, and this was when the car keys (that had been lost about fifteen miles away) turned up. They were found in a spare bedroom.

Wet patches were found on the carpet. At first, Jerry and Elizabeth suspected each other of spilling drinks. But they soon discovered that this was not the case. A dustcap from a timer in the cupboard would often be found on the floor, filled with water from no obvious source. At one time, they watched together as one of Elizabeth's shoes filled with water, apparently from nowhere.

Worst of all was the experience when one of their cats went missing. Although they knew the animal was in the house they could not find her. Upstairs in their bedroom, Jerry and Elizabeth watched as an apparitional cat's paw and leg appeared to come through the bed covers. They tried to grab the leg but found it had no substance, though it was plainly visible to both of them. Both Jerry and Elizabeth were now very scared, and they screamed loudly as they grabbed at the apparitional paw. There was a curious outcome to this manifestation; although the episode was very frightening it did allow them to find the cat – she had been stuck in the divan.

Jerry and Elizabeth called the Salvation Army that night, but they were hardly equipped to deal with the sort of claims they were being offered, beyond comfort and listening.

On the Monday morning Jerry went into work looking as white as a sheet. He could not stop himself from opening up to his boss. The couple were afraid to leave each other for any period of time, and so it was necessary to explain to his boss why he was unwilling to go away on business trips, courses and so on.

'Things continued to deteriorate,' as Jerry described it. Ornaments and pictures moved, one photograph was turned to the wall, plants were uprooted in the back garden, items went missing, money disappeared, and some objects appeared almost as if they were presents. They would be found in the house after coming home from work or after getting up in the morning. These included: a three-tier plastic table (for plants); plants for the garden; mail-order items they did not order and which were unreturnable; a camera; a set of suitcases; a fox ornament; a small green turtle ornament; coloured balls for the dog; a plastic Christmas pudding; a radio; a black jacket for Elizabeth (her size); many presents under both their pillows; and, recently, a Flintstones T-shirt for Jerry. These in addition to the chocolate bars in the fridge. At first, some of the items were thrown away on the advice of the Church.

So much happened on a daily basis that to repeat their 'log' (which they routinely kept for some time) would be boring and repetitious. However, it runs to pages and pages of daily notes on things moving, things appearing, things disappearing, and so on.

One evening Jerry posted a letter. Elizabeth was with him and watched him post it. The next morning it was back in their letter rack, where they leave letters for posting.

Jerry and Elizabeth planned a Mediterranean holiday. A couple of days before they were due to leave they got out their suitcases and started packing, leaving the cases in the spare bedroom. Several times when they returned to the bedroom they would find the contents strewn across the floor. Similarly, they would find items they did not want to take with them packed.

The poltergeist did not stay behind; it travelled with them. Jerry was taking a shower in the hotel when the lid from a perfume bottle flew off. Elizabeth later described the scene to us, as Jerry came flying out, followed by the perfume bottle.

They also discovered that the poltergeist could write. It would complete crossword puzzles for them. Elizabeth told us: 'We had this crossword book, it was so annoying, we would put it down to finish later, we would have half an hour in the sun, pick the book up, and it would be finished.'

On returning from holiday they discovered that the house was just as they'd left it, but immediately after their return the disturbances started again.

The poltergeist also had a predilection for food. The couple regularly found that food had been taken from the fridge; at one time it seemed to have a fondness for cottage cheese. A supply of chocolate bars were regularly kept in the fridge, so that Elizabeth could take one each morning as she left to work. Each weekend they would buy enough for the week ahead, so they knew how many there should be at any one time. There was often an extra bar found in the fridge. More recently, though, for the first time, one went missing.

In the wine rack, bottles would disappear or move, sometimes turning up in a nearby cupboard, right in the middle behind the closed door.

Jerry managed some communication with 'it' after it started leaving written messages in a book of his. He left a note against a magazine rack saying 'Do not move'. It was moved when he got home from work. At one time he wrote a note saying 'Please go!' and, ten minutes later, found 'Get stuffed. You'll pay' written on the pad. Other messages have included a note in a book given to Elizabeth: 'Don't give – Elizabeth hates poetry books!'; also:

'Thoughtless bastard'; 'You'll learn when it's too late'; and 'You move – I was here first'.

Another time Jerry attempted communication was after a badly disturbing weekend. He wrote a note asking, 'What can we do to appease?' Some hours later Jerry took off his trainers and Elizabeth noticed something inside one of them. It was a note saying: 'You f*** off.'

When they took another holiday – to Malta – they both received messages. Elizabeth found written in her book: 'Good holiday'; and Jerry got in his: 'Stay there, bastard'.

On another occasion it was suggested that Jerry should leave a note asking for a response not to himself but to John Spencer (one of the authors of this book). John left a pad and pencil on his desk that day and night. But it was to Jerry that the written reply came: 'Tell John he can get stuffed.'

Jerry and Elizabeth had an additional concern: the possibility of contagion. They worried that their problem, whatever it is, was catching. The effects started to arise at Elizabeth's work; files would go missing, sometimes reappearing in awkward places where nobody would have left them. And there is evidence that other members of Elizabeth's family might have experienced similar – even identical – phenomena. She has tried to talk to them about it, but they would not discuss it with her.

Jerry and Elizabeth also related an account of a time when a friend, Steve, who knew about their problems, looked after their car for a week. When giving the car back he told the couple that he had had some odd experiences, though none very dramatic. When Jerry and Elizabeth offered him a present of a bottle of spirits for assisting them he accepted, but refused to take it into his house, insisting it stayed in his garage.

Money was a constant problem for Elizabeth. The poltergeist appeared to insist that she could not carry money with her. If she took money out of the house, it disappeared. She took to meeting Jerry from work to travel home with him on the trains; if she were to get on a train on her own carrying money for the fare, or a ticket, it invariably would have disappeared by the time she needed it. To her embarrassment, on one occasion this happened and she was fined. Her movements became restricted by this problem, adding to the obvious strain of such an intrusion.

We were invited into the case in August 1993, less than a year after Jerry and Elizabeth had identified their fears. We interviewed the couple, took away copies of their 'log', and arranged a visit on 26 August to set up some monitoring equipment at the house. The object of the equipment was to record any events that happened while the house was empty. Our colleague, Tony Wells, who designed some of the technology we use, joined us for the visit.

Even as we set up the equipment there were some strange coincidences (which may or may not be connected with the investigation; we mention them as there are many claims of electrical and mechanical interference in poltergeist cases). First, on arriving at the house, Tony discovered that his major sensor lead had been severed in half, effectively preventing us from monitoring the two floors of the house at the same time. The EMU (environmental monitoring unit) had to be installed on one floor, but its sensors could not reach the other floor. Tony was quite certain that he had packed the leads carefully. In addition, four magnetic sensors needed to equip the monitors for detection were missing. Tony had specifically checked his equipment before setting out, knowing that he would probably need those instruments. (They were never found.) On later examination the EMU unit was found not to be functioning as usual, though Tony had no explanation for the problems. The radio section of the device was misbehaving; it has never done that before or since.

The gremlins of poltergeist-hunting were affecting us, as is so often the case in this work. During the couple's absence we set up a video camera to point at a pot plant that was often moved. When the couple returned it had shifted to another room, but we discovered that the tape had run out half an hour before they came back, during which time (we presume) the movement took place. The wrong length tape had been inserted. We were left wondering whether, if a longer tape had been loaded, the movement would have taken place. On another occasion, in the kitchen of the house, when the video camera ran out of tape, it was decided to leave the machine off, as the poltergeist seemed to have demonstrated an aversion to equipment; ten minutes later an ornament that had been in its field of view moved to another room. (In the Enfield case some activity took place soon after a tape left recording by Playfair had run out. He states: 'This had to be the night I put in a sixty-minute cassette instead of my usual ninety-minute one.')

Despite our efforts the equipment we used did not detect anything happening during the day.

We spent several more days at the house with members of teams from ASSAP. The first of these was 4 May 1995, when we were present with a team that included Andrew Bathie and Chris Walton. During this time we set up some equipment, including video cameras. Following our arrival at 7.40 a.m., we photographed the rooms of the house in order so that, should anything be found to have moved, we could compare the room to its original photograph. During the morning the telephone rang several times, but was dead when answered. At two o'clock, the comment was made: 'The phone hasn't rung for a while,' and two seconds later the phone rang – but when Andrew Bathie answered it, there was a blank line.

At 2.30 Chris and another member of the team went upstairs, and in the front bedroom found an ornamental china duck sitting in the middle of the carpet. We all knew that this had not been there earlier in the day. The room had been photographed after Jerry and Elizabeth left that morning – and on reviewing the photograph the duck was clearly visible on a shelf. Several members of the team noted the apparently 'perfect placement' of the duck. (See Chapter Four for an explanation of this.)

After Jerry and Elizabeth arrived home we discussed the day

with them, packed up the equipment and left. As we were walking towards our car Jerry called us back and showed us that the duck had moved again to the bedroom floor (we had replaced it before leaving).

Since the poltergeist seemed to have signalled an aversion to equipment, we spent another day there without instruments, but nothing of note arose.

It is difficult to summarise a case such as this, and we can only do so here tentatively. There is the almost certain probability that some of the events attributed to the poltergeist were no more than coincidences, mistakes, and so on. Needless to say, Jerry and Elizabeth are both very sensitive after the years of irritating and intrusive experiences, and they would not be human if they did not sometimes overreact to normal events that in another context would go unnoticed. But there are just too many occurrences that they jointly witnessed, several which are of too strange a nature to be dismissed lightly.

The resilience of the poltergeist is of interest. Although there are many poltergeist cases that have lasted for years, it is generally true that most cases end within three to six months. Why this poltergeist should be so persistent is unclear, but there are two salient points which, if correct, could turn out to give us a clue as to the reality behind the poltergeist. The first point is that Jerry and Elizabeth are a middle-aged couple with no children at home, i.e. none of the classic 'adolescents'. It is possible that when a poltergeist is focused on someone at, say, puberty, it is to do with the hormonal and emotional changes which are taking place; once they have passed and the body has 'settled down' again, the poltergeist activity diminishes. In this case there is no physiological change apparent in the couple, and their stable state may be the reason why the poltergeist also remained steady. Second, we have to consider the possibility that, frightening, intrusive and disagreeable as the poltergeist is, it also meets a need in Jerry and Elizabeth. While dismissing it at the conscious level, they may be holding on to it to some degree at the subconscious level. Elizabeth, for example, could not leave the house to go anywhere where she would need money, and therefore Jerry had to be with her. Indeed, for both of them the activity was more severe whenever they were alone in the house. The result is that the experience has forced them to be together, when perhaps they would otherwise not be. There may have been some part of their subconscious that recognised this need to be together was of advantage to them both. We put this suggestion to Jerry, who accepted the possibility.

Despite these questions we remain convinced that this is a genuine poltergeist case. We have uncovered no evidence that either Jerry or Elizabeth were aware in any detail of hauntings and poltergeists prior to these experiences, yet their story contains many claims that are mirrored in cases down the centuries. Certainly neither Jerry nor Elizabeth seem overly pleased by the attention; they have never wanted us to use their real names and have resisted all media attention. We know for certain that they have never profited by their stories.

In 1995, we asked Jerry to explain how he felt about the intrusions. He explained to us that he thought the poltergeist was ruining their lives, and wondered if they would have any life left at all! They both felt desperate, and wondered if they would ever experience normality again. Elizabeth had been seeing dark apparitional shadows, which she feared might come out and unfold when she opened a cupboard. She often sensed something in the house with her when Jerry was out. He too felt there was something in the house with them, and that it was trying to cause harm. He noticed that, although money had been taken from Elizabeth, the poltergeist took her side in any of their arguments, through the messages they received. Jerry told us, 'Sometimes the abuse I get is just a reflection of her language.' Jerry noticed that after a row the poltergeist seemed to know what had been happening. 'It feels like being watched the whole time.' Elizabeth has said she is much less bothered by the movements of objects than Jerry, and refused to go checking to see what has happened when they have been out, though she notices the differences, of course. Jerry commented, 'Sometimes you laugh it off, sometimes you feel suicidal. How do we feel at the end of the day? We just feel we do not deserve this. Yes, Elizabeth in particular has had traumas, had tragedies in her life. All the more reason for her not to suffer now. Yes, there is tension between us at times – maybe all the time – but it does not mean to say we should be made to suffer this.'

One medium that visited them managed to cheer them up a little. He told them, 'Oh, it tends to be nice people who are afflicted.'

After the above was recorded and written up for this book, Elizabeth tragically died from the sudden onset of cancer. Within weeks of the first diagnosis her condition deteriorated to a terminal level. The poltergeist activity continued up to her death, then ceased abruptly. There was some evidence that it changed its nature during this time; when Elizabeth came home for periods the activity was as before, but in the hospital she had money that did not disappear, and there were only a few small instances of anything strange happening. Perhaps it was the combination of the two people together – as at the house – that really triggered the effects. According to Jerry, whom we interviewed some months after Elizabeth's death, nothing further has happened.

We see, then, in these modern cases, a consistent phenomenon over time. To understand the poltergeist in more detail we shall now look at, and analyse, its specific characteristics.

SECTION TWO

DESCRIBING
THE POLTERGEIST

Chapter 3

Core Phenomena

The presence of certain core (or common) phenomena virtually characterises the poltergeist. All poltergeist disturbances tend to start in a small way, usually with noises, and often grow to a crescendo involving the movement of objects. These two phenomena alone are core characteristics. A third aspect is so commonly present that it deserves inclusion here: that of stone throwing, or lithobolia.

In this and later chapters we shall be examining the manifestations of the poltergeist as they have been experienced and witnessed. These accounts, and the circumstances in which the phenomena occur, confirm in our view that the poltergeist is a reality. We are content to believe that it must operate within our natural laws, of physics and other sciences; however it is obvious that such laws are as yet not fully discovered. In our researches, we have not travelled too far into what would, at this stage, be mere speculation as to how these things happen. What mechanisms allow for the seemingly spontaneous movement of objects, or levitation, or apports, or the host of other extraordinary experiences contained within these chapters, are at best only guessed at. It is clear that such understanding lies in the future, and in the domain of sciences as yet reluctant to take on the examination with vigour.

In the words of Sir William Crookes, talking about the paranormal: 'I never said it was possible. I only said it was true.'

RAPPING AND SCRATCHING NOISES

This is normally the first of the poltergeist manifestations, and the second most common occurrence in poltergeist cases after movement of objects. The noises generally start as scratchings or rappings, and can be heard by everyone in the house. This was true of the Tedworth, Tennessee and Bristol cases. An animal is often considered the cause in the first instance, and the first 'investigation' is often to look for mice, or birds in the attic. In the Amherst case, Esther was convinced there was a mouse under her bedcovers; this assumption may also have led to the disturbances being attributed to an animal in the case of Gef, the Dalby poltergeist.

However, the noises often become so loud that they can be heard from outside the house, and by non-members of the household. In Amherst the loud bangs became a local attraction, with people coming to stand outside the house just to hear them. Sometimes the noises are so loud as to shake the house – or at least to make it feel as if the house is shaking. The 'crack' heard at Dalby was said to have produced this effect; and both Jerry and Elizabeth (at Hertfordshire) reported this separately.

Sometimes the sounds can become positively thunderous. At Cideville in France, in 1850, it is said that 'on some occasions the uproar was deafening, so that it was impossible to stay in the room'.

If the whole neighbourhood hearing the sounds is not proof enough of their objectivity, it should be noted that poltergeist noises have been recorded. At Sauchie, for example, the manifestations were captured on audiotape and film.

The source of the noise is an interesting consideration. They are often thought at first to be coming from the outside surfaces of the house: the walls, doors or roof. The Tedworth case began in this way. As the noises progressed, they seemed to be coming from inside the house.

The poltergeist can also, it seems, mimic noises. Typically, the sound of furniture moving or glass breaking will bring witnesses running to view the chaos, only to find that not a thing is out of place. For example, a South African family in 1901 heard the sound of pots and pans being thrown around, as well as plates being broken in their kitchen at night, but the next day they found everything in its place and no breakages at all. D. Scott Rogo, in *The Poltergeist Experience*, reports that his colleague, Raymond Bayless, was conducting an investigation at an allegedly haunted house when he heard 'what sounded like every dish in the kitchen being broken to bits'. Again, nothing was found damaged. In the Pudsey case the principal witnesses and their guests thought they heard a wardrobe fall on the floor above, but found nothing out of place.

Although 'poltergeist' is commonly translated as 'noisy ghost', not all noisy ghosts are poltergeists. Just as there are visual ghosts, so there are auditory ones. There are many reports of ghostly sounds: voices from the past heard arguing in houses, sounds of battles being replayed long after the event, and so on. These seem to be no more than recordings, but audible rather than visible. The fact that a ghost is noisy does not make it a poltergeist. But how do we differentiate between the two? Probably it is the manifestations of both noise and movement of objects that characterise a poltergeist.

THE SPONTANEOUS MOVEMENT OF OBJECTS

This is the number one event of the poltergeist, so commonly reported that perhaps cases without this phenomenon should not be termed poltergeist. It is impossible to list all the cases and their movements, of course, and many examples will be found throughout this book. The following is a typical account.

York

Don, the manager of a bed shop in York, was not too surprised when some customers complained that they had small coins thrown at them in the upstairs showroom. He was used to it; the shop had been plagued by activity like this for some months. Coins, pens, bulldog clips and staplers had all been flying through the air without apparent cause.

Colin Davies, then an ASSAP investigator, was told of the disturbances by his brother. He spoke to Don, who agreed to an investigation with the proviso that they must not adversely affect the business.

Don told Davies that the first unusual event occurred three months before, when price tickets had seemed to move around on their own. Don hinted that Davies would not have to wait long to see something, as things were now happening daily. He was right. On that first visit Davies was witness to about ten incidents, some of which were very impressive: small items were apparently flying around unaided; as a customer was walking through the shop a marker pen hit a headboard. While Don, Susie (an employee), Davies and the customer were discussing this oddity, two more items fell just outside the office. There was no one else in the shop.

Some fifteen minutes after this, Davies was upstairs when he suddenly felt a shiver and 'knew' that something was about to happen. He moved back downstairs. As he stated in ASSAP's journal *Anomaly* (Issue 8): 'I looked over towards the offices and saw Don in his office on the phone and Susie in her office, writing. Both office doors and windows were closed. [Note: the offices had windows so it was possible to see in with the door closed.] No one else was in the shop. As I was scanning the shop I noticed a marker pen appear about an inch or two below the ceiling. This pen flew across the shop, hugging the ceiling for about ten feet, then arched downwards, hitting a cardboard box. While witnessing this, all my hairs felt like they were standing on end. This was really incredible.' It is very unusual for an investigator to witness an object in motion like this. Quite often the movement of an object is only detected when it is found or heard where 'it should not be'.

Susie, who was by now accustomed to the poltergeist, was not so nervous, and even played games with it. She would put items on her desk and wait to see if any were moved. The objects never moved while she was watching, though they would if she looked away. Sometimes the objects would be thrown in the shop area.

Davies arranged to set up video equipment in the shop to try and record some of the overnight events. During the day before the experiment Davies witnessed some phenomena, similar to what he'd already seen, and set up the equipment with hope of success. Two cameras were recording for nine hours, but unfortunately they did not capture any events. However, minutes after the end of the recording, a pen, a bulldog clip and a plug and lead were seen to move spontaneously. The poltergeist was acting true to type – mischievous and camera-shy.

Few people would buy a bed that might be haunted – so most visitors to the shop were not told of the activity. One salesman, however, interested in what Davies was doing with a camera, was invited to stay around and watch. The man – described by Davies as a 'hardened disbeliever' – wanted proof, and while Susie was talking of past experiences he got it. A small, decorative straw hat slid off a dressing table nearby and dropped on to the floor next to his feet. A number of plastic rods then flew off the filing cabinet and over the salesman's head. The salesman left, apparently impressed by what he saw. Davies was just as impressed.

The telephones in the shop were malfunctioning in a strange manner. Davies, who witnessed some of these problems, spoke later to a service manager for British Telecom. 'I asked him if he would be able to duplicate [the] scenario,' he told us. 'He told me that he could not, as what I had described to him was impossible – but I witnessed it!'

At home, Davies also received some odd calls, and found that his line was sometimes connected to the bed shop – but neither he nor Don had made the calls. Davies had an answerphone, and sometimes heard Don's voice on the machine, saying, 'Hello, The Bed Shop. Can I help you?' Don was apparently answering the same call that was reaching Davies' answerphone.

Don became worried that he was losing business. He turned to the Church for help, and two Anglican priests arrived to give prayers and blessings. As in so many poltergeist cases, this had no effect. Don phoned Davies a couple of days later to report that the problems had not abated.

It is no doubt possible that some of the disturbances were produced deliberately – indeed, they probably were. On one occasion Davies, alert to this possibility and showing admirable objectivity, surreptitiously filmed Susie. He was able to see her cause banging sounds by kicking her desk. (We have also examined the video records, and agree that sometimes she appears to be deliberately causing some of the sounds.) 'Cheating' arises in many cases but, as was apparent in this case, certain phenomena are impossible to fake by 'normal' means under the conditions of observation.

None the less, Susie seems to have quite enjoyed what was happening. Perhaps she also enjoyed the attention it drew from Davies himself, and it is possible she created extra activities to keep him interested. Some of the written messages received seem to emphasise these desires, for example, 'I WANT SUSIE AND COLIN ALONE THEN I WILL GO '. When Davies realised what was going on he decided it was appropriate and responsible to visit the shop less often. The poltergeist activity ended as spontaneously and mysteriously as it had started.

Another workplace incident arose at Air Heating Limited. Employees had to give up trying to work in one of the offices because of poltergeist activity. Mr Caulkett, an executive of the company, spoke to Andrew Green two years after the outbreak.

1. The house in Amherst, Nova Scotia, where Esther Cox and her family lived in the 1870s.

2. Voirrey Irving and her father, with investigator R.S. Lambert at Doarlish Cashen.

3. John Glynn examining the damage to his bedroom in Runcorn, Cheshire

4. Mr Elms and Mr Taylor, of the Bromley poltergeist case. Mr Taylor carries the 14 lb weight which had 'sailed about the room'.

5. Investigator Maurice Grosse with some of the items disturbed at Enfield.

6. Both these matchboxes were scorched yet the matches inside were not set alight. They come from separate poltergeist-infested homes examined by the same investigators.

7. Catherine Kirk together with author Anne Spencer in her home where poltergeist events still occur.

8. Andrew Kirk on a sofa; one of several items of heavy furniture moved during poltergeist disturbances.

Caulkett described how he was originally very sceptical of these two occurrences, but admitted that he became fully convinced a poltergeist had been active in the building. The disturbances included coins being thrown around; telephones knocked to the floor (and constantly needing repair because of this); a tin of paint hurled across the office and spilling its contents on the floor; heavy filing cabinets and a stationery cupboard crashing to the floor; and a very heavy desk moving right across the room. Investigations revealed that a previous owner of the building had conducted seances there. (In our subsequent interview with Canon Carl Garner, he made the point that the holding of seances may well constitute the 'invitation' that can trigger a poltergeist.)

These incidents continued for eight months, even though two 'exorcisms' were carried out by local vicars. The phenomena reduced considerably, though, when one female member of staff left.

There are special features about the movement of objects which are important. For example, things are very seldom *seen* to move; only the fact that they are found in the wrong place makes the occurrence apparent. In the few cases where the object is seen to move it is usually already in motion; in very, very few instances is an object seen to start to move.

The story of the Olive Hill Demon, reported by Roll, is one of those very rare cases.

Olive Hill

In 1968 a poltergeist affected the Callihan family. Tommy and Helen lived with their five children: Beverly (14), Roger (12), two younger brothers and a sister; as well as a teenage girl who had been 'more or less adopted' by the family. She helped Helen to look after the house.

This is an unusual case, where the poltergeist seems to have been 'contracted' from elsewhere. The first manifestations happened to

Tommy's parents and his sister Marcelene. (They had been affected by unusual happenings in two of their previous houses.) It started with a rumbling sound, and the fracturing of glass in a wall-hung picture of Christ; furniture was moved or flung over. Thinking the problem lay in the house, Mr Callihan, his wife and Marcelene moved. But they had hardly unpacked when Mrs Callihan saw an apparition in her bedroom, and objects started moving about.

The case was written up in the local paper, and a psychology student, John P. Stump, went to investigate.

Stump was told that since moving to the new home there had been about ninety incidents, many of which were witnessed by friends (who confirmed this directly to him). The day he arrived was fairly uneventful, but the next morning the poltergeist seemed to be in a mood to show off. Over the next two days, fifty incidents were noted, all while Stump was in the house. Close scrutiny of the disturbances convinced Stump that no one was deliberately causing them.

Occasionally – and this is very rare in poltergeist cases – he had the good fortune to be watching an item as it *started* to move. As was later reported by William Roll: 'On one occasion, while Roger was standing with his grandparents next to the kitchen stove, and John was looking towards the three people and the sink area, which was next to the stove, John saw two bottles and a glass jar containing canned berries, which were standing on the sink unit, move into the sink at the same time, a distance of about two feet.'

(We note that, similarly, during the Seaford case, Mr Herrmann watched as two bottles on a surface started to move – each in a different direction.)

Of a second incident the same day: 'Almost everyone was in the living room, and as Mr Callihan entered the room, looking for a place to sit, John pointed to a vacant chair. At that moment the chair flipped upside down. The closest person was Roger, seated about three feet away, also in John's view. Again, there seemed no way of accounting for this event normally.'

After this, Stump telephoned William Roll, who came to help

the investigation, arriving late on the night of 14 December. After a short time at the house, Roll and Stump went with Tommy and Helen to their home to talk further. After the children were in bed, and the adults were discussing poltergeists and demons, a crash was heard. On going upstairs they found a bowl had fallen from a dresser. Apart from some dubious knocking sounds, this was the first incident to occur at Tommy and Helen's house. There was more to come. The poltergeist continued disturbing furniture, flipping tables around or turning them upside down, often in front of witnesses; even the kitchen stove was found to have moved by six inches.

Helen thought the disturbances were perhaps caused by a demon and that Roll and Stump had brought it with them from Mr and Mrs Callihan's house. She soon asked the investigators to leave, which they did with some regret. The family were Jehovah's Witnesses, and they allowed an exorcism by their local minister, but this was unsuccessful.

Eventually, the family moved away for a while. When they returned, the poltergeist, it seems, had left.

Roll says of the case: 'Though our study of the Olive Hill poltergeist was cut short, it was unique in one respect: it is the only case I know of where two parapsychologists saw the beginning stages of movements of several objects. It was not easy for John and me to believe that we were somehow fooled – or we fooled ourselves – when we saw these objects take off, with nobody near enough to push them, and when we could find no evidence of strings or other gadgets.'

More commonly, though, objects are not seen to move. In the Hertfordshire case, several objects moved virtually every day, and did so for over three years, yet these were only once seen in motion. Mostly the movements seem to have happened when the couple were away from the house. Note that when we have set up recording equipment we have never managed to capture movement –

though twice when equipment has stopped recording movements have taken place shortly thereafter.

The degree of disturbance caused by poltergeists seems almost unlimited. Although in many cases small objects move harmlessly, or only a few objects get broken, sometimes the disruption and damage is extensive. In 1965, the Howell family in Swansea, Wales, fled from their house when furniture and just about everything else in the house was disrupted. Mrs Howell was assailed by two bottles, 'thrown' at her when she walked into her empty kitchen; in fear, she took her children and ran into the street where she met her husband. Immediately he ran into the house and was horrified to find it in a state of almost total destruction. Film taken at the time shows virtually every item of furniture thrown around the rooms; the pictures are reminiscent of bomb-struck houses during the blitz. Mrs Howell said: 'It was terrible, the couch, the television, was just thrown into the middle of the room. When I got upstairs the bedroom was all upside down, my little boy's cot was underneath the bed – if he had been in it he would have been killed. Even the police had to break into the bedroom. It couldn't have been anything human or how could it have got out of the bedroom and down to the kitchen when the police had to break in?'

We can also observe from this case the speed at which poltergeists can 'work'. Presuming the house was in a reasonable state when Mrs Howell was in it, within the few minutes between her leaving and her husband going back in, the whole place was 'turned over'.

Similarly, in 1981 a poltergeist vandalised a house in Bournemouth. Food and furniture were thrown all around the rooms. Photographs taken at the time show virtually nothing in the building left intact.

Thus, poltergeists seem to be unlimited in their degree of movement and their speed; in the following chapter we shall also see that they do not seem to be limited in *what* they can move.

STONE THROWING

Stone throwing in poltergeist cases is so common that, if it must be categorised, it should belong under core phenomena; perhaps it is a sub-set of 'movement of objects'. It may be that stone throwing is common simply because stones are common; the poltergeist seems to use 'local' materials in its manifestations. For example, in one Nottingham garage ball bearings were thrown around, in a Manchester factory steel objects flew through the air, and so on. The stones, though, may have special features. For example, in a continuous bombardment of houses in Birmingham that was investigated by the police, it was they who pointed out that every stone looked as if it had been washed; there was not a trace of dirt on any of them.

Thornton Road, Birmingham

The case that arose in Thornton Road in 1981 involved five houses that were bombarded nearly every night for years. Roof tiles and windows were repeatedly broken, causing costly repairs and necessitating the installation of protective screens. The residents, when they could find no cause for the events, called the police for help. Under the leadership of Chief Inspector Turley, the police went to a great deal of trouble to try and trace a culprit or find a reason. Officers spent nights in the gardens with special equipment and, though the stones continued to arrive, they could not detect who or what had thrown them. Over 3500 man-hours were spent trying to trace the invisible culprit. Turley told a reporter at the time: 'We are completely baffled. We have tried everything we know without being able to find out who is doing this.'

It might be considered that stones, especially those that fall into rooms without openings, are perhaps a part of the apport phenomenon – and, if so, a very large part of it. Apports will be considered in the following chapter.

Stone throwing has a long history. It was reported as early as the Bingen-am-Rhein cases, which occurred in AD 355 and 856.

Port Louis, Mauritius

A typical stone-throwing case is detailed in Mr Cappy Ricks' account of a poltergeist that affected his home, as published in *The Forum* in South Africa. For four days in September 1937, Mr Ricks' home in Port Louis, Mauritius, was disturbed.

The first noted occurrence was on Monday, when a stone landed at the feet of the children's *naneine* (a small Creole girl of about eleven years), which frightened her. During that day forty more stones fell inside the house, and as many outside. The *naneine* was terrified and sent home 'in a state of collapse'.

On Tuesday the bombardment began early in the morning and continued until nightfall, even though the house was now being watched by the police. Stones were not the only projectiles; among the other items was an iron shackle from the courtyard.

On Wednesday more stones arrived. This time Mr Ricks was hit on the shoulder by one, six pounds in weight. In addition, the cook had a dish broken in her hands by a large steel nut falling in the kitchen.

The family were now afraid. Mrs Ricks, their baby, and two servants left to stay with her mother. But the disturbances followed them. They moved on to a friend's house but stones started to smash items there. Eventually Mr Ricks took his family to a hotel. In all, an estimated 300 stones fell that day.

Mr Ricks returned home, where he saw a large stone raise itself five feet in the air, and move off in the direction of the *naneine*. Inside the house he watched a stone heading for himself; it swerved as he was about to catch it and broke some glassware. It was now that he realised the disturbances happened only when the *naneine* was around, and decided she would have to leave.

On Thursday many apports arrived early (as did the *naneine*), and before leaving for his office Mr Ricks piled them on the bed (with a note for a police inspector he had summoned): fourteen stones, up to five pounds in weight, an unripe melon and a quantity of reglisse seeds. Soon after arriving at the office he received a telephone call; apparently much of his home had been wrecked. Many breakable items had been smashed, curtains had been pulled down, and other objects strewn about. Mr Ricks received another call – this time from the hotel – asking him to remove his family at once. He collected them in the car and drove home to find a thousand spectators around his house. He sent them, and the *naneine*, away – and the troubles ceased. It seems fair to assume that the *naneine* was the focus.

In the area of Warren Springs, near Harare, Zimbabwe, many of the homes were built on the site of an old graveyard. During 1983 several people reported that their homes were being haunted by the spirits of those buried below them; the reports included showers of stones and movements of furniture.

In the attacks on Maria Jose Ferreira at Jabuticabal, Brazil, masonry and stones from the house spontaneously flew around, some hitting the girl. The poltergeist had another trick in store: during lunch, 'a stone descended from the ceiling and split into two parts, proceeding in different directions as they fell to the floor'. Needless to say, when put back together they matched, but 'they seemed to snap together as if magnetically attracted to each other'.

In another case from Brazil, a party of six were driving down a road a few miles from the federal capital, Brasilia, when their car overheated. They got out to inspect the engine, and they were suddenly set on by stones flying at them – seemingly from an empty landscape. They managed to reach a police station, and an officer returned to the site with three of the original witnesses – only to be set upon himself by spontaneous showers of stones.

Sumatra

Some instances of stone throwing are very strange in nature, as is this next case.

A report of a stone-throwing poltergeist was sent to the SPR by a Mr Grottendieck, relating his own experience while staying in Sumatra. Certain features of the movements of these stones reveal something of the extraordinary nature of the poltergeist.

Grottendieck and his servant boy were the only people in the house, which was surrounded by jungle. He awoke one night to find small stones falling in his bedroom. After waking the boy and sending him to search the house and surrounding jungle, Grottendieck attempted to catch the stones as they fell, but could not: 'I could never catch them; it seemed to me that they changed their direction in the air as soon as I tried to get hold of them.' He also noted that the stones dropped unusually slowly – almost hovering, before hitting the ground with an exceptionally loud bang – and were warm to the touch.

Grottendieck examined the roof (made of leaves), and found no way the stones could have passed through – yet they continued to do so. The boy returned, looked into the room, and fled into the jungle, never to return.

But Mr Grottendieck was made of stronger stuff, and slept. The next morning he checked the stones were still there. He also found five empty cartridges from a rifle he had fired in the night to frighten anyone hiding; this assured him he had not dreamt the mysterious happenings. He was quite certain that the boy could not have thrown the stones, as he was watching him at the time the stones were falling.

(Something of the strange way in which people deal with experiences of the paranormal is revealed by Mr Grottendieck's summary comment: 'The worst part of this strange fact was that my boy was gone, so that I had to take care of breakfast myself, and did not get a cup of coffee nor toast!')

One of the most famous stone-throwing cases was reported in November 1962 in the *Los Angeles Times*. Again, something of the unique nature of the poltergeist is offered by this account.

Big Bear City

The report stated that a home in Big Bear City had, for the last four months, been pelted with stones. The stones had started falling soon after a family had moved in. They were, typically, of the local variety, 'not unlike other stones in the vicinity', and they felt warm when picked up. But in this case they were seen strangely floating down. In most poltergeist attacks of this sort the stones are described as 'pelting', 'whizzing', or 'ricocheting'. 'Floating gently' is certainly not normal.

Another bizarre characteristic is revealed by the comment of the sheriff who witnessed some of the occurrences. He claimed that 'they didn't make enough noise'. When stones hit a police car, the 'injury to the car was much less than it should have been, considering the size of the rock and its fall'. The sheriff also noted that the stones 'seemed to follow the occupant's children wherever they went'.

The bombardment continued after the family had left and new tenants were in the building; indeed, the second family helped the first to move out – during which time stones were falling around them.

Ghostwatch vigil, London

We once spent the night in a large public building in London. One of the phenomena that occurred that night was stone throwing. Three investigators, including John (Spencer), were stationed together on a landing. At 10.52 p.m. they all heard a loud bang and searched around for the cause. They soon discovered a pebble on the landing, by a locked door. They were all certain it had not been there before, as it stood out very obviously on the empty floor. One investigator, Adam Bailey, was convinced that it had just missed him.

At 11.15 a change of locations was suggested. Immediately, another stone hit a wall, and was spotted still rolling. Moments later an investigator was hit; this pebble was found on the staircase.

Shortly after that another one just missed the same person. Other stones fell throughout the night. At 12.32 a.m., John saw one ricocheting off the wall towards him; he grabbed it as it rolled near him. It was very hot indeed. The angle of its flight suggested it had come from more or less above his own position, or the corridor behind (which had no one in it). All three investigators were certain no one else had entered the area or could have had access to it.

Two other stones were 'received' by other investigators that night, in other areas of the building.

Adam observed that just before each stone arrived there was a 'zinging' sound from the ceiling; John agreed that he too had heard that sound.

During the same period, Anne (Spencer) was part of another watch team at another station in the building; this team heard the sounds of small objects falling, but these were untraced.

Chapter 4

Special Effects

As the previous chapter states, the poltergeist can be characterised by the creation of sounds and the movement of objects. But it can be incredibly imaginative in its array of manifestations; in once sense it seems to be only as limited as the human imagination.

This chapter describes the most common of the 'non-core' manifestations. They do not appear in all cases, but they have occurred with some frequency in reports from around the world and throughout the poltergeist's long recorded history. They are manifestations that also arise outside the purview of the poltergeist, but within the realm of the paranormal.

APPARITIONS
Apparitions have been seen in several poltergeist cases. They are sometimes of people, and sometimes animals. There are also frequent reports of 'misty shapes' or ill-defined forms (in the Hertfordshire case, Elizabeth saw a frightening black shadow when she was in the kitchen).

Perhaps the most striking 'shapeless apparition' was reported in the Runcorn poltergeist case of 1952.

Runcorn

At the Jones family home in Runcorn lived Samuel Jones, aged sixty-eight, and his grandson, sixteen-year-old John Glynn, with whom he shared a bed. There was also Jones' sister-in-law Lucy, who shared a bed with John Glynn's sister Eileen. Other rooms were occupied by non family members. The first poltergeist noises and movements occurred in Jones' bedroom, and seemed to centre around his dressing table. Over the course of time there were many witnesses, and all agreed they could find no explanation for the (usual range of) phenomena: bangings and scrapings; the movement of objects, including bibles, other books and a clock thrown around the room; and furniture smashed. The bed did not escape attention, and one night Glynn and Jones were thrown out of it. Poltergeistery was also reported in Glynn's mother's home nearby.

It was also a responsive poltergeist. One witness, a Mrs E. Dowd, remarked, 'I don't think it will throw anything at me,' to be answered by a book flung straight in her face. When the Reverend Stevens called to the poltergeist, 'If you can hear me, knock three times,' the dressing table shook violently three times.

It could be shy too, and would sometimes refuse to co-operate in light conditions – although some movements of objects were caught by lights suddenly turned on, impressing all witnesses (including church representatives and newspaper reporters who were investigating the case).

The *Runcorn Guardian* editorials stated: 'The manifestations . . . this week have reached proportions that settle any dispute as to their reality. Too many independent witnesses have been present, on too many occasions – apart from our own representative. Two psychic researchers ([from] a body of investigators well known for their logical, not to say sceptical approach), three Methodist ministers and at least two police officers are among these witnesses. Phenomena have occurred in the presence of all these witnesses under conditions precluding the possibility of fraud without their connivance.'

The happenings ceased after about three months. However, it is another part of the story that is perhaps the most fascinating – though whether it can truly be called a poltergeist is difficult to say.

Jones worked on a nearby farm, employed to look after the farmer's fifty-three pedigree pigs. About a week before the disturbances one of the pigs had died. Within a few days several more had died, but the veterinary surgeons could not offer an explanation. Within a fortnight (and now coincidental with the activity in the house) all fifty-three pigs had died without explanation. The farmer stated that, two days after the last pig died, he saw what he described as 'a black cloud' moving around in the yard. He described it as seven feet high, shapeless, but with two prongs sticking out of it. He watched it enter the pigsties and seem to search around. He also saw it in his kitchen on another occasion, and his wife later told him that she had seen the same thing, this time following Jones around. Some poltergeist noises and movement had been noted at the farmhouse too.

On one occasion, when the farmer visited Jones in his 'haunted' bedroom, he saw the same shape on the bed used by Jones and Glynn. The last time the cloud appeared at the farmhouse it was attacked by two dogs; it then rose into the air, never to be seen again.

Interestingly, it appears that animals were reported more in the past than in this century. Animal forms were reported at Willington Mill in the mid-nineteenth century – large white cats, donkeys, monkeys, as well as the misty and luminous form of a human figure. At Epworth, Emilia Wesley wrote in 1716/17: '. . . something was thrice seen. The first time by my mother, under my sister's bed, like a badger, only without any head that was discernible. The same creature was sat by the dining-room fire one evening; when our man went into the room, it run up by him, through the hall under the stairs . . . The last time he saw it in the kitchen, like a white rabbit . . .' At Tedworth, in the 1660s (see Chapter One), an animal was heard, described as 'like a Dog out of Breath'. It was cornered in a linen bag – which was leaping around as if it did indeed contain a real animal – but nothing was found when the bag was opened.

And of course we have the story of Gef, the extraordinary talking mongoose.

When poltergeist events were thought to be the product of witchcraft the sighting of an animal was often expected, because animals were commonly thought to be the form taken by 'familiars' sent by witches to do their bidding.

The move to increased numbers of humanoid apparitions may be because of a general interest in spiritualism, or the belief in ghosts as surviving spirits of deceased people – which for many is an explanation of the poltergeist. Perhaps the scratching and banging noises of early cases naturally led families to expect to find an animal; and perhaps this expectation made 'fleeting glimpses' seem to be just that. Any sighting of a small animal within the environment of poltergeist activity could cause the two to be linked. Nowadays, the association of the poltergeist with 'the dead' has changed our expectations. It is also worth considering that, if a place is thought to be 'haunted', it is more likely that an apparition will be seen.

It is understandable that a variety of paranormal phenomena experienced at the same time are going to be grouped together – if only under the 'unexplained' umbrella. But it is worth pointing out that the human-like apparitions seen in poltergeist cases are usually more of the non-interactive type of ghost, and are very rarely seen throwing things around (which would provide a more obvious link to poltergeist activity). There is a report from 1910 of 'Aunt Leah', who appeared to her nephew the Reverend Tweedale, and was seen taking an object out of his wife's hand. The case involved poltergeist disruptions that are attributed – rightly or wrongly – to the deceased lady. (In the same case an apparitional dog rang a dinner gong.) But such cases are rare. In the Pontefract case (see p. 175) apparitions were reported, but when Diane was being pulled up the stairs by something apparently pulling her clothing, the assailant was not visible.

Apparitions rarely talk. Below, we have included the Berini case as the single example we found of poltergeistery linked with talking apparitions – but it must be considered that the poltergeist activity 'proper' started after the apparitions were seen and heard.

Grant, New England

A case involving apparitions arose in Grant, New England, in 1979. The case was investigated by William Roll and Steven Tringale of the Psychical Research Foundation of North Carolina.

Joe and Rose Berini lived with two teenage children (John and Daisy) from Rose's previous marriage. The family were troubled by the apparition of a small boy dressed in white, and the voice of a young girl calling herself Serena. Joe's father had had a sister called Serena, who had died when just five years old, and the boy was thought to be Giorgio, who would have been Joe's uncle, but who died aged eight.

The disturbances started in May 1979, when Mrs Berini heard the sound of a child crying in the house, and the words, 'Mama, Mama, it is Serena.' This occurred several times, and was also heard by her husband, who confirmed with his father that Serena was the name of his deceased sister. The following night one of Mrs Berini's children nearly died as a result of an anaesthetic mistake during an operation.

When the voice was heard again in June 1979, it preceded a stroke which afflicted Mr Berini's grandmother; it was apparently heard again the night before her death in November.

On 9 March 1981 Mrs Berini was at home with her two children; her husband was on night-shift at a factory. In the early hours of the morning she saw the figure of a small boy. 'It was dressed in a white shirt, white pants and white shoes.' She guessed his age to be eight or nine. Mr Berini and Mrs Berini's daughter also saw this apparition, which started to appear frequently. This young boy –

that Joe thought was the deceased twin of his uncle Carlos –
appeared (and sometimes spoke) as often as three times a week. He
seemed to be trying to get help – he would ask, 'Where do all the
lonely people go? Where do I belong?'

The more traditional poltergeist activity started after this.
Things in the house started to move; the telephone rose from its
table and was thrown across the room; whenever Joe mentioned
Giorgio on the telephone the line would go dead. Taking advice
from a priest, the Berinis tried to ignore the ghost, but other
happenings then occurred: doors would slam, footsteps were
heard, and Rose had a packet of macaroni forced from her hands.
Again the family asked for help, and a mass and blessings were
conducted in the house.

The apparition of the boy was seen less and less frequently, but
another took his place – and this one was quite disturbing. It was
humanoid, but a short, hunched, grotesque figure clad in black,
with very large feet that seemed quite demonic. It spoke of 'really
disgusting things', principally sexual. With its arrival, the poltergeist activity increased. The telephone was still being thrown
about, but many other objects were now also disturbed: furniture
was overturned; small objects were broken; Joe, Rose and her son
John were all hit by flying dishes among other things.

Rose was attacked. On one occasion, her arm was twisted
behind her back and her head pushed to one side, causing her to
choke and turn blue. On several nights, Joe saw his wife pulled
from the bed and dropped to the floor. Rose found marks and
bruises on her body. On one occasion she found gouge marks and
an upside-down cross scratched into her back.

One day in August 1981, soon after Joe had left for his night work,
Rose had perhaps the most frightening time of all. As she later
reported: 'The walls started to bang and the bed was raising off the
floor. I tried to scream and the door slammed so I could not get out of
the room.' At one moment the door opened and Rose rushed out, but
she was dragged back by an unseen force. Somehow she managed to

phone Joe, who rushed home to find his wife huddled in a corner, holding a crucifix and some holy water, while their bed was still lifting off the floor.

The Berinis' priest performed an exorcism in the house, after which the Berinis found a carving knife mysteriously stuck into the kitchen table. It seems though that the exorcism was successful; the family saw no more apparitions or poltergeist activity.

It is unusual for apparitions to be the first manifestation of a poltergeist; but it is possible that seeing them opens up some channel of awareness, or in some way extends an invitation or 'psychic pathway', which encourages the later occurrence of a poltergeist.

West Norwood

A poltergeist that attracted a good deal of attention from the press and the local community arose in Langmead Street, West Norwood. It was a 'typical' case, but the apparitional content was unusually high.

The house was occupied by Mr and Mrs Greenfield (Senior), their sons Cecil and Dennis, Dennis' wife Gladys, Gladys' mother, and two young children, Gordon (8) and Patricia (14).

The phenomena started with unidentifiable scratching noises, gradually getting louder. Later the noises were thought to be footsteps, 'like something walking on the ceiling'. These sounds continued, unusually, for around four years.

Then, one day, Cecil saw the apparition of a grey-white adult figure ascending the stairs towards him. The face was unclear, and Cecil had only the impression of arms folded across the breast. Cecil claimed he felt a coldness, and 'a sort of electric vibration'. When he screamed, the apparition vanished. Five days later Dennis and Gladys saw the same figure, standing a few stairs up. They too were unable to make out the features of the face. They ran to a neighbour, and the figure was gone when they returned. Later, Patricia saw the same figure.

The poltergeistery had stepped up somewhat, to include bangs and crashes, groaning noises and strange lights. The family called in the police. Several times officers examined the house, and on one occasion they heard noises and saw some objects moving. Police Inspector Sidney Candler said, 'I was sceptical when I received the first report of the matter, but after interviewing the Greenfields I am convinced something strange is happening.'

By the end of that summer new apparitions were appearing; for example, Cecil saw a figure standing by his bed, which disappeared after he had hidden beneath the bedclothes for a time.

The case died away, as these things do, and the next family to live in the house reported no disturbances, even though they were well aware of the notoriety of the place from the press coverage.

Sometimes an apparition is of a living person. In Cideville in 1850, a man named Thorel appears to have been seen in bi-location; the 'victim' reported being haunted by a spectre, and later identified Thorel – still alive, of course, at the time – as that spectre.

More recently, in the Enfield case, one witness visiting the house appears to have seen investigator Maurice Grosse in bi-location. As Maurice described it: 'I was upstairs in a bedroom with some of the family, including the girl who was the main subject of the investigation . . . there was a knock on the front door, downstairs. I asked the mother to go downstairs and open the door, which she did. It was her niece. She was indignant, and asked, "Why didn't he open the door?" Asked who she meant, the niece said, "Mr Grosse." . . . She explained that she had knocked on the door, and nobody had answered; then she had knocked again. She told us, "Then the curtain was pulled aside and you [Maurice] looked out of the downstairs window. I expected you to open the door, but you didn't. I looked through the door [the window pane and the letter box] and I could see you going up the stairs, but I could only see the lower part of you." ' Maurice confirmed that he had been upstairs for over an hour, that there had been no one else in the house that could have been mistaken for him, and no one was downstairs at the time.

Apparitions may be an illusion, but poltergeist activity is certainly not. The connection is unclear: if they are *not* illusions, then they lead to the possibility that they are a part of the poltergeist phenomenon; if on the other hand they are, then they may be created by an imagination fired by fear or wonder at the poltergeist. Or perhaps the factor in the mental state of witnesses that 'allows' the poltergeist to infest or arise also 'switches on' other perceptions, inducing sightings of genuine, but unconnected, haunting phenomena.

APPORTS

Another common feature of poltergeists is the appearance of objects (apports) and the disappearance of objects (which we call 'disapports'). We might define an apport, provisionally at least, as 'the spontaneous appearance of objects that have either moved through a solid barrier (such as a wall) or materialised within a room, etc.'. The presumption is that it is not known where the object has come from – if it were known, then the phenomenon would probably be regarded as teleportation. Either way, the same 'mechanism' may be at play in each case.

Apporting is a phenomenon reported by mediums, and features often in physical mediumship. (Notably, many poltergeist victims are said to have mediumistic qualities.) Mrs Forbes, investigated by Nandor Fodor, produced many alleged apports. Unfortunately, she was found to be cheating on later occasions, which rightly means that her manifestations should be regarded with caution – but we should also be wary of ignoring the true phenomena just because she may have felt under some sort of pressure to 'perform'. Some of her apports would have been difficult to fake and would certainly have taken some planning, such as the appearance of Roman pottery. And what drew Fodor's attention to Mrs Forbes in the first place was well-witnessed poltergeistery that seemed quite genuine.

In the Hertfordshire case, apports (and disapports) were very common – even sometimes useful. Their victims received food, ornaments, jewellery, and small gifts placed under their pillows; but they also lost similar objects and frequently money. In the Cardiff case, coins and paper money appeared regularly, to John and Pat in the workshop, and now to Fred and Gerry in their home.

Matthew Manning, whose Cambridgeshire home was for some time affected by poltergeist activity, discovered a few apports. The most unusual was probably bread rolls, one of which was tested and determined to have been baked over a hundred years before.

A very specific apport, which would seem to indicate the involvement of teleportation, arose in the Poona case that surrounded the child Damodar. So many toys were appearing under his mosquito net that he became afraid to use the net. Despite this, he was still subject to several of his toys being 'thrown' at him even though they had been inside a closed wooden toy box. In order to stop this happening, a heavy dictionary was placed on the lid, but toys from within still assailed Damodar and Miss Kohn – who slept in the same room and looked after him. The case records an alleged apport (or teleportation) over considerable distance: a jar Damodar had left at school was suddenly 'flung' into his bedroom at home.

Even more striking was the 1948 case reported by Professor Hans Bender. The witness collected up objects that had been apporting within the house, put them in a box, closed the lid and sat on it. The same items started falling from the ceiling; when the witness opened the box it was empty. This is reminiscent of the Pontefract case, where eggs were apporting. Jean Pritchard took all the eggs out of the fridge, put them in a wooden box and sat on it, but eggs continued to appear in mid-air and were found to be missing from the box. This continued until the eggs were all broken on the floor and the box was empty.

BLOOD

Sometimes the manifestations of the poltergeist imply something to be feared rather than being fearful in their own right. Such is the case of the unusual and rather macabre spontaneous appearance of blood, sometimes in alarming quantities.

In a house in Abidjan, Ivory Coast, in March 1985, blood was found covering clothing, and in pots and pans. Blood spurted from the walls, and while people were walking around the house bloody footprints would appear. No one in the house was in any way injured; and no explanation for the blood was forthcoming.

Mr William Winston and his wife found blood in their home in Atlanta, Georgia, in 1987. Although the couple were type A, the blood found was type O. Blood was found on the walls and floors, and on one occasion Mrs Winston found the bathroom floor covered in blood when getting out of the bath.

During a poltergeist outbreak in St Quentin, France, in January 1986, droplets of blood appeared on the walls, carpets and a bed.

The spontaneous appearance of blood is a rare phenomenon of which we could find few cases, and it is interesting that these cases occurred within three years of each other, though spread around the world. But there have been one or two other connections. Blood was found on the hall table, for example, in the North Aston case outlined in Chapter One. According to Colin Parsons, in *Encounters with the Unknown*, in the mid-1950s Jim and Susan Barker, in their caravan, were affected by a poltergeist experience that included a loud voice, dirt tipped into the caravan, even a bed soaked with the contents of a cesspit. Later, Susan and Jim saw blood pour through the join between the wall and the ceiling in the caravan's living room. The amount of blood was estimated to be about ten gallons (how accurate this is we cannot confirm), and when tested it was shown to have originated from a pig.

FIRES

The Stephen King story *Carrie* is brought to mind when considering the case of a twelve-year-old boy, Willie Brough, who was expelled from school in 1886 after fires were said to have been caused 'by his glance'. He was no longer welcomed at home, and was sent to live on a farm. When he moved to a new school the fires continued there.

Fires during poltergeist activity have been widely reported. The following cases show the diversity of such claims. Just as poltergeists seem able to mimic noises, they can also sometimes mimic visual effects. In the North Aston case, outlined in Chapter One, the whole house was seen to be filled with fire, but there was no burning.

Ramos

In 1989, spontaneous fires broke out around thirteen-year-old Sara at her home in a slum area in central Brazil. She was the oldest of five children who lived with their father and his parents. The children's mother had left the family.

The day before the first fire, Sara had been beaten by her grandmother, Mrs Cardoso, for visiting friends instead of going to church, and for staying out till midnight. This was the first time Sara had been punished by her grandmother in this way, and it has been speculated that it was the shock of this treatment that resulted in the fires.

The next night Sara dreamt of the Devil, who said he would burn and kill her. When she and her grandmother returned to her bed later it was found to be scorched. Mrs Cardoso used a non-flammable oil from the church to anoint the bed. Shortly afterwards, they heard an explosion from inside the mattress and it started to burn. 'There was,' said Mrs Cardoso, 'nobody near the bed when it happened.'

After that first day many fires broke out. It is said that all the clothes in the wardrobe were burned; even wet towels were twice set alight. An explosion was heard coming from a bundle of clothes on the sofa, and was witnessed by Mrs Cardoso and her neighbour, Mrs de Sousa.

Inspectors from the electric company found no electrical fault in the house, and a fireman that was interviewed said he could not explain the fires technically. A Catholic priest visited the house and performed an exorcism; he also suggested that Sara stay elsewhere for a time.

Sara was away for three days, during which time no phenomena occurred. But when she returned the fires started again. Mrs Cardoso had been an eye-witness to some of the spontaneous ignitions, and knew that Sara had not started them with her own hands – but she did realise that somehow the fires were connected to Sara. Thus, she no longer wanted the girl in her house. Sara went to stay for a short time with her maternal grandmother, where fires are also believed to have erupted spontaneously. Only when she eventually moved in with Mrs de Sousa did the phenomena cease. Whether the poltergeist had run its natural course – or whether the change to Mrs de Sousa's care was instrumental – is unknown.

Talladega, Alabama

Twenty-two fires in just a few days during 1959 forced a Talladega family to move from their home. The pyrotechnics followed them however, with five fires starting in their new home. While the police were investigating they noticed a quilt hanging outside had started to burn – but when they tested its flammability by trying to light the material with matches, they could not do it. The activities came to an end as suddenly as they had started. An interesting footnote to the case was provided by a nine-year-old boy in the family, who confessed to starting the fires with matches. But the fire marshal and subsequently the court did not believe him.

Sheffield

One case involving fire hints at the possibility that a poltergeist saved lives. Derek Newman and his family suffered disturbances and noises from a poltergeist for over a year. Then, one night in 1982, the family was woken by an incredible noise, as if someone was 'going round the lounge with a hammer'. Derek got up and opened the bedroom door – and found the house filled with smoke. The Newmans called the fire service, and the whole family was rescued from their burning house.

Derek believes that, had the poltergeist not woken them, they could all have perished in the fire. Given what we know from other cases, though, we are forced to raise the question of whether the poltergeist could have been responsible for the fire in the first place.

Fires have been involved in poltergeist activities since the earliest cases. They are a feature of reports from Bingen, Utrecht, the Dagg case, the Teed case, and the Tedworth Poltergeist. In the Teed case, the poltergeist threatened to set fire to the house before dropping lighted matches on to a bed. They still occur in more modern disturbances, such as Jabuticabal, the Guarulhos case, and at Enfield. In our own study of 136 recent examples, twenty-nine have contained the eruption of fires, mainly small (poltergeists do not generally burn down their own homes!).

The nature of the fires at Enfield is interesting. In 1977, while investigating the case, Maurice Grosse visited another home in Holloway where poltergeist activity had been reported. It included cushions flying through the air, fruit lifting itself from the bowl, and spontaneous fires that had erupted many times. The fire brigade had been called out frequently, but had found no explanation. A box of matches that had been scorched did not catch fire; but clothing, the bedspread, newspapers and a dishcloth had all been burned or scorched. There was also a burn mark found on a wall, with a melted plastic beaker next to it. Grosse interviewed a fireman, who told him, 'In my six years' experience I've never seen anything like it.'

It was shortly after this visit that the first fires erupted in Enfield.

Smoke was seen to come from a cupboard; inside, a box of matches was found charred. Other items were also found burned: pieces of paper, cloths and money. The investigators were forced to question the connection between the two cases, and wondered if the poltergeist was in some way contagious.

Italy

In December 1983 Carol Compton, a Scottish nanny working in Italy, was brought to trial on charges of arson and attempted murder. She had worked in three different homes, and over that period five fires had broken out in the houses (along with various other poltergeist phenomena). As the only link the Italian police could identify, she was arrested and charged. A Professor Vitolo gave evidence, stating that he had never seen such fires before; he was sure they were not caused by a naked flame, but by intense heat. No inflammable materials were located; the pattern of the fires could not be replicated in experiments; Compton had never been caught or seen starting the fires; and she denied having done so.

Despite this, she was found guilty of arson, though the attempted murder charge was dropped. Her sentence was covered by the time she had been held in custody.

Fires could be regarded as a form of assault; certainly they have the potential to be dangerous. Jan and Brian Neven from Daly City, whose case is outlined in the next chapter, found that soon after the birth of their son a poltergeist became active, and most frighteningly took to setting fire to the baby's crib. One crib was ignited several times, and a new one was incinerated on the day it was brought into the nursery.

Such an attack on a baby leads to an important observation about fires in poltergeist cases. They are the one manifestation of the poltergeist that cannot be ignored. A family might attempt to deal with a poltergeist by ignoring, say, moving cutlery, but faced with the outbreak of fire they have to react. Perhaps this attention-seeking is part of the *modus operandi* of the poltergeist.

WATER

Water is a frequent aspect of the poltergeist (earning the nick-name 'pooltergeists' in certain cases). Water has appeared in pools, sometimes in strange shapes, or bursting from walls. Though it seems difficult to draw conclusions from our observations we have noticed a cultural factor that may be relevant: at least since 1950 fire and water have often been reported in the same cases, except in South America (where there are a lot of poltergeist reports involving fires, but no water manifestations).

Jerry and Elizabeth from Hertfordshire (whose case is detailed in Chapter Two) experienced wet patches on the floor and walls and in a cupboard. They called in a plumber, who could not explain where it was coming from. The most unexplainable effect was when the couple watched as one of Elizabeth's shoes filled with water from no visible source.

In the Pontefract case, which arose in the 1960s and was investigated by Colin Wilson and detailed in his book *Poltergeist*, some of the earliest manifestations were pools of water, which appeared in the kitchen and had an unusually neat outline. When the first was mopped up another would appear. When the linoleum on which they were forming was pulled up, the floor underneath was dry. The water board was called in, but could not identify a source.

The Martin family of Massachusetts were plagued in 1963 by a poltergeist that squirted water from their walls. The case was followed up by Raymond Bayless. Mrs Martin explained: 'The water jets out for about twenty seconds, and then there will be a fifteen-minute interval and it starts someplace else . . . There's a little tremor and then a whoosh and then the water.' The family had first noticed a wet patch on the wall, heard a popping sound, and water then gushed from the spot. This continued for days, until the family thought it best to leave – but typically the poltergeist followed them to a relative's house, where it continued to squirt water until they returned to their own home. Even after the water supply to the house was cut off and the pipes drained, the water kept on coming.

Thus far we have identified that the poltergeist has a predilection for stones (earth), fire, water, and perhaps air (in the apports/disapports phenomenon). These are the four basic elements as identified in, say, Wicca (a pagan religion), which is centred on nature. We are not suggesting any direct mystical connection, but the evidence could be taken to imply that the poltergeist is a thing of nature.

ELECTRICAL INTERFERENCES

If poltergeists are adept at using the elements of nature, they have also shown themselves no less capable of handling the intricacies of the modern world. Perhaps they have always been this adaptable. Once they may have got the attention of our early ancestors by banging axes and clubs, then they rang the servants' bells, now they ring the telephone. Indeed, they seem quite at home disturbing electrical equipment.

Interference with the telephone is probably the most common poltergeist-related electrical effect. In the Cardiff case, John and Pat received telephone calls at their home only to find that the line was dead, and British Telecom could not offer an explanation. The calls later started to be received at the 'affected' workplace. Similarly, Jerry in the Hertfordshire case received 'dead' calls at work, then at home. During a vigil at his house, we received several such calls ourselves. In the York case the telephone lines in the shop were malfunctioning in a way that defied their own technology; once again, the service manager for British Telecom could offer no explanation. At home the investigator also received strange calls, finding himself connected to the bed shop.

The most famous electrical and telephone disturbance is probably that of the Rosenheim poltergeist (see Chapter Twelve), where the telephone switchboard was apparently calling the speaking clock. The itemised read-out of the calls showed that the dialling times were faster than would have been humanly possible.

In the Pudsey case, Catherine Kirk told us that, within a few months, virtually every piece of electrical equipment in the house malfunctioned.

Canon Carl Garner told us of an event that took place in a parish mission in Africa. He was assisting one or two white Europeans, who wanted to break out of what they called a 'coven'. They had been into seances, trying to put spells on people and so on. Canon Garner explained: 'While we were praying with one of them, the organ started to play. The only trouble is that the organ was electronic and it was closed – and it wasn't even plugged in!'

Equipment – often the investigators' – has a high rate of failure in poltergeist cases. We have suffered this several times: with normally reliable dictaphones not recording when the indicators say they are; video camera lighting failing in certain 'haunted' areas; an environmental monitoring unit malfunctioning during an investigation, and so on. We have suffered lights and equipment blowing in our own house during poltergeist investigations. (To illustrate the theory of the 'contagion' of poltergeists, one of the effects we noted was an electrical switch on our own cooker changing position while no one was near it. We had just returned from a poltergeist investigation.)

The Enfield case contained a great many electrical disturbances: the cameras of a professional photographer not working (to his great surprise); the tape recorder of a BBC reporter malfunctioning, to say nothing of the investigators' own machines. One or two of these cases of interference are worthy of some attention.

When the BBC reporter's cassette machine malfunctioned they replaced it with a Uher reel-tape recorder, 'one of the BBC's best machines' at that time. It malfunctioned immediately. BBC engineer Don Hitch had never encountered such a malfunction before and commented, 'As far as I am concerned, this particular incident remains unexplained.'

When Professor John Hasted visited the house, a light bulb

broke 'in an unusual way'. Hasted, a physicist, examined the bulb and commented that the break was 'very rare'. Playfair comments: 'It is strange that this happened in the presence of an investigator who would have thought of examining the bulb,' and adds, 'I found myself again reminded of a thought that had occurred to me early in the case: were we investigating a poltergeist, or was it investigating us?'

Perhaps the answer to Playfair's question came much earlier in the case. The team obtained the use of a Pye Newvicon camera and recorder. It failed as it was set up. The fault was rare, and Pye's senior operators were surprised by the failure. Maurice Grosse commented: 'We've got a mechanically minded spook on our hands.' Did Grosse himself see the connection? He is an engineer of some considerable reputation himself – and he was principal investigator of the case.

LEVITATION OF PEOPLE

Levitate: to rise and float in the air in defiance of gravity. The phenomenon has been reported in religious mysticism, and occasionally in poltergeist cases.

Wycliffe Road, London

Wycliffe Road in London was, in 1956, the scene of some poltergeist activity which surrounded Shirley Hitchins, a fifteen-year-old girl who lived with her parents, and who worked in a department store. One morning Shirley woke to discover a shiny new key on her bed. She had never seen the key before and it did not fit any locks in the home. (The key, it seems, was an apport; an unusual start for a poltergeist.) Soon after this, Shirley found her bedcovers being pulled off during the night, and heard loud knocking sounds from her bedroom walls. Noises were also heard during the day, mainly scratching and tapping. Large pieces of furniture began to move about. The poltergeist, after its curious start, was now following a more traditional route of manifestation.

Shirley was losing sleep. She moved to a neighbour's house in an attempt to avoid the trouble but, as in so many cases, the trouble went with her. In the neighbour's house a clock and some ornaments were moved. Shirley's wristwatch was yanked from her, and a poker was thrown across the room.

Back at home one night, in an attempt to discover the cause of these disturbances, Shirley's parents and an uncle watched over her. After a quiet start they heard tapping noises and the bed began to shake. Shirley, who was awake, told them her covers were being pulled from her. The two men took hold of the covers and could feel the force pulling. They had to struggle to keep hold of them.

Suddenly Shirley's body became stiff and – in front of the witnesses – she gently rose and floated six inches above the bed. The men took hold of her and lifted her from this position and away from the bed. Shirley described the levitation later as feeling like a great pressure on her lower back.

This night was perhaps the climax of events. Subsequently, Shirley continued to be troubled by rapping sounds but the other activity was over. The raps were heard wherever she went. At work she was persuaded to see the doctor, who was at first sceptical but then heard the rapping noises in his own room, which convinced him 'something was going on', although he did not know what.

A medium, Harry Hanks, visited the home and made contact with a spirit, who told him that the poltergeist would not trouble Shirley any more. The disturbances had lasted for exactly one month.

This fairly typical case contains one of the most unusual aspects: levitation, the lifting of a person. Objects have often been seen to rise into the air without apparent cause, but a person being lifted by a poltergeist is nowadays almost unheard of.

Stories of levitation are more commonly associated with religious phenomena, and are reported by Christians (most Catholics), Moslems, Shamans and non-Western mystics,

Eastern Yogi, spiritualists, and the practitioners of Wicca. (The phenomenon is examined in more detail in our book *The Encyclopedia of the World's Greatest Unsolved Mysteries*.) In poltergeist cases we have contemporary, witnessed accounts without the possible 'coloration' of religious belief. But there is some overlap, for example in the case of Anthoinette de Grollee, a nun who was the focus of poltergeist happenings (see Chapter One).

Germana Cele (Chapter Eleven) levitated frequently. Even handcuffed she was lifted several feet in the air in front of witnesses. Even her clothes did not seem to obey the laws of gravity; they would stay gathered around her as if she were in a 'normal' position, rather than hang down from her floating body. During exorcism, she levitated for the last time in front of 170 people.

Gauld and Cornell, in their study of 500 cases, found that levitation was reported in 10% of cases pre-1874, and in only 3% of cases from 1874 to 1975. Of these, there were 25 cases in the first 250 and 8 cases in the second 250. We have found, in reports of approximately 136 cases since 1950, levitation of a person occurring in only two cases: Enfield, and Wycliffe Road as described above.

Stratford, Connecticut

Levitation features in one of the oddest cases of a poltergeist on record – the Phelps case. Perhaps the most bizarre aspect of this case were strange figures, formed from clothing, that seemed to create a tableau.

The Revd Dr Eliakim Phelps, his wife and four children (girls aged sixteen and six, boys aged eleven and three) lived in Stratford, Connecticut. Revd Phelps, just days before the beginning of the disturbances, held a seance and received replies to his questions in the form of rapping noises. The church view of the following manifestation would be that he opened an invitation to 'attack' through the seance.

The poltergeist disturbed the Phelps household between March

1850 and October 1851. It made its first demonstration while the family were out at church. They arrived home to find that furniture had been disturbed and the whole place looked as if it had been ransacked. In the main bedroom they discovered a figure made of clothing and laid out as if to resemble a corpse.

After this the poltergeist activity accelerated. The next day objects moved about in front of witnesses. Small items such as cutlery, keys and nails were thrown, and furniture moved. Banging sounds were evident, and there was the sensation of the house shaking.

In one of the main rooms the family found clothing and cushions had been used to form eleven life-sized figures, ten female. They were 'displayed' in devotional poses with bibles open in front of them. Centrally placed was a dwarflike figure, and a final figure was suspended 'as though flying through the air'.

Over the duration of the intrusions the Phelps household was also subjected to apports and small fires. Strange writing was found on one occasion (see Chapter Six).

It was the elder boy that experienced the levitation. He was seen to be 'carried across the room by invisible hands and gently deposited on the floor'. The boy also twice woke to find himself outside, as if he'd been carried in his sleep. On another occasion, while the boy was out with his father, they found their carriage pelted by stones.

The elder girl was hit, her pillow pushed in her face and her neck tied up with tape. And, perhaps strangest of all, a 'vegetable growth sprouted out of the carpet before the eyes of the family'. The leaves were said to be covered with strange hieroglyphics.

Phelps reported in an interview: 'The phenomena have been entirely unexplicable (*sic*) to me. I have followed the slow movement of objects through the air, observing carefully their direction, their slow movement, and their curving flight, and am convinced that they were not moved by any human agency . . . the noises are most violent when all the family are present, especially when they were seated at the table . . . I place no value in any of the messages, and if they are from spirits they are from evil spirits . . . I am satisfied that the communications are wholly worthless, and that they are frequently false, contradictory and nonsensical; the spirits often accuse each other of lying and constantly inflicting injury on persons and property . . . Fifty-six articles were picked up at one time which had been thrown at someone's head. Thirty figures were seen, and twenty window panes broken . . . The phenomena for the past several weeks have been subsiding, and have now ceased entirely, I hope!' (In fact the poltergeist activity came to a full end six weeks later.)

Poona

The case at Poona involved Damodar Bapat, a Brahmin boy aged eight (mentioned above), who was adopted after the death of his parents. There was some of the more usual poltergeist activity – the movement of furniture and objects, and apports of coins – and Damodar was suspected by some of faking; but certainly he was not deliberately responsible for it all.

Mr Jenkins, a medical man, visited the family and kept a diary which included his witnessing of the levitation. 'When I entered, I asked all those present to leave the room. I placed the lad (stark naked) on a small bed, felt his pulse, and told him to lie down quietly. I then closed the door and windows and sat down on a chair in the corner of the room. I looked at my watch; it was exactly 1.30 p.m. I put a sheet over him. In about fifteen minutes I saw the bedclothes pulled off the bed on which the lad was lying, the bed was pulled into the middle of the room, and the lad actually lifted off the bed and was deposited gently on the floor. The lad could feel the arm of the unseen person at work.' Jenkins reports that just after this a paper-weight was flung towards him, and that toys were violently thrown into a corner. This all served to convince him that his earlier theories of mal-observation or illusion were wrong.

At Enfield, Janet levitated, and in her case again we see elements of suggestion or response in the poltergeist. After talking about levitation, and the suggestion by an investigator (David Robertson) that Janet 'just start by bouncing up and down on the bed', it seems that Janet – that very day – levitated. Other people in the house saw Janet seemingly floating up and down in the air, and Janet herself exclaimed, 'I been [*sic*] floating in the air.' She also claimed the most extraordinary experience of all, that during the levitation she had passed through the wall into the house next door.

SHEER POWER OF THE POLTERGEIST

Poltergeists demonstrate a wide range of abilities. Some of their manipulations seem to be so precise and delicate that they appear to have a great gentleness about them; but they can also demonstrate great power, and we might well consider the words of researcher Guy Lyon Playfair, who came across two such cases. He stated: 'It is an appalling thought what poltergeists could do if they felt like it, or were able to. What they do already is bad enough.'

Pontapora

The first case is that of Kenzo Okamoto, who lived with his family twelve miles from Pontapora, Matto Grosso, in Paraguay. The poltergeist that affected them was assaultive in a variety of ways – first almost comically. During a period of furniture movements, everyone ended up evacuating the building except for an elderly lady, who ended up bombarded with tomatoes from Okamoto's tomato patch. She thought he was behind it and threatened to call the police, but he denied having anything to do with it. At a later time his children suffered the same fate.

Spontaneous fires broke out. A damp shirt was burned by a 'fireball' that appeared from nowhere; it also singed the family dog, but failed to raise it from its slumbers. The wooden partition and the thatched roof were also subject to burns.

A reporter, Kazunari Akaki, stayed at the farm for five days. He was unimpressed by the stones and chocolates that seemed to be falling from nowhere, convinced that the children were playing tricks. But his scepticism ended when he parked a heavy jeep outside the house, went in, and within a brief moment came back out, following a loud noise – to find the jeep forty yards away, uphill and in soft mud, with no tyre tracks leading to it.

The phenomena died away without 'resolution' or even, in this case, an identified focus.

The second case is that of Fernando and Mrs Riberio, from Sorocaba. The poltergeist that affected their household demonstrated its power in no uncertain terms. In Playfair's words: 'The most impressive feat of all was the overturning of a concrete water tank, which according to Fernando normally took three men to lift. This had simply been raised from its brick support and dumped on its face in the back yard.'

PERFECT PLACEMENT

One of the least identified 'special effects' of the poltergeist is one we and other researchers have noted time and again in our research. We have called it 'perfect placement', for want of a better description.

Objects found in poltergeist-disturbed scenes, particularly those which appear to be apported or have moved, often have a curiously symmetrical 'feel' to them. This is a very inadequate description for something so intangible, and yet many people have noted it.

For example, in the Hertfordshire case, on one occasion when our investigation team was alone in the house, we found a china duck sitting on the floor of an upstairs bedroom. It had certainly not been there when the vigil began. It stood out dramatically – and in a way that almost no other position in the room would have achieved. It was positioned in open space in the middle of the floor, almost announcing itself, and it faced the door absolutely square on. We noticed its 'perfect placement' as soon as we saw it. Others commented on it too, without our prompting. And there was a curious feeling that it 'belonged' in that place and no other.

In a similar way, we investigated a case in North London, along with researcher Manfred Cassirer (a council member of the SPR who had years earlier investigated the Bromley poltergeist). The witnesses told us of two incidents (among many), both of which seemed to be apports, or perhaps teleports. The first was a packet of cigarettes that was found by the skirting board in the living room. Both witnesses were keen to tell us that 'it was square on to the skirting board, absolutely exactly square on'. Something in this symmetrical placement had struck them as odd. The second incident involved a glass that was found half-way up the staircase – a staircase where the lower half of a human apparition had been seen. The witness described that the glass was 'exactly in the centre of the stair – exactly'.

Examples of such placement also include pot plants lined up in the kitchen at Enfield, and objects placed on the floor in the York bed shop, where the poltergeist used the carpet patterns for its template. The carpet had a repeating design with large flower or medallion shapes, and objects from the office had been moved into the showroom and placed in a line, one on each medallion.

Quite what can be learned from perfect placement is uncertain. However, we believe it is a detail that might not before have been awarded due consideration, and we look forward to receiving reports from investigators of other instances of this phenomenon.

POLTERGEISTS WITH A FIXATION

Poltergeists have a wide range of manifestations, perhaps an endless one. And several seem to be innovative in their actions. The Pontefract poltergeist, for example, developed several unique talents, such as showering a room with white dust that fell from a precise height several feet below ceiling level.

But many poltergeists seem to display a fixated behaviour pattern, centring around one 'preferred' manifestation. Sometimes the reason for this is obvious, for example the case of a woman who had undergone a mastectomy and found that items moved were always one of a pair. But sometimes it is not so obvious – though perhaps this is only because we cannot delve deep enough into the 'inner dynamics' of the focus.

Seaford, Long Island

The poltergeist that visited the Hermann family in 1958 liked to open bottles. Jimmy (12) and his sister Lucille (13) arrived home from school on Monday 3 February to find in Jimmy's bedroom a doll and a plastic ship had both broken. After reporting this to his mother, the family checked the other rooms of the house, and found in the mother's bedroom a bottle of holy water had had its lid removed, was turned on its side and had spilt its contents. Soon popping noises were heard – bottles were popping open all around the house. In a bathroom cabinet two bottles had their caps unscrewed, and the liquid spilt on to the floor. A bottle was found spilling liquid in the kitchen, its lid lying beside it. In the basement Jimmy and his mother saw a half-gallon bottle of bleach lift itself from a box and fly half the length of the room.

There were similar disturbances on the Thursday after school. The same popping sounds were heard, and bottles were found emptied or broken. On the Friday there was just one event, when Jimmy was alone in the house. Saturday was a quiet day; but on Sunday morning the family found seven bottles opened and spilling liquid. One, a bottle of toilet water, had its screw cap and a rubber stopper removed.

James Hermann, Jimmy's father, was rather sceptical, but could offer no explanation, and spent the weekend keeping a close watch on his son in case this was all some kind of practical joke. When Jimmy went into the bathroom to brush his teeth his father followed him and stood in the doorway to question him. Jimmy insisted he had nothing to do with the bottle popping; and as they talked Mr Hermann saw two bottles on the vanity shelf start to move – each in a different direction. One fell in the sink and the other on to the floor. Now convinced that something strange was happening in his house, James called the police.

Patrolman James Hughes visited the house, looked around, and was talking to the family when they all heard a noise from the bathroom. On inspection they found a bottle overturned. Hughes was quite clear that the bottle had been upright on his inspection, and that all the family were with him downstairs when the noise was heard.

Detective Joseph Tozzi listened to Hughes' report rather sceptically. He later visited the house and conducted an intensive investigation before giving the children a serious talk (believing they were somehow responsible).

Objects in the house continued to fall and bottles continued to be spilt. A visitor to the house saw a porcelain figure fall from a table. She described it for the police: 'As it went into the air . . . it looked like a small white feather – then crashed to the rug unbroken.' This figurine became a popular plaything, and was moved by the poltergeist at least twice more. Tozzi meanwhile had checked radio broadcasts for interference, and had an oscillograph installed to check for vibration. Chemical analysis was made on some of the bottles. Tozzi went on to check water leaders, fuse boxes and electrical wiring, and could find nothing untoward. But the poltergeist was not deterred, and continued as before.

But by now it manifested more widely, throwing objects and furniture. A bookcase in the boy's bedroom was found upside-down and wedged between the bed and a radiator. Most of the occurrences were unwitnessed – a crash or loud noise would alert the family or investigator that an event had taken place – but one evening, while in his son's bedroom, Hermann saw the boy's night table twist ninety degrees and fall over.

The poltergeist's final manifestation, after thirty-six days, was to cause a thump and – a good exit, this – open a bottle of bleach in the cellar.

Chapter 5

Assaultive Poltergeists

Norway

At the time of her experiences, Sophie and her two children were living in a small town in southern Norway. Sophie and visitors to the house would often hear banging noises, as if youngsters outside were playing and banging on the walls; there was clear vision around the house with nowhere to hide, but they never could find a culprit.

Sometimes the movement of an object heralded the start to a series of happenings. One night Sophie noticed an ornamental monk figure jump two metres. Suddenly all the lights went out apart from one inside a book-case which started shining in a rainbow of colours. Sophie could hear sounds of movement that she assumed were her children awake and getting out of bed. Thinking they may be upset she went through to the bedroom to find that they were sleeping soundly. Just as suddenly, all the lights came back; the phenomena were over for the night.

This poltergeist does not seem to have focused on the children, as things were happening while they slept, and also while they were away from the house. But they did witness some of the events. On one occasion, zippers on the sofa cushions were seen to open and close and 'movements' were apparent under the covers. 'What is it, Mum?' Sophie's children asked. Not sure what to say, Sophie told them it must be mice. Comically, the children then started to leave food for the invisible mice.

Sophie felt the atmosphere change on one frightening day. She went upstairs to check the children in the bedroom, but could not open the door even though it was not locked. The children were screaming and Sophie was pushing on the door. 'If you hurt my kids I will follow you into hell if I have to,' she screamed. Suddenly the door opened. Sophie entered and immediately felt hands grabbing at her as if to strangle her, though she could see nothing. She fought her way to the children and they all ran from the house and fled to her ex-husband's home. Seeing her, he asked, 'What is on your throat?' Sophie looked in the mirror and saw red marks like fingers on her neck.

The family finally left the house in December 1989. As they left – on a bright, clear day – the flagpole outside splintered and fell into three pieces, as if struck by lightning.

In the Bristol case of 1761 (outlined in Chapter One), two girls were attacked, bitten, cut as if with a knife and assaulted with pins stuck into them. When Dobby was attacked, Durbin believed he saw 'the flesh at the side of her throat pushed in, whitish, as if done with fingers'. On another occasion Durbin saw 'the mark of teeth, about eighteen, and wet with spittle . . . nobody was near her but myself'.

Poltergeists are not generally physically harmful to people, though they may cause considerable psychological damage. But there are cases where the manifestations take on a gruesome, perhaps evil spin. Rare though these cases are, they tell us something about the nature of the poltergeist. This next case involves a frightening series of attacks on a new-born baby.

Daly City

Jan and Brian Neven, with their new baby, Stephen, lived in Daly City in 1972. Brian was a Jew and Jan a Catholic, though Brian converted to Catholicism during the period of poltergeist disturbances.

The troubles started soon after the birth of Stephen. They were so bad that the family moved out to other homes, and even a motel – but it seems that this did not work and they were followed by the poltergeist activity. This included the unlocking and opening of doors, the movement of furniture and other objects, and an eerie apparition. Apports – in this case, coins – appeared.

Spontaneous fires erupted, seeming to centre on the baby's crib. One crib was ignited several times and another was, on the day it was put in the nursery, incinerated. The poltergeist soon began to attack the family, including Stephen, who was hit by flying objects. On one occasion, when Stephen was extremely upset, on removing his nappy Jan found his genitals tied up with a necklace. Brian, on checking his son one day, found his bedcovers wrapped tightly around his face. Other members of the family were also attacked: Jan had a pillow pushed into her face and needed Brian's help to save her from asphyxiation; on another day she was hit so hard she was knocked unconscious. Brian and a family visitor were slapped by the invisible assailant.

Brian's father and brother were with them one night when they tried to communicate with the poltergeist, leaving a pen and paper. They later found words on various pieces of paper: 'he', 'child', 'baby', 'back', 'baby', and 'stay'.

Eventually the events subsided, after fourteen exorcisms by one priest.

Sorocaba

There is some evidence that not all poltergeists reach a high level of attack, but they are frightening and harmful none the less. On

18 July 1972, poltergeist activity arose in the home of Fernando and Alda Riberio and their six children. They lived in Sorocaba, west of São Paulo City. Investigation was undertaken by the Brazilian Institute for Psycho-Biophysical Research (IBPP), under Hernani Guymeraes Andrade.

Small knocking noises heralded the happenings, and eventually the house was ransacked, with 'almost every single piece of furniture in the house overturned'. Special effects included a tyre raising itself three feet in the air and hovering there long enough to scare Fernando considerably. A wooden shelf in the kitchen crashed to the floor. The family moved to neighbours, but they were none too pleased, commenting on the state of their house after the visit: 'It looked as if a tractor had driven through the place.' When the family went back home the poltergeist went back with them. It overturned a concrete water tank which would have taken three men to lift.

But this poltergeist either became assaultive, and potentially dangerous, or was at least brutally clumsy (which is not common). Mrs Riberio was hit by a brick, and one of her daughters was scalded by water from a kettle that was described as 'wrenched from her hands'.

Several poltergeist victims – those who are on the receiving end of the more vicious manifestations earn that title – exhibit bite- and scratch-marks on their bodies. In many cases these have been well witnessed even as they happen. We should consider the possibility that the markings are a form of stigmata, produced by the body in response to a powerful belief system surrounding the focus. They could therefore, at least provisionally, be regarded not as proof of any physical contact, only proof of the experiencer's belief of contact.

We shall later be examining the connection – or similarities, at least – between poltergeists and possession. Poltergeist-like activity is a common part of the first stage of possession – 'infestation'.

Biting and scratching phenomena are part of the second stage – 'obsession'. The similarity is an important one. In possession the term infestation represents 'the demon' causing disturbances in the vicinity of the victim, obsession represents the demon tormenting the victim more directly. Taking this view, the bite-marks and scratches that appear on the skin of the victim may be likened to a message saying, 'I am here'.

In the Mount Rainier case the victim could be described as either the focus of a poltergeist attack or the victim of possession; certainly both aspects were evident, as we shall see in Chapter Eleven. During his experiences there was a time when spontaneous scratches were witnessed. Observers noticed that the scratching seemed to appear as if from inside the skin. Over time the scratches formed letters and then words.

The Jabuticabal poltergeist attacked the focus, Maria Jose Ferreira, leaving bite- and slap-marks on her skin, among other manifestations that included her clothing catching fire spontaneously.

In the Guarulhos case, Marcos awoke and found his arm bleeding. Other people involved in the case were similarly harmed; two visiting children were cut on their legs and Noemia received cuts to her face daily.

A Romanian girl, Eleonora Zugun, became the victim of a poltergeist at the age of twelve. She was at one time sent to a sanatorium, but later studied by Countess Wassilko-Serecki in her home. During that time the poltergeist attacked Eleonora, leaving clear scratches and bite-marks visible on her skin. Witnesses watched teeth-marks appearing, and on some occasions saliva was found in the marks. Examination showed the saliva was not Zugun's. It is clear that some of Zugun's marks were caused 'from outside of her body'. A Dr Walther Kröner tested the scratching by smearing her body with greasepaint, and on examination found that when scratches appeared the greasepaint had been pushed aside by the furrowing.

In 1962 William Roll examined a case in Indianapolis where two people in the same house were attacked – a Mrs Renata Beck and Mrs Lina Gemmecke. Immediately after several small objects had flown around the house, Mrs Beck felt punctures – more like stings, perhaps – on her arms. Mrs Gemmecke got the same treatment seconds later. Mrs Gemmecke was attacked on fourteen separate occasions. When the bites stopped, rapping sounds started. (It is rare for rappings not to be the starting point, but it is possible that they act as an announcement, saying, in effect, 'I am here'; the bites certainly served the same purpose.)

Poltergeists are known to be as happy infesting the workplace as the home. This is the only case we have found that occurred on board a ship at sea.

Mediterranean Sea

On 7 August 1989, the *Francesco*, a Sicilian fishing boat, started the day by firing distress flares off the coast north-west of the Cretan village of Kisamou. After they were towed safely to harbour, the five-strong crew told their eerie story. 'Spectres and evil spirits have been pursuing us relentlessly all night,' they said. 'They attacked us on deck and in the hold, threw gear overboard, destroyed our radio and navigation equipment, broke everything that could be broken and attacked us with stilettos.' The boat matched the story; it was damaged, in disorder, and had stiletto daggers stuck in various points. Captain Falvator Gaimagglin and his crew were obviously in terror, and they would not return to the ship. They requested that the ship be exorcised, and three priests were sent to do this.

In fact the disturbances had been so frightening that the crew still refused to board; they insisted that they be flown home. Months later the ship was still unmoved, and waiting for a replacement crew to take it back to Sicily.

BED DISTURBANCES

Probably the most common intrusive 'assault' in poltergeist cases is the disturbance of the focus – and sometimes others – in their beds. Accounts of beds being rocked, vibrated, bedsheets pulled off, and so on, have arisen in so many cases that they cannot all be listed here.

In the Amherst case Dr Carritte tried to hold down Esther's pillow while it was moving in and out from under her head, and a message threatening to kill Esther appeared on her bedroom wall. In the Sauchie case one witness described a pillow on Virginia's bed suddenly taking an indentation in what appeared to be the shape of a person's head. In the Poona case, Mrs Kohn – who slept in the same room as the identified focus, Damodar – had her own pillow moved, 'gently lifted from its place at the head of my bed . . . and was placed by an invisible hand at the foot of my bed'. In the Mount Rainier case, Robert's bedcovers were disrupted for three weeks; the covers were described as 'being clawed from below', and the bed was shaking. In the Bell Witch case, William Porter discovered that the 'Witch' had got into bed with him.

If poltergeist attacks are to take place at night then a number will inevitably occur in the bedroom while people are in bed. It is also possible that the state of mind in or near sleep is a factor in the 'mechanisms'. However, the bed is also a highly personal place, a 'world' generally occupied by one person only, or in the case of the marriage bed by two people together. That the poltergeist should invade this domain is logical if the poltergeist is associated with individuals at the personal level – which we believe it is. It is therefore not surprising that on occasion the attacks are of a highly personal nature.

Some cases of assault have taken place in bed. In the Daly City case, Jan had a pillow pressed against her face, and it was her baby's crib that was ignited. In the case of Eileen Courtis, the victim woke one night in a haunted room to find 'two skinny but very strong arms extended over her head, holding a large downy pillow as though to suffocate her'; and in the Stratford case, the victim similarly had her pillow pressed into her face.

PSYCHOLOGICAL AFTERMATH

Not all poltergeist assaults are physical, but the psychological impressions left by them can be just as damaging. Stan Conway was the subject of a poltergeist manifestation during his childhood, now forty-odd years ago. The poltergeist affected his family for several years and included some physical attacks. His father went into Stan's bedroom on one occasion when the room was empty and was violently hit on the back of the head. Stan also suffered several unpleasant experiences in that room.

One long-term effect on Stan was that it took years – indeed, into his adulthood and marriage – before he could leave his hands outside the bedclothes and conquer the fear of something attacking him. Stan reflected on his experiences: 'Whatever is locked in my memory is well and truly locked up . . . There are things in my mind which are desperately trying to come out. And if I could handle it I would love to know what it was.'

ASKING FOR TROUBLE?

Many poltergeists are assaultive, but some, it seems, only develop this behaviour in response to a 'dare'. For example, in one case at the Felix Fuld Housing Project in Newark, New Jersey, William Roll, visiting the affected family, announced to them: 'It doesn't hit people.' As he reports, 'At that instant, a small bottle which had stood on an end table by a sofa hit me squarely on the head.'

At Enfield, Maurice Grosse also seemed to challenge the poltergeist. On one occasion he said, 'Are you having a game with me?' The almost immediate response was provided by a cardboard box full of cushions, which 'shot off the floor beside the fireplace, flew over the bed, travelling about eight feet, and hit Maurice squarely on his forehead'.

Perhaps poltergeists just don't like investigators – a notion we shall return to – though it is true that the one at Enfield also assaulted the focus, for example 'holding' Janet by the leg, keeping her rigidly fixed on the staircase crying, 'I can't move. Something is holding me!'

NEAR MISS OR NEAR HIT?

Finally we should consider the question of near misses. Poltergeist lore is replete with such cases, and their meaning must be considered. The question would seem to be: is a near miss a failed assault or a demonstration of precision?

George Hamilton in Scotland, for example, bent over to pick something up from the floor of his flat and a chisel flew across the room and embedded itself in the wall. It was a near miss, and it certainly frightened him; if he had not bent down, he could have been killed. But the fact is that he was *not* killed or even injured, and he *had* bent down. And we know from a variety of cases that poltergeists can be precise, and can respond or act instantaneously the opportunity arises.

If such acts were carried out by one human on another human they would certainly be regarded as a threat, but we might have to be cautious in applying motives to the poltergeist.

Chapter 6

Communication

We have examined various fascinating characteristics of the poltergeist in the previous chapters. Now we begin to move closer into the phenomenon, and look at a further extraordinary aspect: that there have been many times when poltergeists have seemingly communicated information, and in doing so have displayed intelligence.

RAPPINGS

As shown in Chapter Three, noises are a core manifestation of the poltergeist. Usually starting with scratching noises, they often evolve into bangings, or rappings. The rapping noises have sometimes been found to be responsive; the poltergeist uses the sounds as a means of communication.

For example, rapping sounds were part of the phenomena heard at the nunnery of St Pierre de Lyon in 1528. It was found that questions were answered through this form of communication. In this way they confirmed their belief that the communicator was the spirit of an ex-nun, Alis de Telieux, who had left the nunnery and died four years previously.

Derrygonnelly

William Barrett tested the communicative powers of the poltergeist in 1877 when investigating a case at Derrygonnelly, near Enniskillen in Northern Ireland. He was not only trying to find out if the poltergeist could respond, but sought to test a level of knowledge – even ESP ability – on its part.

Holding open a certain number of fingers in his pocket, Barrett found in four separate tests that the poltergeist would rap out that number correctly. This leads to several possibilities: that the poltergeist could see into his pocket; that it knew what he was thinking; or that it was – at least in part – a projection of his own mind.

Barrett was, we know, interested in thought transference. Indeed, he wrote a book on the subject, so it is not surprising that he looked for this in his investigations. And as we have discovered elsewhere in this book, the poltergeist seems to be very good at presenting what is being asked for.

The following case extract illustrates communicative rapping very well.

Southern England

The case arose in April 1974. Mr and Mrs Black shared their council house with their six children. Two of the girls, twenty-year-old Jane and twelve-year-old Susan, shared a bedroom which was the focal point of the poltergeist activity, which manifested as mysterious bangs and rappings.

The case was investigated by Barrie Colvin, who included in his research the assumption that there was an apparent intelligence behind the rapping – since there was some response – which would rule out crepitation, water pipes and so on.

Furthermore, the rappings were only produced when Susan was in the room, in bed, lying on her side, facing the wall, with the light cover over her – and never when she was standing up. The poltergeist activity increased just before Susan went to sleep and ceased once she was asleep, suggesting a connection to her – perhaps that particular brainwaves associated with the entry into sleep were required for the rappings to manifest substantially.

Colvin brought in Dr Reinhart Schiffauer, a research physicist sceptical of the paranormal. Schiffauer became convinced that the rappings were genuine and not the result of trickery. During one curious experiment, Colvin and Schiffauer persuaded members of the family to start calling the poltergeist names and saying that they didn't believe its story. On previous occasions when the family had done this, the banging had crescendoed to the point where the family had to leave the house. It was 'so loud that you could put your hand on the wall and feel the wall vibrating. We went outside to the ground floor below her bedroom window, and you could feel the vibration. It was so loud it was just incredible. In fact we walked down the road and we could still hear it, some fifty metres away.' During the investigation the rappings moved from the wall to the bed-head, which enabled them to better examine it. Eventually the rapping moved around the room to include the exercise book in which Colvin was writing up the case notes.

Colvin and Schiffauer made something of a breakthrough in their study. It appeared that the rapping increased in intensity when not only Susan but also her mother were in the room. Thus Colvin believed that the mother was contributing to the effects. The system of communication with the poltergeist was often employed by the mother, and there were occasions when the observers believed that the 'yes' rap – to indicate that a particular letter was the one to be used – would come *before* the letter had been spoken by Mrs Black. It is worth noting that, when communicating with the poltergeist in the Hydesville house of the Fox sisters, the mother would often contribute to the tests; indeed, it was the mother who suggested that the poltergeist give the age of her daughters as proof of its intelligence. The possibility that the mother was contributing to the intelligence behind the poltergeist cannot be ignored in either case.

ESP experiments were conducted on the family by Colvin. The

test utilised a deck of forty cards, each printed with a number between one and ten. On random selection of cards from the deck, the target cards were viewed by Susan, her mother, the two brothers and Colvin. The poltergeist rapped out six correct calls out of six. In the subsequent two attempts, the cards were seen only by Colvin, but the poltergeist still got sixteen out of eighteen right – a number far higher than chance would have suggested. In a final experiment nobody saw the selected cards, but the poltergeist still got four out of six (see Chapter Ten for more details of this case).

What we can learn from this case is that the poltergeist is not just something throwing things about aimlessly, but seems to have, or use, intelligence. Poltergeist rappings are similar to those heard at seances, and as such we may therefore be considering a form of mediumship, albeit via an undeclared medium.

WRITINGS

Poltergeists also have a history of communicating through writing. In the case of Esther Cox, who in 1878 was the focus of a number of attacks, writing which appeared on the wall above her bed said: 'Esther Cox, you are mine to kill.' At Borley Rectory, during the investigation by Harry Price, paper was found floating in the air with indecipherable marks on it, and later paper was found on which the name 'Marianne' was written in a childish hand. In a case in New Jersey in 1972 there was writing found on walls, written in crayon.

The York case (outlined in Chapter Three) was investigated by ASSAP member Colin Davies. After the poltergeist had been active for some time it started to leave written messages in books and on furniture, many of which concerned the investigator – 'BRING COLIN BACK NEED TO TALK WITH HIM CONTACT 0236879564', for example.

The poltergeist showed a special knowledge of distant events. One paper was found with a message: 'HE IS AT CARPET SHOP 708729 I THINK RING HIM YOU HAVE TO TELL HIM B4 I WILL GO.' That day Davies had been visiting his brother, working in a carpet shop; the number was the telephone number of that shop. (Although this seems strange the numbers were not secret; they were known to both Don and Susie, for example.)

In the Phelps case there is some suggestion that a seance, successfully receiving a response, had 'triggered' the poltergeist. The case also included writings; when the Reverend Phelps turned away from his writing table he heard the noise of his pen scratching across paper. On turning back he saw written: 'Very nice paper and nice ink for the devil.'

Who wrote the note is an interesting question. We have studied 'channellers', who receive automatic writing, usually while in trance. Where the information they receive comes from is debatable – entities, the deceased, aliens, some fragment of their own mind, etc. – but for this purpose it is unimportant. We can be certain that there is something special about the process of channelling; we spoke to one witness who described watching someone fill pages of A4 paper with neat, coherent script, writing 'like Superman does in the films' (i.e. at very high speed). Perhaps Phelps entered a trance state for a moment, and wrote the note himself. We may legitimately open up that question to all written communications from poltergeists.

There appear to be times, however, when the focus is not present and cannot have (even subconsciously) produced the writing. If that is true, then we either have evidence for an outside agency such as a spirit or entity, or we must speculate that writing is possible using psychokinesis (see Chapter Twelve).

In the Hertfordshire case, the poltergeist upset the witnesses living in the house by leaving unpleasant and abusive notes in books and on notepads. The witnesses even tried to communicate back, but the responses received were neither helpful nor meaningful, and appeared to be either mischievous or malevolent. When John (Spencer) offered to be the point of communication, and a note was left for the poltergeist telling it to write to him, the reply was, unhelpfully, 'Tell John he can get stuffed'.

The poltergeist has proven very adaptable – to electrical equipment, for example – and we were not surprised to discover that, in 1991, messages seemingly from a poltergeist had been received through a computer. One not terribly meaningful set of texts was so received during poltergeist activity at Cornish Brassware, as reported to ASSAP and recorded in their journal, *Anomaly*. Messages came up on the screens, such as, 'I have you, I have you, Ha, Ha, Ha.' The company supplying the computers believed it may have been a virus. Given the increasing proliferation of PCs in use, computer-literate poltergeistery is almost bound to increase.

VOICE OF THE POLTERGEIST
Perhaps the most famous form of communication with poltergeists – and the most direct – is when they develop a voice. This has arisen in a number of cases throughout history.

Mâcon
In the case of the 'devil' at Mâcon, in 1612, François Perrault described poltergeist activity first noticed by his wife and maid during his own five-day absence from the house. While in bed his wife's curtains were drawn 'with great noise and violence'. The maid was in another bed in the same room, and was also alerted to the incident. The following night the two lay together in one bed, but the bedcovers were pulled off them. When they checked the doors they were not only bolted from the inside, but also from the outside, and had to be unbolted by another servant in the house. In the kitchen objects had been thrown about, leaving great disorder. Thinking that his wife was the victim of a practical joker, Perrault, on his return, checked the house thoroughly before retiring. He went to bed leaving his wife and maid together 'by the fire, with a lamp upon the table'. Shortly afterwards he heard rumbling, tapping and banging noises from the kitchen. Objects were thrown around. Perrault and the maid examined the house but could find no one. The incident then repeated itself later that night, and

Perrault wrote, 'then did I begin to know indeed that all this could not proceed but from a wicket [sic] spirit . . .'

Six days after the events started, on 20 September 1612, the poltergeist started to make different noises. They began with three or four whistles 'with a very loud and shrill tone'. Gradually a hoarse voice developed, from a source seemingly close to the assembled company, which now included a number of friends assisting in the 'investigation'. Apparently the voice started singing a little tune, 'Vingt et Deux Deniers', a song used to teach whistling birds to sing. Shortly afterwards it progressed to saying 'Minister' several times. All Perrault could reply at the time was, 'Get thee from me, Satan, the Lord rebuke thee.'

Gradually the voice acquired a skill for language and engaged the company in long dialogues, often amusing itself at Perrault's expense. In among the speeches were nuggets of 'special knowledge', revealing information known only to the family. The focus would seem to have been the maid, who seemed at times to be joking and jesting with the 'devil', and it with her. The case ended with classic throwing, of stones up to three pounds in weight; on one occasion the 'devil' returned a marked stone, which was found to be hot.

The development of the voice we see here is very typical. Poltergeists do not seem to come with well-developed voices, but have to nurture them, usually from small noises and whistles, through a stage of a 'hoarse' voice, before becoming fully articulate. As Father Herbert Thurston (who recorded this account) points out, much the same process is gone through with mediums contacting the spirit world. The poltergeist has sometimes been heard to sound like a person prior to full voice development, i.e. breathing noises or gasps are heard. In about ten per cent of cases a full voice has developed from this start.

In the Bell Witch case, the 'audience' persisted in trying to get the Witch to talk, 'and finally it commenced whistling when spoken to, in a low, broken sound, as if trying to speak in a whistling voice; and in this way it progressed, developing until the whistling sound was changed to a weak, faltering whisper, uttering indistinct words. The voice, however, gradually gained strength in articulating, and soon the utterances became distinct in a low whisper, so as to be understood in the absence of any other noise.'

Gef, the 'Talking Mongoose' in the Dalby case, first made gurgling sounds, followed by a bark. Mr Irving found that it could mimic other 'animal noises' he made, and finally it duplicated the human voice by first repeating nursery rhymes.

In the Enfield case, Guy Lyon Playfair witnessed the poltergeist's early attempts at vocalisation. 'Throughout the early evening, we heard the curious whistling and barking noises coming from Janet's general direction that we had been hearing for several days. The whistles were very loud and piercing, and seemed to imitate the way that Nottingham always greeted his wife when he came home from work. Janet vehemently denied making whistling noises on purpose, and her mother assured us that she had never heard Janet whistle. Moreover, she had large teeth and usually wore a brace, which made it almost impossible for her to whistle at all.

'The barking noises were even more mysterious. "Listen," Janet said to me the first time I heard it, "I am not doing it. I can't make that noise." '

After that, the development continued until the voice could converse in full, normal speech. As in many cases it was also abusive, using a range of swear words and demonstrating 'attitude' by giving orders and offering insults. Conversations with the voice lasted for hours at a time, helping to convince investigator Maurice Grosse that it could not have been faked by Janet. The poltergeist in this case was said to be using her 'false vocal cords' and not her normal voice mechanisms.

While studying the vocalisations of the poltergeist, it becomes evident that we do not get 'well-travelled' poltergeists. By this we mean that there are no cases of immediately articulate poltergeists, conversing freely from the time of their arrival as though they developed the ability to speak during some previous manifestation. Indeed, no poltergeist has ever identified itself as one that has been anywhere else before. As far as speech development is concerned, each poltergeist has its own learning curve.

As in the Mâcon case, it is not often clear where the voice comes from. Perrault mentions it being somewhere seemingly close, 'about three or four steps from us'. The voice often seems to come from (or from very near) the focus. In the case of the so-called 'Talking Mongoose' it seemed always to come from the direction of Voirrey, the probable focus, even though this fact was not noticed by the family. In the Enfield case it seems to have been decided that the voice came from Janet, even though she heard it coming from behind herself.

In the Bell case it was thought at the time that the focus, Betsy Bell, may have been something of a ventriloquist, but this was tested by a doctor who placed his hand over her mouth while the voice was being heard. The doctor was thereby convinced that she was in no way connected – directly at least – with the sounds.

The special knowledge of poltergeists is another feature most evident once a voice has developed. In the Bingen case, for example, a farmer and his family were driven from their home by a poltergeist which threw stones, caused fires and shook the walls. But the poltergeist also had a voice, and used it to reveal the secret sexual misdeeds of the farmer. A similar fate befell those around Stephen Wiriet in 1190 in Pembrokeshire, when 'his' poltergeist told people in the locality of their secrets. It taunted them with things they had done in their lives which they would have preferred to keep secret. In the Amherst case of 1889, the poltergeist responded to the question, 'You there, Mister?' Among a stream of obscenities an old man's voice [perhaps a 'hoarse' voice] replied: 'I am the Devil . . . get out or I'll break your neck'. George Dagg and a visitor, Woodcock, had a lengthy conversation with the 'spirit'. Crowds gathered to witness the voice. And again in this case the voice showed 'special knowledge' of the private affairs of many of its visitors.

In each of these cases it was maintained that only something supernatural could have intimate knowledge of one's affairs and misdeeds, and so the early poltergeists were usually interpreted as witches or devils.

In the most recent case of a talking poltergeist (at Enfield), it seemed clear that Janet was not producing the voice deliberately. (This raises the likelihood that the focus is some sort of 'unde-clared' medium.) There is no reason to presume that the 'vocal' cases of the past were any different. However, even if we deter-mine that the voice comes from the person unconsciously, this does not explain the intelligence behind it.

Mediums believe that they are channelling voices from spirits, allowing the spirits to use their body to speak through. This may be true of poltergeist voices. Maurice Grosse is of the opinion that, at Enfield – although much of the poltergeistery may have been recurrent spontaneous psychokinesis (RSPK) – a spirit was involved, presumably the spirit that identified itself using the voice.

An alternative view of mediumship – or the channelling of any messages from 'beyond the grave' – is that the source is actually some aspect of the medium's own subconscious. There is nothing in the poltergeist phenomenon to confirm or refute this; the ques-tion remains open. The information given is rarely profound, and in all cases where 'special knowledge' is given the information is known to other members of the family, or those who have turned up to witness the events. If the medium is also telepathic – the potential link is obvious – then they could as easily be picking up traces from the living as from the dead.

In some cases the language and attitude of the voices could be held to reflect the release of aggression and tension from within the focus.

This is a front-runner theory that helps us to discover the motivating energies of the focus.

What we learn from the communications with the poltergeist is not much more than we learn from the debate on mediums. But, as with mediums, we get closer to a recognition that there are certain people with special attributes, and when they are at the centre of a poltergeist case, the effects can be startling indeed.

Chapter 7

Responsive and Contagious Poltergeists

This chapter picks up directly where the previous one left off. Response is a form of communication – and below we set out ways in which poltergeists have been incredibly responsive to witnesses, onlookers, and investigators. We start by looking at a case from Father Herbert Thurston; although it is a rapping poltergeist, the observation of one of the witnesses was that it responded extraordinarily quickly, almost before the question was asked.

Northern France
Thurston records a first-hand account in *Ghosts and Poltergeists* from a correspondent known as MSL. (We can approximately date the experiences from early in this century.) MSL was living in Northern France, and heard of poltergeist activity in a nearby house where a lady lived alone with her grandson, a boy of fourteen. The boy was being thrown out of bed at night, and when the grandmother slept with him they were knocked out together. MSL visited the pair one evening and heard knockings and rappings, saucepans rattling and so on. On another night she saw the bed rise at one end, so that the leg of the bed was a foot from the floor. The grandmother was very frightened.

As time went on, neighbours heard of the poltergeist and several people – sometimes five or six in the room and as many as thirty outside – came as spectators. As MSL writes, 'The more people came, the more the knockings etc. increased in violence.'

MSL was with a group of people on one occasion when someone suggested seeing if the poltergeist could respond to questions. An interesting suggestion was made: to address the poltergeist as 'tu' rather than 'vous', because 'these things are our inferiors and we must treat them as such'. Asked if it was from God or the devil it rapped once for no, and asked if it was from the woman's family it rapped twice for yes. Then they enquired who had sent it to bother the old woman, and the knocks indicated the age and status of the 'sender'. MSL was unaware of the identity, but apparently the information confirmed what everybody else in the room suspected, having already decided who was responsible.

They asked it certain questions, such as the time by the church clock (which was both erratic and not visible at that time). In the morning they visited the church and were able to calculate that the knocks had been completely accurate. When asked to imitate various noises it was able to oblige (including sawing wood, beating a drum, whetting a scythe, and crowing like a cock). Its responses, MSL noted, were almost more than immediate. She comments: 'Each time it responded perfectly; also if they told it to tap on the ceiling, on the floor, or in the armoire, it did it almost before the words were out of their mouths.' MSL questioned it in English and it responded correctly, although she was the only person in the room who could speak the language. Another person spoke to it in Flamand and again it responded correctly.

In this instance we see that the poltergeist exhibits abilities and knowledge, and responds to the questions of its audience. But that is far from the only type of response poltergeists are capable of. When they combine their ability (or desire) to respond with some of their other manifestations, the results can be startling to say the least.

The Pontefract case, reported by Colin Wilson, shows some remarkable responses. During a vigil to see if the place was haunted, and what the poltergeist would or could do, a Mr O'Donald, together with the Kellys, relatives of the Pritchard family, stayed in the Pritchards' house. Towards the end of the session O'Donald said, 'They do funny things. They're very fond of tearing up photographs, I believe.' Quite why he should have thought so is unclear; it may have happened, but it is not a particularly common feature. None the less, as the Kellys locked up to leave they heard a crash, and found on the floor of the lounge a photograph of the Pritchards' wedding 'slashed from end to end, as if with a sharp knife'. In the same case the house was visited by the mayor and local councillors, and the mayor commented that it was lucky that a grandmother clock on the landing was still intact. It survived just half an hour longer, and then 'fell' downstairs and was destroyed.

In the Jabuticabal case, Maria was out walking with Volpe and a companion when she said she would like a little brooch. One fell at her feet. In the North Aston case, Whing asked for a quoit and received a quoit-shaped stone; he asked for a second and got that too. When he asked for two more, the response was enthusiastic. In the Tedworth case a servant was watched by a roomful of witnesses 'playing' with the poltergeist. Having seen boards moving he asked for one to be given to him, and one on the floor moved towards him. He asked for it in his hand, and it moved closer.

In the Bell Witch case, witnesses 'frequently cut notches on the sticks, casting them back into the thickets from whence they came, and invariably the same sticks would be hurled back at us'.

One of the two most responsive poltergeists of all time must be that of the Cardiff case. When the proprietors spoke of writing down what was happening a pen and writing paper appeared from nowhere and dropped to the floor; when someone asked for a sovereign, a Jubilee Crown appeared, falling beside him; the same person asked for more coins and three old pennies appeared; a carburettor float left in the workshop and 'challenged' to be moved turned up in Fred's change when he went to buy cigarettes; when John said to Pat, 'All we need now are some planks of wood,' planks were thrown instantly (and violently) into the workshop; a heavy brass shell case was fired with blue flames when 'Pete' (the poltergeist) was challenged to 'fire the shell'.

Stones thrown into a certain corner would be 'returned'. Sometimes the stones were marked – and were the ones to fly back. Fontana himself experimented with this. John told us that, as word of the poltergeist got around locally, people would come in to 'play with it'. One old man, apparently with some embarrassment, walked in with a few stones in his hand and asked to throw them into the corner; he did, and was delighted when they were 'returned' to him.

The second such 'highly responsive' case is Enfield. This is a particularly valuable case as it was so thoroughly investigated and written up. For the following details we have drawn from the researches of Guy Lyon Playfair and interviews with Maurice Grosse, the principal investigator of the case.

Mrs Harper and Maurice Grosse went on an LBC radio programme where one contributor told a story of seeing visions (just as the Harper girls were later to do) and another described a woman levitating (as was later to happen at Enfield).

Back at the house, when a chair moved in response to a suggestion from Mrs Harper, she commented, 'Next thing that'll happen the bed'll shift.' It did. Then she suggested the 'books'll come off', and a book flew off the mantelpiece. Playfair suggests Mrs Harper was 'developing an alarmingly accurate gift of precognition' – but perhaps it was the poltergeist developing its responsive powers. (Perhaps it was also developing a sense of mischief; the book was called *Fun and Games for Children*.) Maurice commented at one point that the poltergeist would have to rip the wallpaper off; and it did.

In a long list of paranormal activity, Playfair records spoon-bending. This was in 1977, not long after Uri Geller was making that a famous pastime. '. . . Perhaps to show that it was keeping up to date with trends,' Playfair comments.

Matthew Manning visited Enfield. While he was there he described writing that had appeared in his home; scribbled writing soon appeared on the walls at Enfield.

David Robertson, a student of Professor John Hasted, arrived (Hasted had achieved a great deal in metal-bending research). As Playfair states: '. . . as soon as he [Robertson] had moved in, metal began to bend all over the place.'

The responsiveness was clear to the investigators. Maurice Grosse observed: 'Look at its timing – the moment you go out of a room, something happens. You stay in the room for hours, and nothing moves. It knows what we're up to.'

Perhaps the most controversial comment – but one that we have come to believe likely from our own research – is Playfair's: 'It was becoming apparent that paranormal events only took place in the presence of people who believed them to be possible.' The state of mind of those involved would seem to play a part. Hasted, for example, believed that he got enhanced responses to metal-bending experiments if he was in empathy with the subject under examination.

Where responsiveness leaves and contagion takes over is not always clear, but the evidence is that poltergeists do have an element of 'contagion' attached to them. Those involved find that they 'take a little home with them' after working in poltergeist-infested houses. In the Enfield case, fires broke out after the investigators had visited another poltergeist case where fire was a feature.

In the Cardiff case both families involved had experiences in their homes; one family continues to do so, long after the activity at the workplace has ceased. In the Olive Hill case the phenomena moved from the Callihans' home to their son and daughter-in-law's house. Their son said to them: 'You got nothing to worry about now, Mommy, because whatever was up there . . . is now down here.'

Jerry and Elizabeth (at Hertfordshire) feared contagion from their case for two reasons: because similar events were happening to other members of Elizabeth's family; and because Elizabeth – and to a lesser extent Jerry – were experiencing strange events at work. We also picked up a little of the 'contagion' that Jerry and Elizabeth feared. A cassette player in the car malfunctioned: the cassette loaded itself and started playing. This had never happened before, and has never happened since – and tests to try to make it happen again (e.g. braking sharply) had no effect. Also, in the kitchen of our own home shortly after visiting Jerry and Elizabeth, the extractor fan over the hob turned itself on. Both of us were surprised at the sudden noise (we had been standing several feet away from it). Again this had not happened before, and never since. A year or so later, after a prolonged involvement in the case, we both received coins directly into our laps, John in front of two witnesses when he had no coins with him at all, and Anne the following day when with John in a taxi. (John had not at that point told Anne what had happened the previous day.) The same day, while we were talking on the telephone to the witness, a book on paranormal activity fell from the bookshelves. Also Anne left a pair of earrings in one room, and one of the pair turned up in another room in the centre of the sofa.

Maurice Grosse picked up his own examples of contagion. His car engine malfunctioned strangely during the Enfield case – and the voice knew about it. He heard footsteps upstairs in his house, when no one was up there. He heard a bang near him in the garden, identical to one he had heard in the Enfield kitchen. A diamond ring went missing and reappeared in circumstances suggestive of apporting.

The Harpers' neighbours at Enfield, the Nottinghams, reported phenomena similar to this: a key went missing and turned up three days later on the floor of Mr Nottingham's van. His son poured himself a drink, turned away for only a second and then found his glass empty. A friend visiting the house was 'touched' by a ghostly hand. Mr Nottingham's father reported classic movement of objects in the kitchen. Playfair notes that 'none of the Harpers were involved' in these incidents, but we know, of course, that Janet visited the Nottinghams' house; can the contagion effect linger over time? Apparently, others were aware of this contagion. Friends of the Nottinghams' were no longer visiting; one admitted it was because he was afraid to take 'anything' home with him, and another woman commented much the same thing. The Harper house was showered with stones – common enough in poltergeist cases – but it affected several neighbouring houses, reminiscent of the Thornton Road case.

Professor Hasted also supported the idea of contagion, stating that his wife had suffered inexplicable events at their home after his first meeting with Uri Geller. In fact, contagion associated with Uri Geller has become so widely reported it is known as 'the Geller effect'.

If responsiveness and contagion are true parts of the phenomenon – and the evidence of centuries and several well-examined cases is that they are – then can we learn anything from it? One clue lies in how we deal with cases. In the Miami case the poltergeist never developed beyond the phenomenon of movement and breakage of objects. Was this because the warehouse where this took place was so full of objects that the poltergeist never tired? Or could it be that the investigators, with so much happening around them, never wanted or thought to ask for any other phenomena?

At Rosenheim there was first a great deal of electrical interference, and one or two spurious movements such as swinging light fittings, but classic poltergeistery (i.e. furniture moving, drawers coming out of desks, pictures falling off walls or turning round while still hanging) started only after parapsychologist Hans Bender arrived. When Bender, a poltergeist investigator, examined the happenings, they changed, almost as if responding to his expectations.

The reason we examine the investigators' involvement in the manifestations is illustrated by the obvious difference between the next two cases: Enfield, and our own investigation at Hertfordshire.

At Enfield, as the above examples show, the investigators expected, and asked for, effects. And they got them. Sometimes they were just small movements, sometimes whole developments in the nature of the case. In Hertfordshire we dutifully noted what happened, but rarely commented on what had not happened or might happen. We rarely discussed with either witness the things that might occur, or talked with them about the range of poltergeist experiences. And accordingly the phenomena hardly developed at all over three years; the movement of objects which characterised that case remained more or less the same throughout its duration. For all we know it might have continued for years but for Elizabeth's death (which ended the case). It is worth pointing out that, on one occasion, Anne (Spencer) tested this theory, mentioning that they had not had any water-related happenings for some time (that had been a feature early in the case). The next time we spoke to them they told us that they had found an ashtray full of water just after our conversation. This case, therefore, may have been dictated to, at least in part, by the investigators involved – albeit not deliberately, of course.

This is not meant to be a criticism of either ourselves or other investigators. It is merely an observation, but one that may be useful in dealing with future cases.

In Enfield, what appears to have happened is that the poltergeist eventually 'burned itself out', perhaps because Playfair and Grosse 'exhausted it' in some way. Perhaps our lack of encouragement kept the poltergeist at Hertfordshire at an irritating but lower level of activity; perhaps, had we been more encouraging, the activity might have intensified, but stopped sooner. If it had, it would have been to the delight of the witnesses, a pleasure we were never able to offer them. However, as with most aspects of the dynamic energies behind poltergeists, this is speculation at best.

SECTION THREE

EXPLAINING
THE POLTERGEIST

Chapter 8

Haunts and Poltergeists

In this and the following chapters we shall be exploring further the experiences, examining what might be behind the poltergeist phenomenon – who, indeed, might *be* the poltergeist.

A London Community Centre

The beat policeman of a particular London suburb, PC Paul Doran, contacted us with details of a case that had arisen in a community centre local to him. Pauline, who runs the centre (and a day-care nursery for children), had heard several reports from people in the building of 'sensations' and poltergeist-like events, and had experienced several herself. Her husband and her colleague had also witnessed several events.

On one occasion, the children saw their toy 'sit-in' cars moving up and down the room without 'drivers', and there were claims that the toilets flushed independently. Pauline's husband once opened the door to the office (nobody was in the room at the time) and a paper aeroplane flew directly at him from within the room as soon as the door was open. In the same office papers are often 'moved about'.

PC Doran admitted to being very impressed by one event that he had witnessed. He had placed his hat down (the classic 'bobby's' tall hat), and when picking it up minutes later he found that the badge had been almost ripped off. No one else had been in the room apart from Pauline, to whom Doran had been talking. We examined the hat, and agreed that it took a lot to get the badge off – an inner cover had to be set aside, and then two spring clips pulled hard. PC Doran confirmed that he had never before (nor since) seen anything similar happen.

Pauline believes that one or more 'dead people' are responsible for the events. She identified that there were two distinct 'feelings' to the hauntings: a lighter, pleasant, feeling upstairs and an oppressive, darker, feeling below. The upstairs ghost was named 'Russell', thanks to his habit of rustling papers around. One evening a seance was held, and through a ouija board contact was made with a person who claimed to have died near the centre, the victim of a murder.

With the agreement of Pauline, a medium was brought in to the site. Eddie Burks had recently released a book on his work (*Ghosthunter*), and was well known for his abilities to pick up impressions in haunted locations. Eddie seemed to get a great deal of the background information right, and in particular he sensed two quite separate hauntings in different areas of the centre.

Upstairs, Eddie picked up the impression of an event he thought took place in 1954. *Dark bell-bottom trousers – dark, short jacket – metal buttons – two men struggling – Hit on the head by a plank of wood – Got him on the ground once, then he got up, still struggling – Then the other man hit him – He may not have immediately died.* Burks kept hearing the phrase, 'You've got it all wrong' – but he did not know if this meant that the spirit was telling him he had it wrong, or if it was the victim pleading with the assailants. Eddie believed that the spirit was in distress, and was afraid to move on. It seems that eventually Burks persuaded the spirit to go forward. (Interestingly, while a film crew were with Burks and trying to film him in a trance, three bulbs on the professional lighting rig blew;

the cameraman commented that he had never seen that happen before. All equipment had been working up to that point.)

We stayed overnight and throughout the working day several times, and experienced some of the haunting phenomena. At different times we heard deep thumping and banging noises from, particularly, the bar area; noises that seem to come from within the walls or as if someone was kicking the walls. No one else was present at that location (inside or outside the building) at that time. One very loud sound seemed to come from within a locked free-standing metal cupboard, but no explanation for this could be found.

Downstairs, the centre was used for weight-training. One of the rooms was reported to harbour a strong feeling of a menacing presence, as reported by several people. Together with Chris and Philip Walton from ASSAP, John (Spencer) experienced a very powerful impression of an unpleasant 'build up' there. All three investigators agreed on this feeling of oppression, and its sudden departure when a burst of light 'cleared' the atmosphere. We experienced other strange light phenomena in this location, one of which Anne (Spencer) discovered was at times responsive to an infra-red light flashed at it. And we witnessed the apparently spontaneous movement of objects in that area.

Such cases are very common – but are they poltergeist cases?

The poltergeist has been referred to as a 'haunted person'; certainly it is believed to be person-centred. One person can usually be identified as the focus, and the activity generally takes place around them and when they are present. It diminishes, or is absent, in their absence, and may 'follow them' to other locations. The haunt, on the other hand, has been defined as 'a scene of ghostly phenomena over time with different perceivers'. The haunt is therefore somewhere where phenomena occur independently of any one person. The haunt is also persistent, and can remain so for many years.

A good example of a haunted place is the White House, where there have been various reports of sightings, in particular that of the ghost of Abraham Lincoln. Some fifty years after Lincoln's death Grace Coolidge, wife of President Calvin Coolidge, apparently saw the ghost of the great statesman staring out of the Oval Office window. During the period of office of Franklin D. Roosevelt, Lincoln was seen in a hall in his traditional top hat and garb by Queen Wilhelmina of the Netherlands. One of Roosevelt's secretaries saw him sitting on the bed in the same room Queen Wilhelmina had been in. 'Lincoln' was putting on his boots.

Similarly, visitors to the Tower of London report sightings of Walter Raleigh, several Queens of England, and other apparitions. Reports from this most haunted of locations have been received for well over one hundred years.

These ghosts are all non-interactive, and belong in the category referred to as the 'recordings-type' ghost.

But how do we classify a case such as the Cavendish Hotel in Harrogate? We received reports from two people who had stayed in the same room. The first – Laura – had woken in the night to find a man sitting on her bed. He was facing away from her, and bending over as if putting on shoes and socks. He was oldish-looking, balding, fairly short, and dressed in red and white striped winceyette pyjamas. He stood up, walked towards the window, and literally disappeared.

We can assume that this is a classic 'recording'. From the dress and the actions of the man, we can assume that in life he had once occupied the room, had acted quite normally for a man in a hotel room, and had somehow left behind an 'imprint' that replayed to Laura at that time. We would classify the case as such were it not for Anne.

Anne had stayed in the same hotel, in the same room, approximately three weeks earlier. She had been awoken in the night by a loud bang, and found the bedside lamp on the floor at the other end of the bed – further than she could have knocked it by accident, if she had indeed touched it at all in her sleep. She did not see a ghost, but she had the clear sense of a presence, of someone sitting on the bed next to her. In the morning she had bitemarks on her thumb, which needed a tetanus injection to prevent infection.

The presence on the bed seems to link the two cases, yet only one contains elements that we would find in poltergeist cases. Still, it should not be classified as such; there is no evidence to suggest that it was centred around Anne, and every reason to believe it relates to the room and is therefore a haunting. But there remains some grey area between the two classifications.

Haunts may include several forms of ghostly phenomena – apparitions, sounds, smells, and so on. Indeed, on occasion they seem to contain poltergeist activity: rapping noises and the movement of objects. The London Community Centre case would therefore seem to be a haunt rather than a poltergeist, because of its persistence over time and the lack of a central focus.

Perhaps a poltergeist is no more than a ghost that just happens to want to 'attack' one person. The reason we think this is unlikely is that, outside of the field of poltergeists, ghosts rarely *physically* interact with the environment. The evidence suggests that the ghost is 'appreciated' mentally; even feelings of being touched ('the hand on the shoulder') may be induced directly to the brain rather than physically happening, even though there might well be an intelligence making the recipient feel the sensation.

The second possibility is coincidence – that a haunt happens to be lived in, or worked in, by someone who is a focus, and they manifest or bring with them a full poltergeist. This is almost certainly true in certain cases, but it does not explain the phenomenon we have noticed in public buildings (where there is the greatest overlap between the poltergeist and other ghostly manifestations).

The third possibility, which we favour, is that certain haunted locations set up what we have termed a 'pseudo-poltergeist', as explained below.

Charlton House, Greenwich

Charlton House is a Jacobean mansion, built between 1607 and 1612 in Greenwich, London. The building was designed by Inigo Jones. The house is believed to be haunted, one of the ghosts supposedly being Sir William Langhorne, who lived at Charlton House before his death in 1714. Another ghost appears to be a servant girl, who wanders the grounds with a baby in her arms.

The building is now used as a community centre. Recently the staff have reported to ASSAP investigators (ourselves included) some peculiar happenings. Included in the reports of apparitions and sensations is the movement of objects; for example, plants and their pots have mysteriously moved from their place on the mantelpiece in the Long Gallery.

ASSAP has been interested in this venue for some time and has conducted many vigils and collected many reports of phenomena. Chris Walton, who has led some of these vigils, said, 'The reports involve a huge variety of anomalous phenomena, including mischievous poltergeist-type activity.' It was during experiments involving table tilting in the Long Gallery that the authors were among others who perceived a ghost that appeared, or was of their own 'psychic' making. This raises the question of whether a haunted location can be used to develop psychic ability as well as bring on the more negatively perceived poltergeist effects.

The majority of accounts that combine ghostly phenomena with what seem to be poltergeists – certainly the strange movement of objects – come from buildings that are not private homes but are places open to the public, such as stately homes, castles, community centres or – typically – pubs and hotels. In these places there are often reported apparitions and other haunting phenomena such as the feeling of being watched, or simply the sense of a presence. The activity reported usually includes noises, electrical malfunctions, objects moving around and small breakages. William Roll observed: 'In poltergeist cases there are often daily movements and breakages of plates, knick-knacks, furniture, and other movable household effects, whereas in the typical haunting case such incidents are more rare and more spread out in time, if they occur at all.'

The pseudo-poltergeist, then, needs a focus. In this book, and in the great many accounts not included in this book, there is a large number of people who seem to be at the centre of poltergeist activity. If that number of people exist, then it is highly likely that there is an even greater number who 'don't quite make the grade'. Perhaps the ability to produce poltergeistery is inherent in us all. Perhaps there is therefore a large number of would-be foci who almost produce poltergeists but do not, for some reason.

But what happens if that would-be focus goes into a haunted place? Can the combination of their qualities and the 'atmosphere' of the location produce what looks like a poltergeist? This is what we mean by pseudo-poltergeist; a would-be focus, 'activated' by the energies within a haunt.

This might be why pubs and hotels commonly report poltergeist-type activity. It would also explain why in such locations the manifestations are of a ghostly nature, rather than displaying the characteristics of a true poltergeist. If we assume that some percentage of the population is capable of 'creating' poltergeist manifestations, then over a period of time any one pub is almost inevitably going to have a would-be focus in it. We set out below just three of the hundreds of cases of haunted pubs around the UK, which aptly demonstrate the overlap between the two phenomena.

The Bell

On Tuesday, 27 February 1996, we visited the Bell public house in Toddington, where some months previously the then landlord (a Mr Hyde) had left, saying he was tired of being woken every night by a mysterious presence (thought to be the ghost of a young girl who had at some time in the past been imprisoned in the room that was now his bedroom). A new landlord took over, but he left within two months. When we met Mr Howard, the following landlord of the pub, in 1996, he had been there for fourteen weeks. In that time he had noticed several abnormalities. Three glasses had fallen from the shelves, seemingly spontaneously – this was confirmed by the barmaid, Rose. She also described cups in the kitchen found swinging when one girl walked in, and small bottles falling (also happening around the same barmaid). Rose had been there for some years, and admitted that there had been problems for quite a while. Several regulars had told Mr Howard of happenings in the pub in the past, and he told us also how some strange things had been noticed by him in the bedroom he sometimes uses when staying overnight. He told us he had an open mind but is slightly interested. He suggested that some of the problem may have come from vibrations, the pub being fairly close to the road and passed by some heavy traffic. However, we have stayed there overnight and, despite the heavy traffic, felt nothing remotely likely to have moved glasses from the shelf in question. In April 1996 we spoke to Alan, who has for years run the disco at the pub, and he told us of several instances when normally reliable disco equipment would malfunction in the Bell.

The Grenadier

The Grenadier public house is a superbly atmospheric pub in a cobbled backstreet near Hyde Park Corner. Brightly coloured outside, the inside is furnished with dark wood, open fires, and many military antiques. Printed on the back of their menu is the story of an officer who, one September, was flogged after being caught cheating at cards. The officer died from this rough justice in the cellar, and his ghost is said to have haunted the pub since then; the phenomenon is especially noticeable during September.

Whatever the truth of this story, it seems certain that the pub is haunted. Successive landlords have reported happenings such as apparitions, presences distinctly felt but not visible, knocks and rapping sounds, and the movement of small objects, taps and electrical switches. In 1991 we spoke to the then manager, Peter Martin, who, although not inclined to believe in ghosts, told us of some strange happenings.

He explained how, one evening at around midnight, he was in the bar area with a Mr Edward Webber (a friend of the publican), when they both saw a bottle 'lift' itself from a shelf approximately one foot above floor height, to around head height in the middle of the bar space, where it exploded.

Second, Martin told us that the pub keys would mysteriously disappear from under his mattress where he kept them, and that they would usually be found some time later, somewhere else in the pub.

Alexandra and Paul Gibb took over as publicans of the Grenadier in September 1994. We spoke to them in 1995. The couple knew the reputation of the pub but had not actively read up on it. When we showed Alexandra the report of the keys vanishing she laughed and exclaimed, 'That happens to me!' The keys are now kept behind the bar, but are frequently going missing only to turn up later in a different place. Although nothing specific frightens her, Alexandra will not go to the cellar by herself.

The John's Cross Inn

The John's Cross Inn, near Robertsbridge in East Sussex, is well known for being a haunt locally, and the happenings there appear to include some poltergeistery. We interviewed all the staff at the pub, and have selected the following as the most significant reports.

Bob saw a bottle of tonic propel itself off the bar shelves, pause, then smash itself against the bar. This was also witnessed by three regulars. Bob's son, Peter, had a room upstairs in the pub. When Bob and Sandie (his wife) noticed his window broken they tried to enter the room (Peter was not in it), only to find that the TV had been positioned behind the door and the room was in general disarray. It would have taken some ingenuity to have placed the TV behind the door on leaving the room.

Peter discovered six Perrier bottles in the cellar lined up in a slightly curving line with all the labels facing one way. Bob found that the bottles had come from an empty but unopened cardboard carton. On inspection, he found that it would be impossible to remove the bottles from such a pack without tearing the cardboard.

We could continue with many such reports. Quite why pubs and hotels, and large public buildings, should so frequently be the sites of hauntings is not certain; perhaps we do not have to look further than the fact that many of them are old and they have seen a lot of emotion and history over their time. Perhaps haunts are little more than 'batteries' of energy that build up over the years. And when the would-be focus enters, some small connection is made.

When poltergeists infest homes they tend to build up in activity and abuse, reach a climax, and then cease. The time of infestation is variable – it could be as short as one night or last for several years. More commonly they last a matter of months. They are often attributed to one person. They are not friendly, and not comforting – indeed, they can be frightening.

When poltergeistery occurs in public buildings there are differences. There is usually no build up, no crescendo, rather a long-term, semi-permanent simmering. It does not normally become frightening (except perhaps to specific individuals with certain viewpoints), but is generally regarded as novel, even interesting. Pubs and hotels with poltergeists rarely hide the fact, and are only too pleased to be included in books on the subject – presumably because the publicity brings in more people than it deters. Even the few employees in such places who refuse to go alone into certain rooms, cellars and so on are rarely concerned enough to leave their jobs. We have found that tenants leaving pubs because of poltergeist activity usually do so because the constant low level of activity has worn them down rather than frightened them off.

Inevitably there will be cases of people working in pubs and public buildings who are themselves the would-be focus. In this instance, the manifestations would certainly seem to be those of a true poltergeist; but note that, even in cases where this seems to have happened, there is usually a history of hauntings before they came, and some haunting often continues after they leave. From the three examples above, we think that the John's Cross Inn may well be the site of a true poltergeist (even though it is clearly, from its history, also a haunt). One member of the family seemed to be a centre around which the disturbances were based. In 1996 we discussed with Chris Walton, who maintains an interest in the case, what the current situation was, and he confirmed that the activities had diminished to a very low level – 'normal' pub disturbances only; so the focus may now have passed through the 'poltergeist stage'. The Grenadier, by comparison, is a case where landlords and staff over decades have reported much the same phenomena; here there is no evidence of a particular build-up of activity around any one person or family.

In any disturbance that appears to be a poltergeist, we can often find elements of hauntings. This next case, it seems, started as a haunt and went on to contain poltergeist manifestations.

New Jersey

In 1978 Ted Sinclair bought a two-hundred-year-old farmhouse with the intention of altering it and opening a gift shop. The farmhouse had formerly been owned by one family for several generations. Sinclair was told when he bought the house that it was haunted; at least two people had reported ghostly happenings, including the apparition of a lady with grey hair, wearing a plain house dress.

During the fitting out of the shop the poltergeist-type events started to happen. A workman reported tools disturbed, an employee was struck by a light fitting, and a filing cabinet drawer opened without obvious cause. Electrical equipment in particular was subject to disturbance. In particular, the burglar alarm would go off all hours of the day or night, whether turned on or not! An unwound clock would chime, music boxes began to play by themselves, an adding machine printed rows of zeros for no obvious reason, and a sewing machine started by itself.

The 'poltergeist' was also responsive. Cindy, a niece of Sinclair, shouted a challenge to the poltergeist to prove itself. Suddenly, 'upstairs, it sounded like it was on the roof, there was a pounding: one, two, three, four; one, two, three four – it kept pounding . . . and I yelled out, "I believe you" . . . and as I said that it stopped.'

Karlis Osis (then director of the American SPR) and his associate Donna McCormick investigated the disturbances and the history of the house. They interviewed twenty-four witnesses. Given the nature of the occurrences, the locations of the witnesses, and the timing of the events they could not identify a focus for the activity. Whatever was disturbing the gift shop certainly acted like a poltergeist, yet it was not person-centred. Such a case adds weight to the possibility that some hauntings are the manifestation of an entity or a deceased person with some purpose (perhaps protecting the family home, in this case).

Yet this case, and others like it, cannot alone force us to surrender the hypothesis that poltergeists are person-centred, or even that some poltergeist activity is generated by the focus; there must be connections. The questions raised are interesting.

One is the theory of the learning curve. It is a demonstrable fact that people can perform a task with greater ease when they know it is possible. Consider the number of people who beat the four-minute mile after Dr Bannister broke the 'impossible barrier'; or the number of people who have climbed Everest (including a Japanese grandmother) since 1953 when it was first 'heroically' conquered. In business training and development, a good deal of emphasis is given to leading by example in creative, proactive work – precisely because others will follow once the barrier of 'believability' is broken down for them. The phrase from the business world that is relevant here is, 'Whether you think you can, or whether you think you can't – you're probably right.'

In poltergeistery, perhaps the focus is the one that generates the activity, and perhaps it is something all of us could do if we knew how. The 'natural' focus seems to do it without any knowledge (presumably because he or she has certain qualities). For those who seem to 'develop' the ability, possibly the first stage is believing it possible in the first place. Maybe those around the focus – family, workmates and so on – who are exposed to the happenings become capable of generating a little themselves, based on their new understanding and beliefs. This may help to explain the 'contagion' theory.

It is fairly safe to conclude that ghosts cannot ever move things. Even if we divide ghosts into interactive (communicative) and non-interactive (recordings-type) phenomena, we still end up with two categories of mental 'entity'. Perhaps neither can physically affect the 'real' world. But given the presence of a ghost, a would-be focus can start things moving – and the movements become attributed to the ghost.

Chapter 9

Non-Human Entities as Poltergeists

Pontefract

In August 1966 a house in Pontefract was infested by one of the most imaginative poltergeists on record. Living in the house were Joe and Jean Pritchard, their son Philip (aged fifteen) and daughter Diane (aged twelve). Living nearby was Mrs Pritchard's sister and her husband, Marie and Vic Kelly. When the poltergeist started its activities, Jean, Joe and Diane were on holiday; staying in the house were Philip and Mrs Pritchard's mother, Mrs Scholes.

Philip, on entering the lounge, saw his grandmother being covered in white dust that was falling uniformly from a level half-way up the room. The top half of the room was clear; the lower half was a 'snowstorm' of powder. Mrs Kelly came in, at her mother's request, and was equally amazed.

In the kitchen, patches of water were found on the floor, each with unusually neat edges (a characteristic that has appeared in other poltergeist cases). As soon as they were cleaned up new puddles would appear. The linoleum was pulled up, but the floor beneath was dry. Investigation by the water board could not explain the problem.

Spontaneously, the tea dispenser in the kitchen began shooting tea leaves over the work surfaces. Outside in the hall they heard a crash, and found that a pot plant had moved from the bottom to half-way up the stairs; its pot, however, had made it all the way to the top.

Vibrations were heard coming from inside a locked cupboard. They stopped when the door was opened, but later continued when Mrs Kelly returned at her mother's request. Also, the wardrobe in Philip's bedroom started 'tottering and swaying like a drunken man'.

A local friend, O'Donald, visited the house, inspiring some incredible responsiveness (as mentioned in Chapter Seven), but soon after that the activity ceased.

It was two years before the manifestations started up again. The first event of the revival was when Mrs Pritchard found her counterpane at the foot of the stairs; after returning it she found Philip's had been moved to the same spot. Plant pots upended on the carpet; decorating materials acted strangely, brushes and buckets flying about and a roll of wallpaper swaying 'like a cobra'. A brush hit Diane with a force that should have hurt; yet she seems hardly to have felt it.

The poltergeist was very disruptive, banging as if on a drum, turning lights off, and moving various objects around. On one occasion all the crockery in the china cupboard was thrown on the floor, but none was damaged in the slightest. Diane was pinned against the stairs by a sewing machine on a huge oak stand that had floated up towards her; it could have crushed her but it did her no harm. It could not be moved by Philip or his mother when they tried, but when Diane relaxed they were able to remove it.

In the bedroom Mrs Pritchard's bedcovers were ripped off, then her mattress and herself were thrown off the bed and on to the floor. This happened four times, though she was never hurt.

The poltergeist also ate. A sandwich was found to have been bitten through by something with 'enormous teeth'.

When Joe's sister, Maude Peerce, arrived, she told them they should seek a logical explanation. She was not able to provide one herself when the fridge opened, a jug floated out, and poured milk all over her head. She didn't seem to find one either when her gloves started 'acting', peering round spookily from behind the door frame. She concluded in the end: 'You've got the devil in this house.'

The poltergeist then really started showing off, with apport/teleport phenomena, as described in Chapter Four.

Attempts to exorcise the poltergeist did not work; indeed, after holy water was used, water was found trickling down the walls, almost as if the presence were making a point. Several 'religious based' manifestations followed, including a crucifix sticking on to Diane as if she were a magnet.

In terms of ingenuity, probably the cleverest manifestation was a white mohair coat that was found buried in a mound of coal; when it was pulled out it was completely clean.

Most frighteningly, Diane was seen being dragged up the stairs. 'Her cardigan was stretched out in front of her, as if Fred [the name the family had given the poltergeist] was tugging at it; his other hand was apparently on her throat.'

An apparition of a tall, dark, monk-like figure was seen by at least six people, members of the family and neighbours; two people together on the last occasion. This final sighting of the apparition was when it seemed to disappear into the kitchen floor – the room and indeed the part of that room that had been the central point of many of the manifestations.

The manifestations ended as abruptly as they had begun.

It is possible that the two-year break between activities could be related to the two children. Although Diane seems to be the focus for the second outbreak, she was in Devon for the first – and Philip seems to have been the focus at that time. Perhaps characteristics or dynamics running in the family can extend to poltergeistery. Or perhaps they were simply inspiration enough for the entity to visit them.

The action of Diane being pulled up the stairs was something of a turning point for researcher Colin Wilson. He states: 'What really changed my mind about the psychokinesis theory was Diane's description of being dragged up the stairs by the entity. Nobody in the house on that evening had any doubt about her terror and confusion. It is just conceivable that Diane's unconscious might throw her out of bed – by way of demanding attention. But by no stretch of the imagination can I imagine it grabbing her by the throat and dragging her up the stairs.'

The identification of the energy behind poltergeists as either the spirit of a human being now deceased or a 'living agent' using recurrent spontaneous psychokinesis (RSPK) are modern interpretations, based in the former case on the spiritualist belief of survival of spirit and, in the latter, on studies including psychological observations. The earliest recorded poltergeist manifestations were attributed to non-human entities in one form or another. Perhaps even before this, early man perceived these manifestations – and would almost certainly have attributed them to his gods or to mischievous elementals in nature.

For a period prior to the birth of spiritualism it was thought that devils or demons were responsible for the poltergeists. Names such as the 'Demon Drummer of Tedworth', the 'Devil at Mâcon' and the 'Demon of Spraiton' were used at that time. But these days it is difficult, if not impossible to define a case which demands to be explained as the action of non-human entities. However, Colin Wilson believes that this could be the case with the Pontefract manifestations. Such an array of activities, a degree of responsiveness, is perhaps most easily identified as an entity. Another obvious criterion to use in searching for possible entity cases would seem to be, quite simply, when the poltergeist identifies itself. In the Quebec case of 1889 the entity identified itself as such: 'I am the Devil. I'll have you in my clutches. Get out of this or I'll break your neck.' Later it said: 'I am an angel from Heaven sent by God to drive away that fellow.' It spoke as if it had a will of its own, threatening to steal Woodcock's pencil when he criticised it. It was seen in many forms, as 'a tall, thin man with a cow's head, horns, tail and a cloven foot, at another time as a black dog and ultimately as a man with a beautiful face and long white hair dressed in white, wearing a crown with stars in it'.

Belief in non-human entities is long standing, but has seen some revival more recently with New Age thinking. (Certainly the deliberate desire to achieve a close oneness with the Earth has revived a belief in elementals and so on.) If we look into fairy lore, we find several characters who demonstrate many of the attributes of the poltergeist – for example, the Boggart.

The Boggart was a mischievous trickster and is probably best described in the story of Yorkshire farmer George Gilbertson. The Boggart played tricks on everyone in the house, particularly the children, snatching away bread and butter, upsetting soup bowls, pushing them into cupboards and so on. Characteristically, no glimpse of the Boggart was ever seen. The children would play with the Boggart by thrusting sticks into a hole in a cupboard and watching them shoot back out again. One of Gilbertson's sons apparently pushed a shoe horn into the hole and it was pushed back so hard it hit the child on the forehead. Gilbertson and his family decided to move, packed up their carts and rode away, telling a neighbour that they were leaving because of the Boggart. They then had the shock of hearing the Boggart in the cart saying he was following them. The family turned round, deciding that if they were going to be haunted, it may as well be in their own home. According to the story the Boggart continued playing at the farm until it was 'tired', after which it was no longer felt to be present.

We think it is fair to acknowledge the probability that these early interpretations are just that: interpretation. Almost certainly, poltergeist activity came first: strange sounds, stone falls and movements of objects, mischievous interference in people's lives and so on. In the case of such paranormal activity with apparent intelligence behind it, it is common for people to attribute a human or animal creature to the disturbance. This personification can be seen in all cultures through the ages. In the European legends the explanation given for thunder and lightning was originally Thor in the heavens rolling his chariots or sparking his hammer on an anvil. Later, scientific analysis of thunder and lightning provided a different explanation, which has in no way diminished the reality of the weather phenomenon, but which in this case has made redundant the original beliefs about the Norse gods. We suggest that the poltergeist is in a similar situation; first came the phenomena, then the personification, and now there is a gradual move towards a greater understanding which is leaving the non-human entity and fairy theories behind.

Even modern researchers, however, do not fully accept this rejection of an external force. D. Scott Rogo, for example, in *The Poltergeist Experience*, comments: 'Cases such as the Amherst Mystery indicate that, whatever the true nature of the poltergeist may be, the force in some cases is to some degree independent of anyone in the disturbed family. In other words, *in rare instances* the poltergeist may be a true psychic invasion.' And Colin Wilson comments (in his book *Poltergeist*) that he originally believed 'that poltergeists are probably a creation of the unconscious mind' but, following discussions with Guy Lyon Playfair (and in particular the case of the Black Monk of Pontefract), 'changed my mind and convinced me that Guy Playfair was correct. Poltergeists are, for the most part, spirits of the dead.' In fact, Playfair takes the view that poltergeists are spirits or elementals which use psychic energy exuded from disturbed teenagers for mischief-making, abandoning it when they are bored. Although Wilson refers to spirits of the dead, it would seem that the wider definition of spirits (to include other entities) was in Playfair's mind.

In the Guarulhos case there are several occasions when the poltergeist is perceived as an apparitional entity; sometimes almost werewolf-like, also as a hairy arm with a claw. Also, Pedro claimed to have fought an invisible entity, slaying it with an invisible sword. Brazil in particular has many religious beliefs and cults which believe in demons, spirits and so on, and of course these are going to be interpreted in poltergeist cases by some analysts. Andre

Perciae de Carvalho, in 'A Study of Thirteen Brazilian Poltergeist Cases and a Model to Explain Them' (*Journal of the SPR*, Volume 58 No. 828), comments: 'Several groups, like spiritualists, evangelicals and Afro-Brazilians, believe in the existence of non-physical entities such as spirits, devil(s), angels, Oryxas, etc., which can communicate with our world through sensitive [mediumistic] people.' Because of the mix of religious beliefs in Brazil, poltergeists in that country can provide justification for Spiritist, Protestant and Roman Catholic beliefs in the devil and the spirit world, as well as representing black magic in action.

In Chapter Four we made the point that poltergeist cases in Brazil do not seem to produce water phenomena, at least according to the reports we have found. Might this be because the interpretation put on poltergeist activity in that country is one of attack by demons or spirits? Water is regarded as a symbol of purification and would certainly not feature in the 'work of the devil'.

There is some ground of reconciliation between a belief in entities and a belief in the power of the human mind: that of the mental construct of thought forms. We recently spoke to a psychologist who believes it is possible that a thought form created by the mind can take on a life of its own independent of its creator and, indeed, sometimes contrary to the creator's wishes. It is worth considering the Dubthab Rite of Tibet (as described by both W. Evans-Wentz and Alexandra David-Neel). Through this rite it is apparently possible to create a human-like apparition, known as a Tulpa. David-Neel, experimenting, created one, a monk-like figure that was seen by many other people. However, she describes how the control of the Tulpa slipped away from her; it became independent, reflecting her fears, and even changed its facial expression to a look of sly malignance, before starting to touch and rub itself against David-Neel. It took some considerable reversing of the rite to rid herself of the Tulpa.

Evans-Wentz recalls Milarepa, who projected so many Tulpas of himself that many of his followers believed they met him in various parts of the world after his death.

We can speculate that the archetypal adolescent youth – full of repressed energies and seeking subconscious effect out in the world – creates a Tulpa which is, to suit the circumstances, invisible but highly effective. Perhaps that Tulpa even begins to act independently of the will of the creator, even turning on him or her at some point.

But are all these interpretations just attempts to personify or stylise the otherwise difficult-to-grasp abilities of the human mind? Of course, we do not know at our present level of knowledge. It may be that when we have analysed the poltergeist effectively we will discover that 'it' is not one thing but several – that some poltergeist phenomena are the product of RSPK, some are Tulpa-like thought forms, some are spirits of the dead, some are hobgoblins from the fifth dimension, etc. What we can state at this stage is that the dependence on external entities to explain poltergeists is unnecessary (even if it turns out to be true).

Let us take a simple poltergeist movement, such as the pushing of a plant pot across a table. We can perform that feat in the purely physical world by applying our finger to the pot and pushing it. When it happens apparently spontaneously, and if we attribute it to an entity, then there would seem to be three broad ways in which the entity can perform this:

1. By being physical itself
2. By its own mental power
3. By being physical in another dimension in a way which can affect the physical world in this dimension.

There are some cases which not only suggest that an entity is present, but that it has physical form. In the Bell Witch case Porter held something, but it was only a weight. Several reports include people being throttled, scratched or bitten, acts which imply physical contact. In the case involving the Conway family, Stan felt the presence of 'something horrid'. As a boy he would scream in fright while in bed, and tell his parents that something was touching him. 'I do remember the feeling of an entity and it was not a kindly entity. It was a big, big, black entity, almost human, but black.' His father, at a seance in the house, also felt there was an entity present.

However, we cannot be certain whether the perception of physical form (i.e. weight, density, apparent contact) is objective, or imposed directly into the witness's mind. If the latter is true, then it may be imposed by an entity or by the witness themselves.

Many poltergeist activities simply do not reflect what we can do in the physical world; using known senses and physics alone we are not able, for example, to pass objects through matter. On this basis we must assume that the poltergeist, if physical, is not the *same* physical as us.

Propositions 2 and 3 rely on the ability of the entity to operate beyond the known laws of physics (or to operate the known laws in unknown ways), using what we might broadly and inaccurately describe as 'mental energy'. The question that arises from this is a simple one: why do we need the entity?

If entities are thought to be using 'mind power', then why can we not speculate on 'human mind power'; why do we need another source of mental energy? We know that certain poltergeist activity meets the needs of individuals, or has been said to match the repression of, usually, the focus. We can certainly speculate with some confidence that some poltergeist activity would seem to be generated by psychokinesis. Although there is difficulty in reconciling the abilities of RSPK in poltergeist cases with laboratory-tested PK, we can be relatively safe in accepting the possibility of the existence of this energy to some degree. Even the Playfair/Wilson belief in discarnate entities relies on them 'kicking a football' of human-generated psychic energy. If it is found that a human can generate psychic energy in this way – and we know humans exist – then we do not need to rely on an entity to explain it.

So why would we want to attribute poltergeist activity to a third party?

First, there are some obvious advantages in believing that a non-human entity is causing poltergeist activity. The most obvious is that it means it is not the focus or the family doing it, and thus they become the victims rather than the perpetrators. The claimants are therefore pleading for sympathy rather than risking the blame of others. Needless to say, it must be difficult for foci to believe they are creating the effect themselves as none of it, presumably, is done consciously.

Second, to believe in poltergeists means that we have to believe in some realm of ability beyond the known physical laws of science. By pushing the poltergeist into the category of a third-party entity we get the benefit of acceptance of a larger world around us with more exciting possibilities than we presently imagine, without having to revise our beliefs in our own powers. In short, we can remain comfortably human while all around us is chaos.

Third, humans (particularly in the Western world) are lacking in mythology. Our cultural beliefs have been shaken by dependence on rationalism, and we are left with a 'real world' which satisfies our scientific needs but none of our spiritual needs. The poltergeist becomes one way in which we can re-create our gods and spirits and populate our planet with entities to provide us with the myths we lack.

But we must return to the question of whether an entity is *needed* to explain poltergeistery. The views of researchers such as Rogo and Wilson, mentioned earlier, appear to be no more than the point at which their 'boggle factor' (i.e. what they find believable) is exceeded. But is it fair to set a personal 'boggle factor' in this way (even though we all do it, of course)? If we can push an object away with our minds, or pull it towards us with our minds, or throw ourselves out of bed without using our muscles, then does it really take so much more of a stretch of the imagination to choke our own throat and extend our cardigan out ahead while forcing ourselves up the stairs? There is really no logical reason why this should be any less possible. We might speculate – and it would only be speculation – on how such a mechanism would work. We can assume that Diane did not consciously want such a thing to happen, and so we need not speculate on why her subconscious might need it; but people do some very curious things to get attention, and the subconscious probably acts in an even more curious way as it is free of the social and other constraints with which the conscious is controlled. However, we might assume that at some level Diane believed herself to be in the grip of an entity. If her mind could generate some activity without muscular control, then is it not possible that she subconsciously constructed an entire 'theatre of the mind', in which a self-generated entity grabbed her by the throat and dragged her up the stairs? And would not the physical disruption of her clothing correspond with the images her mind was using?

In the Bromley poltergeist case (investigated by Manfred Cassirer) there was some indication that movements in the fertiliser had left the marks of a hand. This leads to speculation that it was something physical rather than a mental power. But the same arguments as above must apply. If the image used by the mind to move the fertiliser was that of a hand, would the resultant imprint not resemble one, even if it were only internally generated and externally projected?

Most of us have a point beyond which our will to believe cannot continue. We might be able to accept that we can push a coin across a table by the power of our mind, but we stop short of believing that we can cause one to appear in thin air. When the 'boggle factor' is passed, and we can no longer accept that something for which we have reliable witness evidence is within the power of people, then we do as humans have done since the dawn of time – we personify that strange power and attribute it to a demon.

Perhaps all that is needed to remove our dependence on demons and spirit entities is to relax our boggle factors and consider the possibility that man is a collection of talents, some of which we can only dream of and many of which are yet to be discovered. Or perhaps we have yet to understand a world that is not wholly the domain of Mankind.

Chapter 10

Poltergeists as Contact with the Dead

Hydesville, New York

In 1848 Maggie and Katie Fox were living in Hydesville with their parents, John and Margaret. They had moved there in December 1847, and it was to be a temporary home. In March 1848 the family was disturbed by a series of thumping noises in the night, which Margaret believed may have been made by a ghost. The effects varied: unaccountable shaking of walls and furniture; sometimes light knocks, sometimes very heavy thumps as if furniture was being moved, frightening the children to the extent that they insisted on sleeping in their parents' bedroom.

The Fox family was not the first to hear these raps. Michael Weekman, a former occupant of the house, had also heard such noises, but had left the house without discovering the cause.

One evening it was noticed that when the father made some noises they would be repeated. Mrs Fox described the night they first attempted communication with the raps, Friday 31 March 1848: 'It commenced as usual. I knew it from all the other noises I had ever heard before. The children, who slept in the other bed in the room, heard the rappings, and tried to make similar sounds by snapping their fingers. My youngest child said, "Mr Splitfoot, do as I do," clapping her hands. The sounds instantly followed her with the same number of raps. When she stopped the sounds ceased for a short time. Then Margaret [Maggie] said, in sport, "Now, do just as I do: Count 1, 2, 3, 4." Striking one hand against the other at the same time; the raps came as before . . . I then thought I could put a test that no one in the place could answer. I asked the noise to rap my different children's ages, successively. Instantly each one of my children's ages was given correctly, pausing between them sufficiently long to individualise them until the seventh, at which a longer pause was made, and then three more emphatic raps were given, corresponding to the age of the little one that died . . . I then asked, "Is this a human being that answers my questions?" There was no rap. "Is it a spirit? If it is make two raps." The sounds were given as soon as the request was made.'

The children soon discovered that if they clapped their hands the rapping noises would respond to them. Using a code, rapping for yes and no and the letters of the alphabet, the ghost identified itself as a murdered pedlar, Charles Rosa [or Rosma], who offered details of his family and claimed his throat had been slashed by an occupant of the Fox sisters' house five years before. He claimed his remains had been buried under the cellar floorboards.

A maid was found who had previously worked in the house; she confirmed that a pedlar had spent the night in the house. But as no missing pedlar was known to the police no murder enquiry was pursued, though digging in the cellar revealed some human teeth, hair and bones. (In 1904, a skeleton was found in the cellar with a tin box, allegedly a pedlar's box, nearby; the remains were discovered by school children following the collapse of the cellar wall.)

According to Catholic priest Montague Summers, Mrs Fox made some enquiries about the claims and discovered that there was a story about a pedlar – named Charles Ryan – murdered in the bedroom occupied by the two girls. Summers adds that the person named as murderer later turned up in Hydesville and 'threw very hot water on the story'.

Neighbours witnessed the rapping communication, and very soon hordes of people were turning up at the house, sometimes up to three hundred at a time, and the story was sensationalised in the popular press. It became the catalyst for bringing together the loose strands of a new religion of Spiritualism. This was almost a religion waiting to be born; the writings of Emanuel Swedenborg a century earlier, and of his devotee, Andrew Jackson Davis, had paved the way for a belief in contact with the dead. The Fox sisters' claim came at a time when channelling messages from the dead through mesmerism was a popular belief. They became a focus that crystallised a collection of beliefs into one new religious movement.

It was obvious that the noises were affiliated in some way to the children, as they only occurred while they were around. Investigators stripped the children in a search for contrivances; they also made the girls stand on pillows, and the noises continued. The children were split up and sent to different homes: Kate went to Rochester and stayed with her sister, Leah, and Maggie went to Auburn to stay with her brother, David. The noises continued at both places. While Kate was in Rochester, Leah found that she too could communicate with the spirits. A lodger at the house who gave little regard to the happenings found objects 'thrown' at him. Family members at Rochester had pins jabbed into them while they prayed; Mrs Fox's cap was pulled off, and the comb was pulled out of her hair. In Auburn, the noises were also apparent; a teenage girl visiting the house heard them and – an echo of the contagion theory – later found they were also present at her own home twenty miles away.

Back at Hydesville, noises heard were thought to represent the murder of the pedlar: '. . . horrible gurglings [presumably as the man's throat was cut] and the sounds of something being dragged across the floor.'

The family moved to Rochester; the knockings continued unabated; sometimes said to be loud enough to be heard a mile away. One day, while a visitor was asking questions of the spirit, a message in knocks was given: 'Dear friends, you must proclaim this truth to the world. This is the dawning of a new era . . .'

It was a considerable success. Inevitably, the sisters became the victims of a polarised media, some totally supporting them and the rest denouncing them as frauds. The 'stage show' became a 'road show', travelling various cities. The seances became more complex, with objects moving, tables rising, and members of the audience discovering that they too had mediumistic powers.

Very soon many others were attempting such communication, and by 1850 there were 100 mediums in the Rochester area. The craze quickly spread to Europe, where taking tea and moving tables became quite the done thing.

Shortly after this, Leah acted as the Fox sisters' manager, presenting them as – in effect – a stage show. By 1855 both Maggie and Katie were suffering from alcoholism and Maggie dismissed Spiritualism, now a recognisable religious force, converting to Catholicism. Katie continued the performances, which now included mirror writing. In 1871 she impressed the British Spiritualists in England, and Sir William Crookes in particular.

In 1888 Maggie – for a large sum of money – publicly denounced Spiritualism, confessing that she and her sister had created the rappings by cracking their toes. (This would hardly explain the earlier manifestations at Hydesville that shook the furniture and were heard 'a mile away'.) Katie sat silently by her side, not commenting. Maggie claimed: 'Spiritualism is humbug from beginning to end. It is the greatest rubbish of the century . . . Every so-called manifestation produced through me in London or anywhere else was a fraud. Many a time have I wept, because, when I was young and innocent, I was led into such a life.' The next moments were described by the *New York Herald*: 'There was a dead silence. Everybody in the great audience knew that they were looking upon the woman who is principally responsible for Spiritualism, its foundress, high priestess and demonstrator. She stood upon a little pine table with nothing on her feet but stockings. As she remained motionless, loud distinct rappings were heard, now in the flies, now behind the scenes, now in the gallery . . . Mrs Kane [Miss Fox's adopted name at the time, following her relationship with one Elisha Kane] became excited. She clapped her hands, danced about and cried: "It's a fraud! Spiritualism is a fraud from beginning to end! It's all a trick! There is no truth in it! Stop!" A whirlwind of applause followed.'

Elisha Kent Kane, an Arctic explorer of some repute, also seems to have believed her to be cheating, as he wrote to her in two letters: 'Are you never tired of this weary, weary saneness of continual deceit?' And also: 'Do avoid "spirits". I cannot bear to think of you as engaged in a course of wickedness and deception.' (Although often referred to as her husband, Maggie and Elisha may never have been married.)

Maggie also blamed Leah, indicating that she believed her elder sister had wanted to found a new religion. There may have been some jealousy of Leah; the sisters were hardly on speaking terms with her by now and, while they battled with their alcoholism, Leah continued the Spiritualist work, becoming involved in early 'materialisations'.

Although Spiritualism was already on the wane and rejected in the mainstream, devoted Spiritualists did not believe the confession, believing instead that Maggie was simply a very sick woman. Katie had not spoken at the public appearance, but later said she did not agree with Maggie's claims. In 1891 – notably the same year that Leah died – Maggie withdrew her confession. 'Would to God that I could undo the injustice I did the cause of Spiritualism when, under the strong psychological influence of persons inimical to it, I gave expression to utterances that had no foundation in fact.' She referred specifically to 'persons high in the Catholic Church' trying to force her into a convent.

Katie died in 1892 at the age of fifty-six as a result of alcoholism, and Maggie died less than a year later in Brooklyn, a destitute.

The house at Hydesville burned to the ground in an accidental fire in 1955, but in 1968 was rebuilt as a tourist attraction. At the rear of the rebuilt Fox house is the cornerstone of a shrine, which was never completed but which confirms the house as:

THE BIRTHPLACE AND SHRINE
OF MODERN SPIRITUALISM

Although the events at Hydesville are very much of a poltergeist nature, and apparently included occurrences at other houses, many of the phenomena around the seances were more to do with Spiritualism, rarely encompassing more of the poltergeist activities.

Analysis of the claims of the Fox sisters is generally thought to have confirmed the legitimacy of their paranormal experiences (without reference to what those experiences may mean in terms of survival of spirit). Certainly many investigators approached the Fox sisters with a view to proving them fraudulent, but ended up concluding that they were not. For example, William Crookes stated: 'For several months I enjoyed almost unlimited opportunity of testing the various phenomena occurring in the presence of this lady, and I especially examined the phenomena of these sounds . . . it seems only necessary for her to place her hand on any substance for loud thuds to be heard in it, like a triple pulsation, sometimes loud enough to be heard several rooms off. I have heard these sounds proceeding from the floor, walls, etc. When the medium's hands and feet were held – when she was standing on a chair – when she was suspended in her swing from the ceiling – when she was enclosed in a wire cage – and when she had fallen fainting on a sofa. I have tested them in every way that I could devise, until there has been no escape from the conviction that they were true objective occurrences not produced by trickery or mechanical means.'

It is quite possible of course that the Fox sisters faked some of the phenomena, possibly under the pressure of their commercial interests or their sister Leah's desire to start a religious movement, but some phenomena was genuine.

The Hydesville case may have come at a key point in history to trigger the religion of Spiritualism, but it was certainly not the first time contact with the dead had been claimed. The following case comes from around five hundred years earlier.

Provence, France

Guy de Torno had died, and a voice that claimed to be his was being heard in his bedroom. A prior, Goby, from Alais, wrote a report and described his investigation. He examined the whole house, left guards on the roof, and even persuaded an independent woman to sleep with the widow. Goby and others sat on the dead man's bed in vigil, and after prayers they heard some sweeping noises. The watchers then persuaded the widow to ask if this was the spirit of her husband, which a feeble voice confirmed, 'Yes, I am he.' The spirit spoke of the afterlife and purgatory, as well as his past sins, and was able to demonstrate its knowledge about a religious object carried by Goby that the others were unaware of. It was asked what form it took, and replied, 'A dove.' To prove it, the room was showered with white feathers.

This was Spiritualism long before the religion was founded; the events took place in 1324.

It is possible that the Provence case is not one of a poltergeist, though we might liken the shower of feathers to showers of materials in other cases; but the following story, from 1620, is one that more clearly relates to the rappings and communications of a poltergeist. After Humbert Birck had died in 1620, in Oppenheim, noises were heard in a house that he had lived in, and now belonged to his brother-in-law. This man, when he heard the noises, said, 'If you are Humbert, my brother-in-law, rap three times on the wall,' which happened. The noises were apparent for about six months, then stopped, and restarted some months later. This time a voice was often heard speaking of sorcery and malediction. In the presence of a curé, rapping answers were given to his questions. We also refer to the case of St Pierre de Lyon, where the activities stopped after the nun's needs were met.

These cases are very early, and it is difficult to comment on them because of the unreliability of the source material and the predisposition of time. And it must be remembered that not all poltergeists have identified themselves as spirits of the dead; indeed, the Bell Witch specifically stated that it was not, and that there was no such a thing.

However, we shall now go on to examine a few contemporary cases, where better records have been kept of their genesis and development.

Ardachie, Scotland

The Ardachie case of 1952 contains several characteristics suggesting an identified spirit. Mr and Mrs MacDonald were working as housekeepers at Ardachie Lodge, at Loch Ness in Scotland. On their first night the MacDonalds heard footsteps which they could not explain, and Mrs MacDonald saw a vision of an old woman beckoning to her. The MacDonalds moved into another room and were soon disturbed by rapping noises. Looking outside the room they saw an old woman with a lighted candle crawling along the corridor. Several people knew that the previous owner of the house, a Mrs Brewin, was an arthritic woman who had tried to catch out her servants (who she believed were stealing from her) by crawling around at night with a candle. During investigation by the Society for Psychical Research, investigators heard several loud knocks, and Mrs MacDonald saw a woman in a doorway again. In an apparent state of trance, she declared that Mrs Brewin was 'complaining' that her favourite tree in the rose garden had been allowed to die – a fact verified by the gardener.

There is a similarity between this case and the report from Newark Street, where noises were heard that the witnesses thought resembled the tapping of a walking stick. This seemed to be validated later when the family were told a former occupant (who had died there) had had a bad leg.

In Cardiff, the poltergeist activity had continued for years before Fred Cook – who had not been involved at the start but who now has the poltergeist in his own home – saw an apparition on three occasions of a boy in a peaked cap. Some connection was suggested, though never substantiated, to a boy that had died in the area in a traffic accident.

The tapping noises at Newark Street tell us very little, as they could well be part of the early stage of poltergeistery, but they were interpreted at the time in the context of a surviving spirit. The apparition, rappings and footsteps at Loch Ness perhaps indicate Mrs Brewin's spirit's survival after death, but may not point to a true poltergeist. At Cardiff there was no doubt of the existence of the poltergeist – but no direct connection to the apparition.

One occasion where the poltergeist appears to have identified himself as the spirit of a dead person is the Enfield case of 1977. The first suggestion came from Mrs Harper, who believed it was a child after seeing a 'child-sized' dent in a pillow. This confirmed what she had been thinking for a while. Apparitions were seen; the first was a grey-haired old lady (seen by two people). Janet saw the apparition of an old man in a chair in her bedroom. But it was through communication that the identities started to arise. The name Watson (a pseudonym used in *This House is Haunted*) first appeared on a drawing made by Janet while in a trance; and the name Frank Watson came to her sister Rose, also in a sleep-like state. They knew that a man called Watson had died in the house years before, but were aware of few other details. Rose said he'd died in a chair downstairs; months later they discovered from a neighbour that Watson had indeed died while sitting in the living room. All of this happened before the voice had learned to talk.

When the poltergeist identified himself as Joe Watson using speech, the investigators asked him if he had once lived in the house, and he replied that he had. Repeating a question Playfair had asked earlier, Grosse asked, 'Do you know you are dead?' The voice stated that he shook Janet's bed to get her out, as he used to sleep there. He stated that he had come 'from out the grave'. By now he was calling himself by another name (the pseudonym 'Bill Hobbs' is used in the book). He claimed that he went blind, haemorrhaged, and died in a chair.

John Burcombe, brother of Mrs Harper and living just a few doors away, much later saw the solid-looking apparition of a man in a chair in the living room.

These more recent cases seem to be bringing us close to the idea that poltergeistery is the work of the dead – but some caution is needed here. In the Berini case, although the events started with apparitions, traditional poltergeistery was yet to follow. In Enfield there are three basic phenomena at work: poltergeistery, apparitions and a voice. The apparitions never spoke, nor were they seen manipulating objects. The voice claimed to be a dead person and took credit for the poltergeistery – stating it had shaken the bed, for example – but the voice was not the apparition. In any case, we cannot be certain that it was not lying for effect; had it really created the poltergeist activity? We may still have a case of a haunt – perhaps involving the dead – *and* a poltergeist, which may have nothing to do with the dead. There is one thing of which we can be certain: a lot was going on at Enfield and it is possible that whatever came first may have opened 'psychic doorways' to the other phenomena, that may or may not have been directly connected. By the time the case was at its peak, sorting out one from the other would probably have been impossible.

We should consider the mediumistic component in haunts and poltergeists. In the Loch Ness case it seems that Mrs MacDonald became mediumistic during her time at the lodge. At Enfield there were several suggestions that Janet was an unconscious medium – indeed it is speculated that all poltergeist foci have some mediumistic qualities.

Matthew Manning, now well known as a psychic healer, seems

to have started on that road after an outbreak of poltergeistery in his own home, which was perhaps his introduction to, and awakening of, these abilities.

During the outbreaks of poltergeist activity in his house, Manning received messages on the walls, seemingly from spirits of the dead. In a locked room where pencils had been left, scratching noises suggested the action of writing. Over a seven-day period over five hundred signatures – some dated – appeared. The names have been authenticated from the parish records. These signatures concurred with a channelled message received by Matthew from Robert Webbe, who died in 1733 and had originally lived in the house, that he would bring 'half a thousand signatures of friends and family'. The 'promise' seemed to be the result of an argument; Matthew's father had asked Matthew to tell Webbe not to write all over the walls – 'We've got enough to do without him making more work.' But Webbe argued that it was his house, his walls – and he'd do what he liked!

Mediums brought into cases have sometimes offered the link between the poltergeist and the dead, as in the following case.

Nottingham

In 1972 Alan Gauld investigated a case in a council house near Nottingham. The family had been troubled to the point of anxiety by relatively common poltergeist activity: smells both pleasant and unpleasant, rappings, smashed crockery and so on. The family appeared to have identified the source as 'Granpa Jim', partly because of the smell of his pipe tobacco, and partly because a six-year-old boy in the house stated he had been talking to Granpa Jim (who had died some years previously). It is worth pointing out that Granpa Jim did not ever live in the house.

A medium brought to the house seemed to sense, without foreknowledge, a great deal of detail which corresponded to the old man. On the face of it this might suggest that Granpa Jim is correctly identified as the source of the poltergeist, but a number of questions arise. If the spirit of Granpa Jim was present in the house and responsible for certain haunting phenomena, this does not guarantee that he was responsible for the poltergeist phenomena. Also, we have to consider that the medium could have picked up the information about Granpa Jim from the family or the surroundings without it being any part of the phenomena under investigation.

There are similarities here to a case that arose in 1977, also in Nottingham, when a medium visited a house and gave details of a man she said was causing a range of 'low level' poltergeist activity. It appears that elements of the description offered were recognisable as a person formerly known to the lady of the house, but the lady chose not to take the investigation further.

In the Pudsey case, a medium visiting the house described a man in spirit. From the description he was recognisable as a deceased relative of Andrew Kirk. However, he was not identified as the cause of the poltergeistery, and his being there was said to be to comfort the couple.

Sometimes, mediums produce evidence that proves to be of little value.

Hannath Hall, Near Wisbech

In 1957 Alan Gauld and Tony Cornell investigated Hannath Hall; reportedly the new occupants were being bothered by strange noises. Before long both investigators heard rapping noises in the 'haunted room', and found that by using a code they were able to communicate. The spirit claimed to be a woman who had been murdered in the house in 1906. The investigators were unable to validate the claim.

In April 1959 (by now Gould and Cornell had made around twenty visits to Hannath Hall), they brought with them a medium and held a seance. A lady 'came through', and claimed that she had made the rapping noises. She said her name was Eliza Cullen [or Culler] and that she had buried her baby in the garden. Again the investigators were unable to validate this claim, although of course this does not mean it is untrue.

One instance where the poltergeist claimed to be a surviving spirit is the Black family case of Southern England (see Chapter Six). Like the Fox sisters, the Blacks worked out a rapping code and communicated with the poltergeist. It identified itself as Eric Waters, attempting to contact people in authority on earth in order to describe how he had been murdered (similarly to the Fox sisters' murdered pedlar).

The claims do not, of course, prove whether or not Eric Waters was a dead person communicating through rappings. Indeed, no record of him could be found despite extensive searches. From his communications he has been described as banal, inconsistent, simple-minded and child-like. Terry White, in *The Sceptical Occultist*, suggests he appeared 'more the fragment of a personality than a disembodied intelligence'. There is no record of a murder on or near the site of the Blacks' house. Terry White concludes: 'Colvin's investigation showed how a person-centred poltergeist case could masquerade as a ghost.'

Grosse and Playfair, in discussing the Enfield case, speculate that the tensions in the family allowed spirits to use the energy created. They do not specifically identify one of the communicators as the likely suspect, but Playfair suggests they were more like 'fragments of confused minds that once belonged to perfectly ordinary men and women who just don't understand their present condition . . .'

What we see from these few examples, and other cases, is that there is only a tenuous connection between the spirits of the dead and poltergeist phenomena. Very often that connection cannot be proven even at the rudimentary level, i.e. the person identifying themselves cannot be located in historical records and certainly no deeper proof can be made in any individual case.

We notice that, where a connection is made between the two phenomena, there is often someone present (sometimes one of the investigators) who believes in that connection, or is open to its possibility. In other words, there is either a medium who specialises in communication with the dead or a researcher who believes in it. It could be suggested that the connection has occasionally been brought about by seeking it in the first place. Bearing in mind the fact that poltergeists have displayed both intelligence and ESP – shown in the Black case – and also responsiveness and mimicry, then they might be able to 'pick up' on the beliefs of the family and investigators, and take them as a cue to impersonate a dead person.

There is an inherent illogicality between the manifestations of the poltergeist and the claim that they are brought about by a surviving personality following death. The actions of the poltergeist are often unreasonable, illogical and childish. Perhaps that is too judgemental – people trying to attract attention, people in panic, and people angry with others sometimes do strange things, and there are modern therapies that actively encourage people to 'find the child within' and fool around in illogical ways. Perhaps that is part of life on 'the other side'. Nevertheless, the poltergeist often seems to be *so* bizarre that something beyond the normal human condition appears to be at work.

This might be reason enough to reject the idea of a poltergeist being a surviving spirit and move on to other possibilities. However, we should not be too easily dismissive. Perhaps there are ways to reconcile the dilemma. Treat the following suggestions as 'mind games' only; we do not have the slightest evidence in their support . . .

We might consider that the world after death is sufficiently different from this one that it somehow merits such apparently childish behaviour. However, this would not seem to be a very sustainable argument; what purpose could a spirit possibly have in sticking a carburettor float in someone's garden umbrella?

The poltergeist may only be a fragment of the surviving personality;

it does not have to be the whole personality. It might be just the anger, or the frustration, or the confused, or combinations of these, without the wisdom, or the reasoning, or some other governing component.

We might liken the 'newly dead' spirit to a new-born (or even disabled) person. Rather as a baby does not have full motor function control in its first months, and there are some illnesses that impair the motor functions, so the spirit might be still trying to manipulate this physical world as it used to, but not yet able to realise it must use its mind rather than its muscles. The result may be perfectly intelligent intentions which manifest in the physical world as meaningless, clumsy acts simply because of a failure to perform them successfully. Perhaps the poltergeist activity ends when the spirit 'finds its feet' in its new environment.

Perhaps the interaction between worlds is naturally very limited. The spirit seeks a comprehensive signal to alert a former friend or relative that they have survived, and finds that they can only drop a few coins or break a few glasses; so the spirit tires of the limitations and goes off to do whatever more mature spirits do, and the phenomena stop.

Perhaps language as humans know it is a peculiarly human invention, and one that we shed at death in favour of something more intuitive or emotional, but it takes time for the surviving spirit to get used to not being able to make itself properly understood through words. Writing in poltergeist cases is limited in communicative value, and mediums often make the point that they receive impressions they must do their best to interpret.

We must remind the reader that these suggestions are at best speculation. There are probably hundreds of other possibilities, and one day we may find that the truth lies in none of them.

One obvious criticism of the possible link between poltergeists and surviving spirits is that, despite the fact that mediums claim to be truly in contact with the spirits on an intelligent basis, the one message we never hear is something along the lines of: Thank goodness you've got in contact with me. I was having a terrible time trying to get myself noticed by sticking carburettor floats in umbrellas, breaking bottles, etc. etc.'

At our present level of knowledge we must leave this line of argument, simply because there are too many unknowns. There are however other possibilities that need to be examined. The main line of enquiry must be: if poltergeists are not the dead, then what else explains the apparent connection?

We should first consider telepathy. There is of course much speculation about the existence of telepathy, but whether or not we can argue for its existence we certainly do not know the mechanism which enables it to work. One assumption often given or implied is that it is an instantaneous transfer. However, presumably it does not have to be instantaneous; it may be possible that a person who exits a room may leave an impression which can be picked up 'telepathically' later on. A sensitive person perceives this, and translates it as a surviving presence occupying the place, when in fact it no longer does so. This of course does not explain poltergeist phenomena, but may explain why researchers who favour spiritualist survival and seek a surviving spirit may be able to 'lock into one'. In the Loch Ness case, for example, if Mrs Brewin was present in some way then she may well have been communicating, but, equally, if Mrs MacDonald was mediumistic she may have been picking up, by psychometry, traces of Mrs Brewin's presence from long ago, which she 'translated' as visual images. Indeed, many mediums use psychometry, the picking up of impressions left behind.

The same argument might be put forward for traces left within a collective unconscious (if such a mechanism is accepted). If we ignore survival of spirit completely, then we might also argue that the apparent identification of someone who once lived in the room or died in the room is known to someone still alive. The person searching for a contact may telepathically pick up the impressions from someone else rather than from the now-deceased. Again, this only confuses the issue of investigating poltergeists, because of the predisposition of witnesses and researchers towards any particular interpretation.

There is a further possible connection to be considered: that all poltergeists are the result of activity generated from within a person (perhaps using PK), but that some of these people are dead. After all, if the living can move objects with mind power, and if the dead survive in a mental state after death, then perhaps the dead can do the same thing. This would explain in a very simple way why some poltergeists appear to focus on a living agent, and others seem to be active in haunted places where the dead seem to be at the centre of activity. It could also account for those cases of poltergeist activity where the focus is either not identified or is absent during activity, such as in the Cardiff case, where the probable focus, John, was not always present. The activity there even happened when David Fontana, the SPR investigator, was on the premises alone.

And there is always the possibility that a mental, self-aware, ghost can use the energy of a focus, or would-be focus, to manipulate the physical world.

But if we can speculate that the dead are able to use the same abilities as the living to create poltergeists, then we have one other obvious point to consider – why look for the dead? (Ignoring for the moment that some poltergeists have indicated they are – or masqueraded as – the spirit of the dead.) While we cannot be certain that the dead exist after death, we do know for certain that the living exist. And it is to them that we must now turn. In doing so we leave this chapter with a fascinating poltergeist and communication case that arose in Glasgow in 1975. Archie Roy describes the case in his book, *A Sense of Something Strange*. The events, described as violent, surrounded two boys aged eleven and fifteen. Rapping noises were heard, and communication was found to be possible. The rappings spelled out information about the early life of an occupant of the house. But in this case, during the time of the poltergeist activity, the man was still alive! Indeed, he was living downstairs, ill with cancer. The poltergeist activity stopped when he died.

The dead may be the driving force behind poltergeists, but we believe they have not yet proven their case. With that in mind we must now explore other avenues of enquiry.

Chapter 11

Possession

Mt Rainier

In 1949 a young boy, Robert Mannheim (Douglass Deen in some accounts), lived near Mt Rainier in Washington State, USA. He was thirteen when he experienced poltergeist-like noises for the first time.

(Interestingly they seemed to be linked to Spiritualism, and arose almost exactly 100 years after the movement's birth. Robert had been influenced up to that time by an aunt, Harriet, who was an enthusiastic Spiritualist. On the 100th anniversary they might well have discussed these matters in some depth.)

Spontaneous and unexplained noises were heard – first, what sounded like water dripping. The sounds seemed to come from his grandmother's bedroom, and when investigated by the grandmother and Robert (whose parents were out for the evening) they saw a painting of Christ shaking as if being 'bumped' from behind. When Robert's parents returned the dripping sounds had stopped, but the sounds of scratching and clawing could be heard. The sounds appeared to come from under the grandmother's bed, and continued for several nights.

Eleven days after the first sounds had been heard Robert's Aunt

Harriet died. When she had visited the Mannheims' house she had introduced Robert to the ouija board; and Robert now used the board to try to contact his aunt. (Considering what was to happen later, we must consider the definition given by some who have studied mediumship, that it is a benign form of possession – allowing a spirit to temporarily take over the body of the medium. Many believe that playing with such devices leaves the person open to psychic attack.)

At the time of Harriet's death the scratching sounds had ceased, but in Robert's room the sounds of squeaking shoes and marching feet were heard. Robert, his grandmother, and mother were all together on the bed, and Robert's mother, Phyllis, asked, 'Is this you, Aunt Harriet?' and suggested three knocks for 'yes'. Three knocks responded. Phyllis asked for four knocks as confirmation, and got four knocks. Shortly after this, the bedcovers were disrupted strangely, as if being clawed from below, and the bed was shaking.

The scratchings continued for three weeks. Over time, furniture and objects in the house were upset and sent flying around. Robert was thrown out of a large stuffed chair in which he was sitting. Things also happened when Robert visited other houses. At school, Robert's desk would move itself into aisles and cause quite a disturbance banging into other desks.

The family, now worried, asked for help from their local Lutheran church. The Reverend Luther Miles Schulze spoke to the family and witnessed furniture moving and dishes flying around. He agreed to take Robert to his home, where he was sure that no poltergeist activity would take place. He was wrong. That night the bed shook violently. Then the priest saw the boy tipped from a chair and slide stiffly, still under his blankets, under the bed. Beneath the bed, and apparently in trance, the boy bounced up and down, scratching his face on the bed springs.

After this Schulze realised he was unable to halt the happenings, and took Robert back home.

At home an awful manifestation started to occur. Robert was found to be suffering from scratches to his chest, arms and legs, but the scratches seemed to be coming from the inside of his skin. These scratches would later form letters, and then words. They even spelled out answers when questioned, causing the boy much pain.

The family were advised, 'You have to see a Catholic priest. The Catholics know about things like this.' The time had come to consider that a case of a poltergeist had become a case of possession.

When the priests visited Robert it seems he was able to speak some Latin – regarded (when unknown to the victim) as a sign of possession. He also spoke with what was described as 'a deep, gravelly voice'. This voice claimed to be the devil, and continued to torment the boy and his priests. An attempt to sprinkle holy water around Robert's bedroom resulted in the bottle being flung and smashed.

The Catholic Church identified the boy's case as one of demonic possession. Robert was exhibiting some of what, in their eyes, were the classic symptoms: speaking and comprehending languages (especially Latin) unknown to the person; clairvoyance; the knowing of secret matters; excessive physical strength; blasphemy; aversion to holy objects; and levitations.

Over time the case followed the pattern of the accepted stages of possession:

Infestation: demonstrated by the poltergeist-like scratching and rapping noises, then
Obsession: tormenting the subject (the skin markings could be regarded as a sign of this), and finally
Possession: the demon using the body for himself. (The demon sees through the subject's eyes and speaks using the subject's vocal cords.)

The Catholic ritual of exorcism was performed by a Father

E. Albert Hughes, but during the ceremony Robert slashed Hughes' arm, leaving it needing one hundred stitches and, it seemed, permanently injured. (Hughes may have been over-keen to forge ahead with the service of exorcism without proper research or preparation.)

The family moved to avoid publicity, and for a time the activity stopped. When it restarted the family were unsure about calling in the Catholics again; after all, the poltergeist activity had only turned to violence during the last exorcism. So they contacted a Jesuit minister, and eventually a Father William Bowdern was appointed as the exorcist to rid Robert of his demons. (The exorcism became famous after the story was dramatised in the film *The Exorcist* by William Peter Blatty.)

Interestingly, the exorcism was sanctioned before possession was believed to have occurred. As Thomas Allen (in *Possessed*) states: 'Bowdern decided to ask Archbishop Ritter to find and appoint an exorcist to perform the rite *before* a demon entered Robbie [our emphasis].' Allen goes on to point out that: 'Ritter had no conclusive way to prove that Robbie was possessed or in imminent danger of being possessed. The boy showed none of the traditional signs cited in the Roman Ritual.' (Note: some of the signs were in fact present, such as the talking in Latin.) 'So Ritter faced a dilemma: if Robbie were suffering from mental illness rather than from diabolical possession, evil was not involved. An exorcism would do no good and could even worsen his condition. But if this were diabolical possession, then evil, a terrible form of evil, was present and Ritter had to order a priest to risk his soul to save Robbie's.'

We see then that what became a possession case started as a poltergeist case. It was so classic a poltergeist case that we must consider the following questions:

1. Was it coincidental that someone surrounded by poltergeist

activity should also apparently become possessed?

This seems unlikely. The number of people affected by poltergeists is a fraction of the population. Even less, the number possessed. That both things should affect one person without connection seems statistically unlikely to say the least. We can safely assume that there is some link. Most cases of possession have poltergeist activity during their early stages. The Church also believes there is a link, based on its examinations of possession cases.

2. Did one develop from the other?

The Church believes there is a progression, and it seems logical that there was such a progression in this case. The poltergeist seems to have developed, acquiring different manifestations over time, and it seems to have progressed from infestation, through obsession (i.e. scratch markings on Mannheim's body), and eventually into possession, as depicted by the voice claiming to be the devil and the use of 'unknown' Latin.

3. If it did develop, then how and why?

Either the progression was 'natural' in evolution, or it was the product of an intervention. It may have been the introduction of the priests that caused a boy suffering from a poltergeist to believe himself possessed, because their belief system accepted the reality of possession, and they took the poltergeist activity – infestation – to be an early stage. Robert was considerably influenced by his spiritualist Aunt Harriet. He might have been equally susceptible to the suggestions of the Catholics, who were subliminally 'telling' him he was affected by demons.

4. Was development inevitable?

If poltergeist foci can become possessed, why do they not

all become so? If there is a restraining factor is it external to the focus, or something within the person? Is it an attitude, a belief, or perhaps just a level of response? For example, for some an increased level of fear might lower resistance ('psychic barriers') and either allow in an external possessor, or create a growing belief in one. Arguably the 'irritation' of poltergeist activity might lower the psychic defences in some way, and allow the intrusion.

If this is so, then there could be a danger that, treated carelessly, any poltergeist focus could become possessed. However, the fact that it happens so rarely shows that it is not inevitable.

5. Given the above, why do some poltergeist foci go on to become possessed?

It has been said that in all possession cases the possessor needs some kind of opening or invitation. In *Deliverance* (edited by Michael Perry), the point is made: 'Possession . . . cannot just "happen" unwittingly. Man cannot catch demons as he catches the common cold. He has to put himself at risk and in a vulnerable position. The greatest risk is that of straightforward invitation.'

Perhaps the use of a ouija board by Mannheim was a way in which he extended that invitation.

6. Finally, was the poltergeist in this case a 'real' poltergeist?

Of course we have no way – yet, at least – to define a 'real' poltergeist; at best we can describe it as a collection of manifestations. While there is always the possibility that two sets of identical manifestations may not come from the same cause, in this case there is too much similarity to other poltergeist cases for this not to be regarded as one. Apart from the nature of the manifestations themselves, one important aspect of poltergeists is that they are responsive not only to the needs or fears of the families affected, but also to the investigators. Poltergeists respond to the knowledge and beliefs of the investigators; and in this case the investigators were priests.

We should examine some of these similarities in a little more detail. Apart from starting with scratching noises and so on, the case contains many factors that have arisen in other poltergeist reports. Voices, apparently speaking through the focus, have been reported in a number of instances. In this case voices emanated from Robert's mouth, and were attributed to the devil. There have been cases of what seem to be telepathy, or acquired knowledge, in poltergeist cases, which might go some way to explain the knowledge of Latin that arose in Robert's case. Many poltergeist victims tested have shown high ESP scores.

We must further note that the second stage leading towards possession – that of obsession – also contains aspects seen in many poltergeist reports. Victims often report being hit, bitten or scratched and display the marks of these attacks, for example in the Bristol and Guarulhos cases. These effects were present in Mannheim's case. The possessed develop a hatred of holy items; the poltergeist has also often shown a marked dislike for religious paraphernalia (although not as intense as that shown by the possessed). One clear difference between possession and poltergeists – at least in this case – is that exorcism in the case of possession works. Religious exorcism in poltergeist cases can make matters worse. In this case an early sprinkling of holy water aggravated the situation.

But we would stress again that perhaps the most important distinction is in the belief systems – primarily of the focus, but also of those around him or her. If a person believes the devil is attacking, then it might manifest outwardly in that way; if a person believes ghosts are running amok in a house then they are more likely to see apparitions; if a person believes the poltergeist results from psychological disturbance, then they might find an unhappy or disturbed person to act as focus. By giving Robert instruction in the Catholic faith he was in one sense trained to believe in evil and demons which, of course, helped him to believe in the power of exorcism and thereby facilitate the release from his tormentor.

In the end, Robert became a devout Catholic. Perhaps his beliefs helped to make the process of exorcism work. But perhaps that same belief first helped make the process of possession begin.

Such a link between focus and 'investigator' may well be apparent in this next case, which first appeared in the 11 October 1925 edition of the *Sunday Express*.

Keighley

Nineteen-year-old Gwynneth Morley was reported as being 'haunted' for over a year by a poltergeist. Everything in the room she stayed in would be thrown about and smashed. Furniture, including heavy settees, was lifted and turned over or broken. During meal preparation, water and butter was spilled on the floors. Half a grapefruit disappeared, to be replaced with bananas. When the grapefruit reappeared 'whizzing past her ear', the bananas disappeared, and reappeared later on another table. The poltergeist activity was tremendous, and Morley's room 'looked as if a tornado had swept over it'.

The case was examined by Montague Summers, a Catholic priest, who was critical of the 'cure' that was – in this case – effected. He comments that 'the main cause of this apparent cure is said to be the mediumship of Mrs Barkel'. Mrs Barkel's spirit guide apparently helped in finding the cure for the girl; a band of Indians (in spirit) were to protect Morley from the disturbances.

Summers comments: 'It is an ordinary instance of obsession, and will be easily recognised as such by those priests whose duty has required them to study these distressing phenomena. That the interpretation put upon some of the occurrences is utterly false I am very certain.' Summers believed that the forces that 'helped' Morley were actually evil in disguise, and sums up by saying that she 'should have been exorcised by a trained and accredited exorcist'.

If the spiritualists who assisted Morley are guilty only of using their own interpretation, then surely so is Summers. In the light of the Mannheim case, and the responsiveness of the poltergeist at Enfield, we must consider that Morley may have had a lucky escape, and could have had to go through possession before cure.

We might learn a little more by examining a different case of poltergeist/possession, which arose just after the turn of the century.

Umzinto, South Africa

Germana Cele, a sixteen-year-old Bantu girl who attended Marian-hill Order Mission School, was, in 1906, thought to be possessed by the devil. She announced it herself, showing Father Horner a written pact she had made with the devil. From that point, her character changed dramatically. She became violent, exhibited great and unusual strength, growled in an animal-like fashion, and appeared to be in conversation with beings not apparent to others.

She appeared occasionally to 'break free' of her possessor, calling out to the nuns to help her to confess, or 'Satan will kill me'. Guarded by two sceptical nuns, Germana berated them angrily, and 'with a giant's strength' threw them across the room and beat them.

Her head or mouth would become burned when touched with holy water (though never with ordinary water, even when substituted without her knowledge), and she showed an aversion to the cross.

Many manifestations arose during this period of diabolic possession that arise in poltergeist cases. She showed some ESP ability in telepathy and clairvoyance; she was able to describe in great detail a journey taken by Father Erasmus while she had stayed behind in the mission. When made fun of by one man she humiliated him by revealing highly intimate details of his personal life. Certain phenomena surrounded her: at least twice, fires burst out nearby; once, as she walked into the kitchen, a huge flame leaped into the air frightening everyone except herself. Indeed, throughout the poltergeist activity she laughed a good deal, and sometimes seemed even to be in control of the manifestations. On another occasion, after she shouted in her sleep, huge flames shot from the bed. The boards and bedpost were half burned – though she was untouched by the heat.

Germana was moved from the dormitory into a house and given a private room, but once there banging and pounding noises started. Continuous thumping on the door happened each night. When a monk and a Reverend Father stayed up on guard, they reported: 'Suddenly at ten o'clock there was a sound like a thunderclap at the door. Inside, everyone cried out in fear and horror. We hurried outside to find out what was going on. Then again one, two . . . five tremendous blows. We went out once more and again there was nothing in sight. Banging and pounding could be heard on several doors inside the house. We went to investigate and found nothing. The noise and poundings continued in the rooms of the religious brothers, in the smithy, in the storage section, and even in the shed, where the animals had become restless, but nowhere was there anything to be seen. The noise stopped by eleven fifteen.'

Germana frequently levitated, floating three to five feet in the air even while handcuffed and also while sitting in a chair. Observers noticed that her clothes did not seem to obey the laws of gravity; they would stay around her as if she were in a 'normal' position, rather than hang down from her floating body. Her last levitation was in September 1906, during exorcism, and in front of 170 witnesses. The ceremony took two days to complete. In January of the following year she lapsed, apparently making another pact with the devil, and was exorcised for a second time in April 1907. The final departure of the devil was accompanied by foul smells – perhaps the last poltergeist-like feature of the case.

Here we see that the poltergeist-type activity seems to have started

214

after the possession, of which the girl seems to have had fore-knowledge. The interesting point is that the poltergeist activity seems to have been used by (rather than heralding the arrival of) the 'demon'. It is possible that the nature of Germana's 'pact with the devil' makes her a very willing, voluntary subject, and there-fore she may have missed out – or gone through very rapidly – the early stages of infestation and obsession. Alternatively, if we consider poltergeists to be the manifestation of RSPK, then we might conclude that Germana not only convinced herself she was possessed, but 'used' the energy so released to produce poltergeist phenomena. There are instances where she seems to have enjoyed the effects, perhaps demonstrating a power beyond that of others. It is unclear, but very thought-provoking, whether she actually con-trolled the manifestations, or merely knew that she was the focus of them. As we have seen, 'poltergeist power' could be an awesome power indeed were it ever to be in a person's conscious control.

We should not overlook those rarer cases where the poltergeist is blamed as a manipulator. Michael Williams, in *The Supernatural in Cornwall*, relates the story of a poltergeist in St Issey, near Wadebridge, which occurred during the Second World War. Fol-lowing the death of a baby in the family there were several reports of poltergeist activity, and the baby's older brother – then aged nine – was identified as the focus. The boy seems to have been aware that he was the focus, but he insisted that 'something' was making him do it. Under scrutiny the child picked up an object and threw it across the room, but the witness then saw the object lift of its own accord and throw itself back! In a later test by his mother, the boy was placed in the kitchen with his hands tied; still witnesses watched objects thrown about as if by some invisible force. The case implies some form of possession, the possessor making the boy do things, but true paranormal effects were also present.

It could be said that mediumship is a form of controlled, volun-tary possession. Certainly poltergeist-like activity is associated with physical mediumship; table rapping and bangings, table tilting, and other manifestations are common in that situation. Possession is a mechanism of transfiguration mediumship. However, mediums do not go on to become 'truly' possessed, and so perhaps the comparison is unfair. We must of course recognise that mediums are 'possessed' by deceased humans, not demons. And the element of control is important – the fact that the person knows what is happening may reduce the 'fear factor'. Maybe that is what feeds the growing poltergeist/possession situation in a 'normal' case. If so, then there is at least some link between stress reduction and the reduction of poltergeist activity. Perhaps it also prevents possession taking hold.

The Church believes that poltergeist infestation can be cured by their approach. Canon Carl Garner described to us many successes in halting poltergeist activity. He has dealt with many cases in the UK, and more during his thirty years in Africa. He believes that the person should come into the Church. 'In the long term,' he stated, 'you need to be in a supportive context.'

But what if there are no possessors? We must consider the possibility that demons do not exist. Perhaps everything in possession and poltergeist activity is internally generated. Many believe that it is a mental illness. Does our evidence hold true if that is the case?

In fact, yes it does – and very well. The key would seem to be belief, and expectation, influenced by others who have beliefs and expectation. Such abilities are dependent on proving the existence of much that we call paranormal, and that would be true in either case.

There is some value in discussing not just *how* possession progresses from infestation through obsession till finally reaching possession, but *why* it should do so. There would seem to be two main possibilities regarding demonic possession: either an external entity (a demon) genuinely possesses a person, or alternatively a person *believes* that they are possessed.

If we consider first the possibility of a genuine external entity,

9. John Matthews of the Cardiff poltergeist case talking to author John Spencer.

10. Fred and Gerry Cook of the Cardiff poltergeist case who are at the time of writing still experiencing poltergeist phenomena in their home.

11. The community centre in North London;
a haunted building with poltergeist-type events occurring.

12. Pauline and Dawn, managers of the community centre, who have
both noted disturbances and the strange atmosphere.

3. One of the 'early morning' photographs taken at the start of a vigil in the Hertfordshire poltergeist case showing the porcelain duck in situ.

14. During the day, with the occupants of the house absent and only the investigators on site, the porcelain duck was found standing on the bedroom carpet.

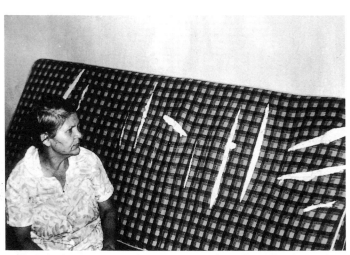

15. Sofa showing cuts made by the poltergeist at Guarulhos in Brazil.

16. Stones which fell near investigators, including one of the authors, during a vigil in London.

why is it not simply capable of possessing its victim 'unannounced', as it were? It is too far-fetched to believe that it is obeying either a code of ethics or a code of morality (like some kind of Prime Directive that keeps it in check until an invitation is extended), so we would have to assume that the build-up phase, i.e. infestation and obsession, is some kind of natural process necessary for possession to take place. If that is the case, we might speculate that poltergeist activity is the first salvo in a battle of attrition; the demon frightening and wearing down its potential victim, who is gradually lowering their psychic shield and allowing full possession to take place. Perhaps in another way the victim becomes open to the possibility of paranormal activity, and that openness becomes a vulnerability which allows the possession.

If we take the view that possession is a mental condition generated by the victim, then the build-up phase is presumably something of a credibility factor, i.e. it would be difficult to go straight from non-involvement in the paranormal to full possession without some personal exposure to lesser effects (albeit being generated unknowingly by the victims themselves). In this case the poltergeist activity might be, as is commonly speculated, a form of RSPK that reflects some kind of deep subconscious need on the part of the witness.

Chapter 12

The PK Potential

Rosenheim

Investigators, police and reporters were, in 1966, called to a lawyers' office in Rosenheim in West Germany. They had been called in after electrical disturbances could not be traced to a natural fault by engineers. Lights were 'blowing', bulbs were coming out of their sockets or exploding, and the telephone system was seemingly making calls on its own.

Professor Hans Bender was called to the office. He identified the focus, a nineteen-year-old girl named Annemarie Schneider. There was good reason to single her out. Light fittings would swing spontaneously as she walked beneath them, and the disturbances would only begin after she had arrived at work in the morning. Just before the Christmas holiday some intensity of activity was reached; light bulbs exploded, lamps were set in motion, pictures would swing and fall to the floor, drawers opened by themselves. Annemarie was becoming tense and upset; she would sometimes be found sobbing or shouting.

The office was quiet for the holiday period, and there were no disturbances even though there were people there. Activity resumed on 9 January, when Annemarie returned to work. Just eight days later the climax of activity was reached: several workers (including Annemarie) received electrical shocks, and chairs were rising into the air even when occupied.

The police were called in to investigate the damage. They were sceptical and suspected trickery, and kept a close watch on Annemarie. But they were shocked into belief when a heavy oak cabinet moved, and realised this could not have been done by her even if she had had help. It took two strong policemen to return the cabinet to its original position.

Annemarie was noticeably the most tense of the staff. This may have come from realising she was the focus rather than the other way round. 'I never had influence over anything. I was very hurt indeed,' she said. Bender commented: 'Annemarie seemed to instigate psychokinesis in response to her emotional problems.' Terry White in *The Sceptical Occultist* comments of the degree of her condition: 'She reacted to the disturbances around her with hysteria and muscular spasms which temporarily paralysed one of her arms.'

Annemarie was dismissed from her job; the cost of the damage had totalled 15,000 Deutschmarks. Her notoriety was hard to shake off, and she felt obliged to leave other jobs when phenomena occurred. There is no evidence that any disturbances happened at Annemarie's home.

In later experiments, she was found to be a poor PK subject but her ESP ability was high – a profile which fits most poltergeist foci.

One of the most prominent theories to explain poltergeist activity is that of RSPK – recurrent spontaneous psychokinesis. This explanation dispenses with, at least at its face value, the need to depend on the spirits of the dead or discarnate entities to perform poltergeistery, and suggests that the activity is generated by as yet unclassified forces emanating from the human mind.

We can see from the many cases in this book that the poltergeist is 'person-centred', and seems to cluster around one individual.

But is there any evidence to suggest that the poltergeist is 'person-generated' (i.e. a product of the mind rather than an outside agency)? There are a few cases that give us very specific clues. In certain instances the manifestations are of a nature that accurately reflect something highly personal in the life of the focus. For example, in the book *Deliverance* there is a report of a poltergeist that disturbed or destroyed only objects that were one of a pair. The woman in the case had had a mastectomy (the removal of one breast). Following a second operation removing the second breast, the poltergeist still occurred but not so specifically. As the woman came to terms with her condition, so the poltergeist activity faded.

Canon Carl Garner told us of a case he had investigated where a woman found a knife from her kitchen in her bed; he anticipated a Freudian element, until he discovered she was about to remarry, and had, in a previous marriage, been stabbed by her husband.

There are several cases where the focus seems to be unhappy at work; and the manifestations centre around them while they are at work. The Cardiff poltergeist started after John had been worried about the success of the business; perhaps significantly its activities included the spontaneous appearance of money. *Deliverance* contains the account of a man who had considerable work-related problems, and seemed to be causing poltergeistery at the workplace, until he confided in and sought help from his partner.

There are less specific speculations we can add to the argument. In the Hertfordshire case the poltergeistery worsened whenever Jerry or Elizabeth was alone; this factor brought them together, and we might argue that it served a purpose as such. But we can only guess at that; we have no confirmation from the couple that they needed an excuse to stay together. In most cases – and in particular the historical cases that were never examined from a psychological point of view – we do not know the driving frustrations of the focus specifically enough to know if the manifestations match them accurately.

It is not inconceivable that an outside agency, an entity or spirit of a dead person, could produce such specific manifestations, but for the time being we shall examine the potential of the focus as the 'generator' rather than just 'attractor' of events.

Before speculating that poltergeistery is mind-generated we need to examine whether or not there is evidence in any circumstances that the mind can generate anything beyond the physical body. Some definitions are required. PK (psychokinesis) is the apparent ability of a person to affect the physical world by mind power alone, without the use of known physical forces. There is the implication in this definition that PK is deliberate, or at least arises with the knowledge of the subject. However, there is a belief that PK can be generated 'accidentally'; this is termed RSPK (recurrent spontaneous psychokinesis), and is held by some to be the driving force behind poltergeist activity. (There is some debate about the technical definitions of psychokinesis and tele-kinesis. The latter avoids reference to the source of the 'movement at a distance'; thus we use the former in this book, as we are referring to 'mind power'.)

To avoid being over-pedantic about the source of such human powers, we use the phrase 'the human mind' loosely, to encompass an image of a human-generated force capable of acting on physical objects without apparent physical connection. That such abilities might actually generate not from the mind but from the soul, the astral body or some other component, is for this purpose ignored.

One of the first people to experiment scientifically into PK was Dr Joseph Banks Rhine, who set up the first laboratory studies of parapsychology at Duke University in North Carolina in the 1930s. The work started when Rhine was approached by a gambler who claimed that he could influence the way dice fell at the gaming tables. Rhine set up statistical experiments. The basis was simple: volunteers were asked to influence the roll of a die; PK would be suggested if, statistically over a long period, a high number of correct throws could be shown, more than that which would be expected by chance alone. Rhine believed that his experiments confirmed the reality of PK, but his techniques have been questioned and debated ever since, particularly on the grounds of lack of supervision.

Physics professor John Hasted, of Birkbeck College in London University, also experimented with PK in the 1970s. One subject, teenager Nicholas Williams, apparently bent keys while he was at some distance from them; recording equipment indicated that several keys were being affected at the same time. Strips of aluminium sheet were left in a room and Hasted and Nicholas left the room. When they returned they found the aluminium 'rippled' like a concertina. Another experiment Hasted undertook was to see if subjects could bend paper-clips enclosed in glass; this was only successful when a small hole was left in the glass. Hasted believes that his experiments were sufficiently controlled to ensure that fraud, while mechanically feasible, was not possible. As poltergeist researchers we have noticed that, even when the most spectacular of events happen, there is always room for a small percentage of doubt, almost as if the agency producing the effect does not wish to be completely 'pinned down'. If we assume that PK (and RSPK) are manufactured by the human mind, then perhaps there is a limiting mechanism in most people which prevents them creating an effect that would be too overwhelming for their own beliefs. Hasted recognised that he got more positive results in his experiments if he was emphatic, working with rather than challenging his subjects. Similarly, the state of mind of the poltergeist focus may also be of importance. Empirical scientific method is suspicious of these sorts of problems, perhaps rightly, but science may one day have to recognise that 'if that's the way the world works, then that's the way the world works'.

Princetown Engineering Anomalies Research (PEAR) was started in 1979 by Robert Jahn to test whether or not human minds could upset sensitive equipment used for information processing. With help from psychologist Brenda Dunne, many controlled experiments were set up. One of these experiments tested the ability of subjects to influence binary signals on a random event generator. The volunteers were asked to will the machine to produce either a greater number of pluses or minuses – in effect, 'heads' or 'tails'. As a control, other volunteers were asked simply to watch the machine in action. After around two million tests (taking twelve years) the PEAR researchers concluded that nearly one hundred of the volunteers seemed to be able to affect the outcome, if only slightly. The control group produced results conforming to chance. Jahn and Dunne were able to state that they had found 'scientific evidence that human consciousness plays an active, albeit small, role in the creation of physical reality'.

Another series of experiments which shed light on the PK debate were those conducted by psychologist Kenneth Batcheldor. He conducted around two hundred sittings in a seance-like atmosphere. (Significantly, however, these were experiments undertaken without recognised mediums, and were not seances in the sense that no attempts were made to contact the dead.) After around a dozen failed sittings, eventually a table rose from the floor while the only hands touching it were on the top surface. As Batcheldor put it, 'It seems that we had stumbled upon a genuine paranormal force.' Over successive experiments levitation was accompanied also by rapping sounds, rotation at high speed, and the table 'walking' around the room. In some experiments even the chairs that the people were sitting on were suddenly moved. Guy Lyon Playfair sat in on some of Batcheldor's experiments and was considerably impressed. His report in *If This Be Magic* is based on audio recordings made at the time. He comments that after his first sitting he had 'witnessed more PK activity in a single session than I had in ten years of investigating poltergeist cases'.

Playfair described one session where they used a four-foot-wide table weighing 46 lbs, that took some effort just to lift at all. Batcheldor asked for raps by first knocking on the table himself. The table responded with raps and all manner of other sounds.

Then it vibrated very loudly. When Playfair sat on the table he described it as feeling like a vibro-massage and quite enjoyable. In the end they conducted several experiments with the table, which included all four witnesses sitting on it while it slid around the room. They stopped the session after that. As Playfair said, 'If PK could move more than a third of a ton, it could have knocked the house down.'

In later summarising his experiences at a talk in Czechoslovakia, he summed up the requirements as, 'a table, darkness, and a minimum of two people. The mental part is more complex. You must have total faith in the possibility of generating PK, and a total lack of resistance to the idea of doing this yourself.' Too much analysis might be unwise, but he also adds: 'PK tends to behave as if directed from a level of the group mind, far beyond any individual's conscious reach.'

Similar experiments to Batcheldor's, but with a unique twist, were conducted by the Canadian research group led by Dr A. R. G. Owen, when they created a spirit called Philip. Theirs were similar to Batcheldor's experiments, except that the group was focused towards one purpose. They convinced themselves of the existence of a fictitious ghost called Philip who, they decided, had lived in seventeenth-century England. According to the script Philip had committed suicide after letting down his mistress, who was burned at the stake for witchcraft. By focusing on a belief that they could contact Philip, they were able to produce rappings and also a 'walking' table (which performed even under the bright lights of a TV studio, where Philip happily responded to questions from the audience). Interestingly, belief played a major part in this experiment: when, in a fit of anger, one of the experimenters shouted at Philip, pointing out that he was only 'made up', the responses stopped until the group had reconfirmed its belief.

Perhaps the most extraordinary claims for PK were made by the group SORRAT in the 1960s and 1970s. The Society for Research on Rapport and Telekinesis was formed by Professor John Gneisenau Neihardt. The group was largely composed of those who seem to have some psychic ability, and much of the approach was 'seance-like'. Over a period of time SORRAT produced, they claimed, a wide range of events we associate with poltergeist activity: vibration and rappings, and levitation, for example, of a small picnic table. Many experiments were witnessed by the whole group and were photographed on several occasions. The table also 'walked'. On another occasion a planchette 'hopped like a frog' for well over half a mile in front of two astonished but delighted researchers. Once, Dr Neihardt's chair rose into the air while he was sitting in it, apparently in response to his desire to levitate as D. D. Home had done decades before. Dolls and toys were also seen to levitate.

In order to validate the experiments, deliberately targeted PK was directed at objects in sealed glass boxes. There was a whole range of claimed successes, which included objects moving spontaneously and the appearance of spontaneous writing. They even filmed a pen in a glass box writing a message on paper at high speed. A toy train that had been placed in a box was found outside it – apparently teleported. While being filmed three rings apparently linked together, further suggesting the passing of matter through matter. Apports during the experiments included objects from locations well away from the farm in which the experiments were being conducted, as well as the recovery of items thought lost, including a maid's ring, which apported into the hand of one experimenter much to the surprise of the maid, who had lost it some time before.

Dr John Thomas Richards comments: 'The assumption has often been made that gross movements of heavy objects are somehow different, at least quantitatively, from the PK movements of very light objects . . . I do not choose to make this distinction when dealing with the SORRAT PK experiments, because both light and heavy objects have moved paranormally to about the same degree . . . apparently the weight of the target object makes little difference.'

Dr Richards also points out that the experiments frequently 'failed', but phenomena that had not been intended or expected would happen. In effect, SORRAT created poltergeist-type events – demonstrating RSPK better than they did PK.

One experiment involved a stainless steel spoon suspended inside a sealed glass bottle. Two members of the team stroked the bottle, willing the spoon to bend. They were not particularly impressed with their initial results, although they thought the bowl of the spoon may have flattened slightly; but when the following month four members of the team put the bottle on the table and stroked it, repeating the words 'bend, bend', the handle twisted and the bowl of the spoon flattened. The proceedings were photographed, including the spoon gradually jamming in the bottle, unable to swing freely.

Two famous experimental subjects have been Nina Kulagina and Felicia Parise. Kulagina, a Russian housewife, has been described as 'one of modern science's greatest puzzles'. She has been filmed and observed causing small objects to move by PK. These abilities were first noticed in the 1960s by psychologist L. L. Vasiliev at the Institute for Brain Research in (what was then) Leningrad. Vasiliev tested his observations and found that Kulagina could move objects by willpower, even if they were under glass. From this he went on to conduct many experiments, often filmed. Kulagina's abilities were real and well attested to. In February 1996 a British television audience was able to see for the first time some of the film – which was impressive, but the object and movements, although obvious, were insignificant when measured against the disruption caused by a poltergeist. (This difference between PK and the apparent power of RSPK we will consider shortly.) Probably the most spectacular experiment was when Kulagina successfully separated the white and the yolk of an egg without physical contact, again recorded on film. Equipment monitoring her physiology recorded loss of weight, and pulse and blood-sugar responses consistent with stress. This may be significant, as stress is believed to be a factor in the production of poltergeist activity.

Felicia Parise, who had watched film of Kulagina, attempted in 1971 to replicate the PK movements in front of witnesses. Although she seemed to have some difficulty and required much practice, she did find some spontaneous events would occur. Objects would fly about or fall from shelves around her. Because of this, she decided not to continue with the work and allowed her abilities to subside.

Kulagina also had similar effects. Once, following a bout of anger, 'a picture moved to the edge of the shelf, fell, and smashed to bits'. She learned to control her abilities, whereas Parise decided to deny them. Just as Kulagina and Parise found that PK could arise spontaneously, so there is a famous version of this exteriorisation attributed to an argument between Freud and Jung. The two were together in Freud's study, and Jung was getting angry at Freud's intransigent position. Jung began to feel a change come over his body, as if his diaphragm hardened and heated. Suddenly there was an explosive sound from a bookcase. Jung indicated it: 'There, that is an example of a so-called catalytic exteriorisation phenomenon.' Freud dismissed it, possibly angering Jung even further. Then there was a second sound. This time Freud admitted that he was impressed. (There is a lesser-known sequel; the sounds arose again when Jung was not there. Does this suggest that Freud had been angered enough to produce his own RSPK, or had Jung left some residual energy behind?)

Digressing slightly from PK, but perhaps tangential to its understanding, was a report in the *Daily Mail* of Friday 17 May 1996. Scientists at the University of Technology in Sydney had demonstrated how brain-waves were being used to turn on lights, operate toy cars and so on. Electrodes placed on the subject's skull were hooked up to an amplifier and transmitter. The subject, physicist

Les Kirkup, 'closed his eyes and relaxed, raising the voltage from his brain-waves from 0.9 to 3.5. The desk-lamp across the room clicked on. As he opened his eyes, the voltage dropped and the light switched off.' Professor Ashley Craig commented: 'What we have done is to identify signals within the brain which we believe everyone can control, and devise some novel technology to pick and analyse those signals. Once analysed, those signals can be made to activate any device such as a household appliance.' Scientists had found what was described as a 'mind switch' between alpha waves (associated with relaxation) and beta waves (which occur when a person is drowsy). It was that mind switch which was harnessed. It was further commented that 95% of people tested were able to control their mind switch without training.

Interestingly, many paranormal phenomena occur at the transitional stage between sleep and wakefulness or vice versa (hypnopompic and hypnogogic). Although this is the point at which people are subject to hallucination we have always argued that it may also be the point at which the creative, intuitive part of the brain is functioning and perhaps more open to genuine paranormal phenomena. The study at Sydney suggests that the same point, between relaxation and actual drowsiness, is also the point at which the 'mind switch' comes into operation.

We believe there is sufficient evidence to suggest that PK has been proven to exist, even though there is a great deal yet to be understood about it. But we are left with a wide gulf between this and the power of RSPK associated with poltergeist phenomena.

Influencing the fall of dice, and the cleverness of separating the egg white from the yolk, hardly compare to lifting several tons of concrete (as apparently happened in the Sorocaba case). An examination of poltergeist claims shows that the power used is far greater than anything that has been demonstrated in laboratory conditions. For example, in the Rosenheim case a heavy oak cabinet was found to have moved; the focus, Annemarie Schneider, could certainly not have moved it by normal means without help.

One possibly naive explanation of the difference in power between PK and RSPK may simply lie in the difference between a controlled experiment and genuine anger. When the unconscious, irrational mind takes over, it appears to be able to call on more extreme resources than otherwise. There are several accounts of parents performing incredible feats of strength, physically lifting objects in order to rescue or safeguard their children, when, in 'normal' conditions, they would not be able to show such extreme strength. Perhaps the same is true of 'mental strength', and perhaps RSPK is generated by a part of the brain beyond conscious or rational control where much greater potential lurks. Indeed, maybe those parents were being assisted by some form of PK or RSPK when they acted in those extreme situations.

Actual injury, though, at the hands of a poltergeist (and in the context of this chapter, therefore, at the hands of the uncontrolled power of an individual's mind) is very rare. Stones moving at great speed hit people with hardly any impact and rarely any injury. It is conceivable then that there is for the poltergeist a 'governing factor' which, even when out of control in the literal sense, still allows for human respect, tenderness or restraint. The strange quality of impact by poltergeist-thrown objects was mirrored in some of the SORRAT experiments. Dr Richards comments of the table levitation experiments: 'When the table levitated, it usually did not simply fall to the floor like a stone. It frequently seemed to float down very gently, and while it might strike one of the experimenters, it rarely caused even a minor contusion.'

One other noticeable difference between poltergeist cases and PK experimentation is that, occasionally, events happen when the focus is not present. In the Hertfordshire case, for example, objects frequently moved when the couple were not in the house. This may not be particularly significant, however, as we have no knowledge of the 'distance', or time delay, over which RSPK can 'work'.

Curiously enough, when we look for PK ability in poltergeist foci (as opposed to RSPK), we find little evidence of such. We do, however, find a high ESP factor. Annemarie of Rosenheim was found to be poor at PK though good at ESP. Similarly, Felicia Parise was first tested for ESP and found to be a good subject. In 1966, after disturbances at two workplaces, a teenage boy named Heiner was tested by Hans Bender and found unsuccessful at PK but high on both telepathy and clairvoyance.

Julio, from the Miami case, produced some interesting results in a laboratory. Firstly, a decorative bottle 'fell' when he was around, and a few other events occurred, suggesting something of the poltergeist was still with him. On PK tests he generally scored badly, barely above chance and certainly not enough to merit a positive conclusion. However, in tests at influencing the fall of dice he scored way above chance; whenever the dice machine broke and the dice fell out, they fell mostly to the appointed numbers. The experimenters were surprised the machine broke at all, as it was a very sturdy device, but during the experiments it broke four times. Did this suggest that Julio's RSPK was more prevalent than his PK?

The state of mind involved is probably the most important unresolved question. Before we go on to look at the mental state of the focus in particular, we can consider what might be learned by examining two situations where poltergeist activity, or at least PK, *ought* to be present if it were 'that easy'.

There are many claims, primarily from within the Catholic faith, of 'moving statues'. The claim, briefly summarised here, is that statues, mostly of the Virgin Mary, are seen to vibrate or rock or make other movements, often in front of large crowds. This is thought to be a sign of the Virgin's presence. One religious affairs analyst pointed out that, in one case of 'moving statues', many people in one place on one night looking at one statue reported movements – but all reported them at different times. In addition physical evidence is absent; there is no evidence of scratch marks or stresses in the stone or its surroundings. We might ask ourselves why a large group of people – all of whom would probably love to see the statue move, all of whom have a vested interest in seeing it move from their own religious point of view, and all of whom exhibit the very wishful thinking that investigators believe can create an illusion of movement – are *not* able to summon up enough PK to make the statue move. The fact that this does not appear to be the case suggests that the crowd's state of mind is the wrong one. The degree of passion and desire is not enough, or is not appropriate; perhaps it requires the negativity of anger or stress to exteriorise itself.

The second example relates to children. If PK were 'that easy', then there ought to be large numbers of children making their cuddly toys, dolls and other games play for them without touching them. We are not inundated with reports of spontaneously marching soldiers or dancing teddies, and so we must conclude that, again, the state of mind (rather than mere desire or opportunity) is important.

What have we shown with this chapter?

As the manifestations of poltergeist phenomena bear similarities to the manifestations of controlled experimental PK, we believe that at least part of the mechanism of the poltergeist relates to RSPK, and will one day be explained in those terms. Even so, it is difficult to reconcile all poltergeist activity in this way; there is no evidence that PK can produce voices, for example. And some manifestations stretch the abilities of PK to the limits of credulity – for example, the spontaneous starting of fires or the appearance of water. Perhaps in these cases PK (masquerading as RSPK) moves the gases and molecules to the right place and then mixes them in appropriate ways. But we must be cautious of attributing too much to one ability; even if we conclude that the poltergeist is person-generated, perhaps a whole range of talents were needed, some of which have yet to be 'dreamt of in our philosophy'.

We must also consider the views of those who believe that 'mental powers' may be a factor in poltergeist activity, but not the only factor, and that the powers of the human mind are linked with, or used by or in conjunction with, discarnate entities or the spirits of the dead. Nothing in this chapter eliminates that possibility with certainty, but as Roll comments: 'I do not know of any evidence for the existence of the poltergeist as an incorporeal entity other than the disturbances themselves, and these can be explained more simply as PK effects from a flesh-and-blood entity who is at their centre. This is not to say that we should close our minds to the possibility that some cases of RSPK might be due to incorporeal entities. But there is no reason to postulate such an entity when the incidents occur around a living person. It is easier to suppose that the central person is himself the source of the PK energy.'

Gauld and Cornell, in their 1979 book *Poltergeists*, commented on the PK experiments that had taken place in the previous forty years: '. . . they have yielded no clear or certain evidence as to the nature of PK. Thus to explain poltergeist phenomena by reference to PK is to explain the unknown in terms of the unknown.' We believe that this statement still holds true.

The Scottish judicial system has a verdict not available to the English courts: that of 'not proven'. This is generally accepted to mean that the suspect is thought to be guilty, but that the evidence is too little to convict. We believe that RSPK is almost certainly behind some elements of poltergeistery, but until more is understood about the nature of this and other attitudes of the mind, the verdict must remain 'not proven'.

Chapter 13

Eliminating the Poltergeist

The most common dilemma for investigators is the conflict of interest they will encounter when called out to a poltergeist case. They will arrive, interview members of the family, and note down all the fascinating manifestations of the case. It takes a certain level of interest – even passion – to commit so much personal, unpaid time to these studies in the paranormal. Inevitably then, investigators feel a certain sense of excitement when confronted by a 'good' case. Eventually they will nod their heads and confirm, 'Yes, we would love the opportunity of studying this case,' and the family will look at each other briefly, with slightly puzzled expressions, and one will turn to the investigator and say, 'Study it? We don't want you to study it – we want you to get rid of the wretched thing!'

Investigators learn very early on that poltergeists are not just noisy; they are, to quote Harry Price, 'mischievous, destructive, noisy, cruel, erratic, thievish, demonstrative, purposeless, cunning, unhelpful, malicious, audacious, teasing, ill-disposed, spiteful, ruthless, resourceful and vampiric.' And if you have such visitors in your house your main concern is that they should leave!

The removal or eradication of poltergeists comes in many forms, based largely on the belief systems of the investigators dealing with the case (naturally taking into account the belief systems of the families affected). There are a few instances of people who have learned to live with their poltergeist. With acceptance the manifestations can be viewed from a different perspective. In the Cardiff case, John came to accept that there was a poltergeist in his work premises; once he realised it was not adversely affecting his business (only one or two stories reached him of people afraid to visit the workshop) he switched from finding it worrying to finding it quite an interesting experience. Nevertheless he admitted that, once it ended, he was glad it was all over – and he did not want it back. Fred, who had also been affected by the poltergeist, still has incidents arising in his home. He has said that he regards the poltergeist as 'a privilege', and seems untroubled by it. Both he and his wife say they would like it to end, particularly as it worries their children (adult children who do not live at home), but Fred admitted that if it did stop he would worry that he had offended it in some way. Several of his comments suggest a certain affinity to 'Pete'.

Catherine Kirk, whom we interviewed just prior to finishing the research for this book, was very upset by a poltergeist that moved objects, furniture and keys. She was even more concerned by some manifestations she was experiencing at night. But after a visit from a medium she has come to accept that she shares the house with spirits, and now finds it far less bothersome than before.

All these people, however, would be happier if the poltergeist left. Most affected families are in no doubt or ambiguity that they want the manifestations to stop, and speak of wanting to resume a 'normal' life, of which they feel they have been deprived. Jerry and Elizabeth, for example, found they were increasingly unwilling to have friends round in case anything happened while they were there – or, worse, in case the friends 'imported' some of the activity back to their own home.

Many people turn first to the Church. In some cases this decision is based on a strong religious background, and the Church is a natural point of call; for others it seems appropriate because, through one means or another, they have come to believe that the poltergeist is in some way connected with the spiritual world, or the world beyond death – and that seems to be the province of the Church.

THE CHURCH AND POLTERGEISTS

It is generally accepted that many approaches by the Church are known to be unsuccessful, but this observation may be biased because we do not hear of cases that are directly and successfully dealt with. Canon Carl Garner told us that he receives an average of two calls a week relating to the paranormal. If a churchgoer is troubled and the local priest visits and sorts the problem out, then there is no need for anyone else to know what has happened; the Church, of course, do not file their statistics with paranormal research organisations. The cases where we or other investigators have asked for help from the Church are less likely to be success-ful, as approaching them does not necessarily reflect the families' first or primary belief. And perhaps belief has something to do with successful eradication.

The Church does not take the service of exorcism lightly, nor does it believe it appropriate for poltergeist activity. *Deliverance*, the 'handbook' of the Christian Exorcism Study Group, starts with the general caution: 'Not everything that is popularly described as "the occult" is properly so called, and many requests for the removal of evil spirits have to be refused because they are mistaken and inappropriate.' However, they point out that exposure to the paranormal has brought people to the Church: '. . . many people have come to religious faith as a result of some such experience.'

However, do not be under the illusion that they fail to take poltergeist reports seriously. In fact, they note that the polter-geist 'is the single most frequent cause of appeals to members of the group for help', but believe that 'exorcism is never an appropriate cure for such cases'. (They add that there may be other situations arising within the confines of poltergeist claims, which might make exorcism appropriate, but not of the poltergeist itself.) Their reasoning is simple: 'There is no evil spirit to be cast out.' A blessing is thought to be more appropriate. When the Church is dealing with those who have no understanding of the Christian faith, they warn that even these 'approaches may do more harm than good'.

Agincourt Road, Portsmouth

New Statesman and Society reported the case of a poltergeist that, in 1991, affected Susan Greggs. She lived with her daughters, Nichola (23) and Sarah (8), and Nichola's daughter Jasmine, aged two. Poltergeist activity began shortly after moving in, when the family were decorating. (Although repair and renovation is often associated with the onset of some ghost phenomena, it is not generally so with poltergeists, and the connection here is likely to be coincidence. However, poltergeist activity is often reported within six months of moving house.) It appears that Jasmine befriended a ghost and the family asked to be re-housed. Two mediums who examined the house believed the ghost was 'a miserable old sod' called Percy who once lived there. Whether 'Percy' was truly a poltergeist is debatable. Certainly the family experienced poltergeist-like activity: cups of tea snatched from people's hands; clocks suddenly advancing several hours; clothes strewn over bedrooms; furniture thrown at Nichola; Nichola pushed down the stairs; the oven door opening and shutting on its own; cutlery flung around and taps being turned on. They turned to the Church for help, and the house was blessed by the Reverend Len Fox, vicar of All Saints, Portsea. The result was that the poltergeist activity got worse.

Why matters should have worsened is uncertain. If the poltergeist is generated from within the mind, perhaps certain people are less tolerant or believing than others; perhaps it comes down to no more than the family having (or not having) a rapport with the minister concerned. The focus either respects, disrespects, or couldn't care less about the Church, believes or does not believe in its powers.

There is a hint of this puzzle in the Olive Hill case reported by W. G. Roll in *The Poltergeist*. In 1968 a Kentucky family who had suffered poltergeist activity agreed to an exorcism by Jehovah's Witnesses. The group believed that the activity was in some way connected to the clothing of one of the family, so they piled it all up in the yard and burned the lot. A pity, since, as Roll states, 'the poltergeist ignored the ceremony and continued as before'.

Sometimes the unexpected response arises. In the Seaford case, the family affected were Catholics and might have expected their bottle-opening poltergeist to be dealt with by the rituals of that belief. They put out bottles of holy water – but the poltergeist seemed merely to take a delight in popping those too.

In the case of the Pontefract poltergeist an amateur exorcism was performed by layman Vic Kelly. A Catholic priest, Father Hudson, had been consulted but had declined, suggesting that the job could as well be done by an amateur, but warning that matters could be made worse. Kelly said prayers and sprinkled the house with holy water. After the ceremony was completed one of the family, Jean Pritchard, asked, 'Did Father Hudson say how long it would be before we'd know it worked?' The response was a huge crash from above, and Jean continued, 'Never mind. It didn't.' Then water started spontaneously trickling down the walls – the poltergeist perhaps showing it had a sense of humour and certainly an indifference to holy water.

Two cases where the intervention of the Church succeeded are reported in *Ghosts of the North* by Melanie Warren and Tony Wells. The first arose in Lucas Road, in Durham. Paul and Mary Clayton moved into the house in 1965 with their baby son. They shortly began work on building a new kitchen. The first hint of strangeness came when Paul noticed unpleasant vegetable smells in the house, like burned cabbage (there were no vegetables cooking). On entering the kitchen Paul found the place totally disrupted; all the cupboards had been emptied on to the floor. Ten days later Mary called Paul at work from a neighbour's house to tell him they were being burgled (they and the police had suspected burglary after the first incident), and she could hear smashing glass from the house. On investigation – with a police officer – they found no breakages at all, though the smell was so bad Paul was almost sick. People began to suggest a poltergeist, and the couple turned to the Church for help. The local vicar decided to perform an exorcism, which took four hours. The smells were eradicated immediately, and the couple reported no further disturbances.

The second such case was at Hobstone's Farm. Following poltergeist activity the Church of England were consulted, and the Reverend Noel Hawthorn decided to perform 'an exorcism'. A ceremony of a blessing with holy water and a banishment of the 'tormented spirits' was enough to end the disturbances.

In dealing with poltergeists the Church is urged to reassure the victims about the position they are in. In particular the counsellor dealing with the situation should remind those involved that: 'The "poltergeist" is in itself incapable of inflicting spiritual harm on anyone or anything, that it is certainly not a demon or demonic, that the "owner" is definitely not possessed by it, and that he is in no danger of suffering a mental breakdown because of what is going on around him.' The guidelines continue: 'It thrives on tension and fear and shrivels when normal relations are uppermost . . . Poltergeist phenomena which disturb certain families are another form of dissociated mental activity or energy, not the activity of a geist who is poltering about. This often bizarre form of the acting-out of interpersonal tensions is always unconscious and of human origin.'

Father Thurston, an authority on religion and the paranormal, offered some tips for success through certain approaches: 'Experience has shown that exorcism and comminatory [i.e. threatening, denunciatory] rites of the Church are not always, or indeed generally, effective in putting an end to poltergeist disturbances, though they sometimes produce a temporary mitigation. On the other hand, I have come across a few cases in which a special novena [special prayers over a nine-day period] or the saying of Mass seems definitely to have got rid of the nuisance.'

Suitable approaches might include a prayer and blessing, and the laying on of hands. Exorcism is to be avoided. Even in cases of possession the Church does not believe in exorcism for human spirits, but reserves it only for demonic and non-human situations; humans in spirit 'need, not banishment to hell, but love . . . and pastoral concern'. And the Church further holds back from excess by pointing out that minor exorcism – a prayer to God – is usually all that is needed. Only in very rare cases should major exorcism – a command to an unclean spirit – be used.

Finally they point out that: 'An exorcism should be short and sharp; God (even when he acts through sinful humans) does not require hours and hours of cajoling and repetitious formulae in order to expel evil.'

What *Deliverance* does say about poltergeist activity is: 'The most obvious correlation within the data available on poltergeist disturbances is the link between emotional stress and the phenomena reported . . . There seems to be predisposing features which lie behind poltergeist cases; for example, a change in lifestyle, puberty, menopause, sexual malfunction, a drastic change in personal relationship such as a death or a birth in the family, worries about employment, promotion, or threatened redundancy, stresses between the generations in a family or at work (especially if there is an adult present), or stresses within the marital relationship. There appear to be peaks at about the age of seven, and at puberty – particularly if there is a child with uncaring parents. Retirement is another time at which the emotional stresses may mount to such an extent that it discharges in the form of a poltergeist.' (Given the list it is a wonder anyone escapes poltergeist activity!)

We interviewed Canon Carl Garner, asking him for his view on identifying and dealing with poltergeists. He described how he begins from the point when someone comes to him, reporting disturbances in their home.

'You do what very often a priest or a minister will do which is to say, "This is in the house." We will do a house blessing. Sometimes the fact that it finishes then indicates that you weren't dealing with a poltergeist; I've never known a poltergeist lie down just like that.

'If it is a poltergeist normally the house is quiet for, say, three days and then it starts again. And when it does resume, it can resume much more dramatically. Therefore the other side has to be looked at: that's the person.

'I would look for the person around whom these things seem to circulate, or to be focused, having ruled out the possibility that it's people playing tricks, the "phoneygeist" thing. Then we look for, in that person, two sets of traumas. We look for trauma in the past and we look for stress or trauma in the present. The trauma can be stress, the trauma can be guilt. And the trauma can be hurt. One is looking first of all at the person at which it concentrates. And secondly what's been going on with them; you are following, in a sense, a psychological approach.

'The third leg I look for is the thing that switches this unusual circumstance from what would either be depression or depressing thoughts to a poltergeist; that is some form of occult contact or involvement. In the poltergeist it doesn't seem necessarily that it is overt involvement. It can be close contact. It can be in the family. Even if they said, "I don't like this," it's been in the house. It's been around. It's been in their background.

'I say to them, "You call us or me or the priest," and we talk about God. And I will ask them what sort of belief they have. Whether they have any belief in Jesus, whether they are prepared to express what belief they do have in a way that's honest to them. Whether they are prepared to subsequently work to go on the path of trying to find out more about the good. That will be my particular line. Long term they need to be in a supportive context.

'But my experience would suggest that if people don't follow it

242

through it will knock at the door again. They have gone so far; you might say they have swept the house but they haven't fully cleaned it. They need a bit of protection inside, not just outside.

'The other thing I would do after praying with the person is always to bless the house. And I would do that dramatically. I want to say: if you have experienced something which has had the element of the symbolic in it then to do something which declares the alternative in a symbolic way is always appropriate.'

We should now look at alternatives to the Church's approach, which others have found appropriate or effective in certain situations.

FROM OTHER CULTURES

An example of exorcism from the aboriginal culture was reported in Raymond Bayless' book *The Enigma of the Poltergeist*. In 1963, a guest house in Wellington, New Zealand, was subjected to a stone-throwing poltergeist over several days. Despite police investigation no 'obvious' cause could be found. A Samoan visitor insisted that the trees around the building, which had been cut back to tall stumps, should be cut down to ground level. Shortly after this a Maori made much the same claim, explaining that evil spirits hid in the trunks. The trees were cut down to ground level, and the Maori performed an 'exorcism', with food that 'fed' the evil spirits to remove them; finally she sprinkled blessed water around the house. After prayers, the Maori announced there would be no more trouble – and the disturbances ceased from that day onwards.

A colleague, Judith Ja'afar, related a similar, personal experience from the time when she lived in Nigeria. She had awoken during the night many times, 'petrified, because there was this face lying right on top of mine'. Judith had been sleeping in a newly built room in her house, and the nightmares had only started after moving in there. She would always awake and find herself looking at a particular spot in the room. This continued for several years.

A local man explained her problem; there was a particular type of tree next to the extension that evil spirits liked to live in. The tree had grown huge, and was hanging over the building. The man told her to chop the tree down, and then she would be all right. Her husband was unimpressed, not believing in such stories, and although the tree was not cut down it was severely pruned back, so that it longer hung over the room. Judith summed up: 'And we didn't have any problems after that. It never happened again.'

SENDING TO THE LIGHT

Although the Church clearly believes that they are the appropriate spiritual authority for dealing with these matters, there are many alternative groups and people who believe that they can undertake a similar service.

One of the alternatives is spiritual mediums 'helping the spirits to see the light and move on'. Many mediums believe that the poltergeist is an unquiet soul seeking to gain attention – perhaps an angry spirit not fully realising he or she is dead and wondering why people are ignoring them, or a guilty spirit responsible for their own or another person's death. (*Deliverance* acknowledges the Church's belief in 'unquiet spirits of the dead'.) The medium approaches the case on this basis, and seeks to send the spirit 'to the light'. This means, in effect, explaining to the spirit that it is now deceased, and that it should move on and cut the ties to the former life. The spirit is helped to understand that he or she is dead and is shown how to move on to the next phase; they are directed to look for the 'light' or for a relative they know has died who can help them 'pass over'.

We reserve judgement on what is actually happening at these ceremonies. Perhaps it is just as described, and the 'sending to the light' actually moves a former human on to the next world; or maybe it only convinces the family – and the medium – that that is what has happened, and the internal change in their attitude stops the poltergeist events. Perhaps some other mechanism – objective or subjective – is happening. But there can be little doubt that there are many cases where this intervention has 'cured' the poltergeist, or removed an apparitional spirit.

STRESS COUNSELLING

There is strong evidence that stress is always present within families affected by poltergeists. The Church recognises this and believes that stress and personal difficulties are behind all poltergeists. If tension within the family is managed, or altered, then it appears that either the poltergeist fades away or, if entities are involved, they are no longer able to feed on the energy they need. The result is the same; once the stresses are managed, the poltergeist stops. For a time it appears to go through a diminishing stage where the activities continue at a low ebb; but by now the family usually has a more positive attitude towards it and finds it more bearable – the start of permanent eradication.

Maurice Grosse maintains that, whatever the cause, stress management is part of his approach. Members of the Enfield family recently related (in LWT's *Strange But True?* programme) how much Grosse had helped them get through the strange experiences they had. They were in no doubt as to the debt they owed him.

EXORCISM THROUGH REFOCUSING

One way that we have found stresses can be reduced is to get the families affected to take a different view of the poltergeist, to see themselves as part of an investigative team rather than victims.

If the poltergeist is generated internally, then by changing the internal dynamics we might expect the poltergeist energies to change, and, in doing so, generally to abate. This was the effect in a case reported in the 1960s by Nandor Fodor of a family from Baltimore.

Baltimore

The family were disturbed by a 'typical object-throwing-type' poltergeist. Ted Pauls, a seventeen-year-old, was identified as the focus. Fodor, who was convinced that a 'psychodynamic process was at the heart of every outbreak', met the family and looked for a way to help them. He noticed Ted had a preoccupation with science fiction, and decided that this was his way of escapism. But it was Ted's writing about his hobby that gave Fodor an idea. Fodor announced on television, and broadcast on radio, that while he had been visiting and investigating a poltergeist case he had discovered a 'near literary genius' in Ted Pauls. Fodor later admitted that this was not, in his real view, the case. The ruse worked, however: after the broadcasts Ted was appreciated more by his family and others; his writings – which had been viewed as an obsession – were now seen as a talent. Pauls, who had not been popular with his peers, found a new standing. The poltergeist activity quickly became more pronounced (it often gets worse before it gets better!) then gradually stopped. (We must bear in mind that the case had lasted a month, and many disturbances only last that long anyway – so the 'cure' could have been coincident; however, the cure has a logical ring to it when set into the context of many poltergeist cases.)

Ted perhaps had an artistic talent searching for expression. He was possibly frustrated that he was not being appreciated by others in the way he appreciated himself. We could extend our thinking on the poltergeist a little, given what happened in this case. Perhaps the poltergeist can be looked on as a form of 'pavement artistry' – a temporary means of expression while the creativity in the focus is finding a more 'acceptable' form. Of the Sauchie case, Dr Owen noted that Virginia was very creative with her hands. Perhaps Fodor got Ted's poltergeist over in a short time by offering encouragement in just the right form to just the right person.

There is some evidence that stress control is a useful weapon for 'curing' (or at least reducing) poltergeist manifestation. In the Hertfordshire case, we suggested to the couple that they rethink the way they perceived their poltergeist. We asked them to think of themselves not as victims but as investigators 'on site', working for us within their own house. They should be pleased when 'something happened', we told them, because it would be something for us to study – and they should note it down ready for scientific study. Our premise was that, if – as we believed – the paranormal was most active within the 'artistic' part of the brain, then by getting them to use their 'scientific, rational' side they would be less susceptible. By the same token, they should feel less stressed – and even perhaps as excited as we might be as researchers. In the end they did as we asked, and reported that the following day they had their first 'clear' day for over a year. That said, things went back to the same level of activity the next day; perhaps because we could not sustain this change, or they were unable to believe in what we had asked them to believe. But we seemed to have scored a minor hit. Maurice Grosse has always maintained that even if there are entities, poltergeists need a level of stress before they can 'operate'.

If the poltergeist is natural – in that it is a genuine part of the human condition – then we might assume that it evolved for a purpose (as did most physical and mental attributes). In that case we should be looking to finding out what useful purpose it was intended to serve. Perhaps 'eradication' should look less towards stopping the poltergeist but more to 'using' it, when it will of course disappear as a poltergeist but perhaps leave behind an enhanced person.

EXORCISM THROUGH DREAMS
Psychoanalysis, it seems, has its own form of exorcism.

Chelsea, London
Nandor Fodor, in his book *The Story of the Poltergeist down the*

Centuries (written with Hereward Carrington), describes the case of a Miss Whalen, who was affected by a poltergeist in her 300-year-old cottage in Chelsea. The phenomena included footsteps, apports and disapports, movements of objects, and so on. According to another person living in the house, when Miss Whalen was absent (in hospital having an operation), the activity ceased, only to resume on her return. The poltergeist seemed to be people-centred, and centred on her. Fodor states: 'I was convinced . . . that the creepy atmosphere of an old house lends itself to an unconscious projection and dramatisation of one's own conflicts into ghostly manifestations. I decided to ignore the dynamics of the reported happenings and informed Miss Whalen of my considered opinion that she was haunted by her own past . . .' Fodor explained to her that the footsteps represented the arrival of 'the message', and that the disappearance of objects represented a 'troublesome complex' that she must attend to. Miss Whalen apparently accepted this immediately. Fodor states: 'Deep within herself, she felt that in some way she was involved in the phenomena.' Fodor described working through Miss Whalen's dreams with her, and bringing out the various repressed beliefs and history that were causing her problems. In doing so, the hauntings ceased.

PLACEBO

Poltergeists have been cured, at least for some time, by the use of a 'placebo'. Providing the victims believe that 'something is being done', the poltergeist is reduced in activity, or eradicated. It is believed that – if the poltergeist is generated from within individuals, or feeds off their emotional state – they take from the placebo either comfort, and believe something is happening, or they see the attention given as 'permission to heal themselves'. This phrase, more often applied to healing – conventional and alternative – reflects a belief that all healing of disease or injury is done 'from within', and that 'good' doctors or other healers are those that can instil in patients a desire to heal themselves. So it may be with poltergeists.

Tony Cornell described one case where he acted virtually like a kitchen-based white witch! He used bleach and earth from outside the house to prepare a mixture that (he assured the family) once spread around the house would remove the poltergeist. They had to act in certain ways as the material was laid down, almost as though a spell was being cast. In the end the poltergeist was eradicated. Since Tony had made the whole thing up at the time – and it seems unlikely that he accidentally hit on an ancient piece of magic – we must assume that the family did all that was necessary themselves.

As all of these exorcisms reflect certain beliefs about what lies behind poltergeists, and since all of those beliefs are possibly interpretations that provide a framework for action rather than an objective reality, then perhaps *any* cure – psychoanalysis through dreams, exorcism, 'sending to the light' and so on – may be no more than a placebo. At this stage we really do not know. Perhaps, however, the placebo – if that is what it is – takes effect more quickly if both the investigator (or priest, or medium) as well as the family believe in what they are doing. At the practical end, we might argue that, providing it works – who cares why? From the investigative end, we would like to know the reason, of course, because if nothing else it would give us further clues as to the origins of the poltergeist.

CRYSTALS

Many believe that crystals contain energies that are beneficial (for example, they are often used in healing). Thus they are used by some mediums in the eradication of poltergeists. In one case (where we worked with the mediums concerned) they positioned the crystals in order to eradicate the poltergeist, but within a short time the crystals had gone. The family believed that the poltergeist had eradicated the crystals! But crystals were used with success in one poltergeist-infested pub which we investigated for some months. The result could, of course, have been a placebo effect, but several aspects of the case imply that it was not – not least, the sceptical attitude of the proprietor to what turned out to be the cure. For this reason we have set out the case in more detail below.

Rye, Sussex

The Union Inn was run by Stephen Dartnall. The pub was being troubled by phenomena that were preventing him or his family from getting a peaceful night's sleep. The investigation was instigated by our colleague, Tony Wells.

There were rumours of the building having had a troubled history. It was thought to date back to the 1400s, and the local historical society believed that in Victorian times it was owned by the local mortician, whose daughter broke her neck falling down the cellar steps. Further rumours included an illegitimate baby walled up in the chimney.

Stephen, his wife Anne and their two young children had taken over the premises in July 1992. The family rarely stayed at the inn, preferring to live in their house nearer the children's school. Stephen, though, used to stay occasionally, when his work demanded, but preferred to sleep at home after the manifestations started.

The disturbances at the inn included women in the bar area experiencing the feeling of being 'touched'; loud noises at all hours for no obvious reason; sightings of a ghost – believed to be the mortician's daughter; a male figure seen by Stephen walking through the closed door of the main bedroom; thumping and bumping noises from above the bar area; doors opening and closing; strange smells; and apports and disapports.

The investigating team also experienced strange phenomena. On the first visit, Tony and his partner heard someone go into the toilet upstairs – but no one was there. Another time, John (Spencer), Robin Laurence and Tony (Wells) were standing together at the top of the stairs, near an open bedroom door, when they saw a light go off inside the room. Nobody was in the room and no one could have touched the switch without being seen. (The light switch was indeed now in the off position.) At the same time, in the room below us, others were reporting banging noises coming from above, where the three of us were standing – but we could hear nothing, and had not been moving about.

John and Tony – and eventually all the members of the vigil – watched the bar door to the kitchen opening and closing spontaneously. There was no breeze or vibration to cause the movement. When Tony approached the door to close it, it slammed shut in front of him in a way that left every team member astonished.

Exorcists were invited by a medium who had visited the inn. They described negative ley lines, and proposed placing crystals around the building. This, they claimed, would eradicate the lower-level entities that cling to such power lines. They said they could counterbalance the negative energies with quartz crystals, which were placed on the positive lines. Quartz amplifies energy, they explained, and the nine crystals they used would restore the inn's energy balance.

What is important in this chapter is the fact that Stephen was not at all impressed with the exorcists (their term for themselves) when they arrived – and seemed to become less so as the evening wore on. It seems that he had expected a 'bell, book and candle' ceremony performed by a priest dressed appropriately. He did not take to New Age exorcists turning up in well-tailored suits with briefcases. Frankly, Stephen did not expect the exorcism to work (and, given the experience of cases before this, neither would we have done).

However, it did work. One of Stephen's children had sometimes reported a 'friend' he had nicknamed 'Postman Pat' (because he was blue). The children had not been present during the exorcism, nor had they been told about it – but shortly after returning to the inn the boy told his father that he couldn't find Postman Pat anywhere. The disturbances had stopped. When we checked with Stephen in 1995 he confirmed that he had never again been troubled.

UNDERSTANDING THE POLTERGEIST

Chapter 14

The Focus

It is clear that in almost every poltergeist case there is a focus, a person around whom the poltergeist centres. Examination of the focus provides us with our closest understanding yet of the poltergeist. Jacob Bronowski, a British scientist, said, 'Ask an impertinent question, and you are on your way to the pertinent answer.' In this chapter we set a few impertinent questions.

OBSERVATIONS

Cases we have related in earlier chapters give a great deal of information about the focus, but there are a few further observations that need to be highlighted.

Differences in foci

It is widely believed that poltergeists are associated only with adolescents. This is not the case, and we have started this section with the following case to demonstrate this.

Bromley

In his analysis of the Bromley poltergeist (*The Persecution of Mr Tony Elms*), Manfred Cassirer points out that 'the poltergeist is classless and equally at home in castles and council houses; it knows no national boundary or restrictions of any kind. In the present instance it inflicted itself on a modest commercial venture run by three ordinary men in Kent.'

Investigations started in October 1973, when Manfred Cassirer received a call at the Society for Psychical Research from an agitated Mr Alf Taylor, one of the people who operated the Kentish Garden Guild, a small garden shop attached to some allotments. Manfred and his colleague, Pauline Runnalls, visited Taylor for a preliminary interview.

The first incident was recorded on 26 April 1973, when Taylor arrived at the shop to find his colleague, Tony Elms, somewhat agitated. Powdered substances were hitting the ceiling; a pewter jug on a shelf shot across the floor (even when sealed inside a plastic box); pellets of fertiliser were lifting themselves out of a bin and moving up to the ceiling, some even hitting customers. Perhaps more alarming, a seven-pound weight came off a set of scales. At one point the two men and their colleague Clifford Jewiss were forced to abandon the shop early because of the disturbances. On another occasion Elms' shirt was cut to shreds by a saw forced down his back.

Manfred notes that poltergeists are generally not harmful, though they can be mischievous and disturbing. He comments on this case: 'However that might be in general, there had been a quite disturbing incident in which Mr Taylor had been hit on the head by a box of trowels and forks, while Mr Elms had fared even worse and was in fact a rather frequent target of spiritual spite.'

With the poltergeist's usual creativity in using immediately available resources, caps of bottles in the shop would come off mysteriously, and the contents spill to the floor; over a hundred-weight of Maxi-Crop fertiliser had to be destroyed when containers were found to have been tampered with. Manfred noted 'the impressions of hands' – as if the fertiliser had been scooped out prior to being thrown at the ceiling.

It appears that Taylor was at least one of the foci of the poltergeist, as he experienced attacks in his own home and in the presence of friends. Elms was another. (Alternatively, one of the men was the focus and the other suffered from 'contagion'.)

The shop was subject to apports – in particular, showers of matches – on one occasion, half a hundredweight of peat.

Perhaps inspired by certain crosses and religious symbols that appeared, Elms attempted an amateur exorcism. The result seemed to have been an increase in the level of sound and violence of the poltergeist, and further attacks on Taylor.

Fertiliser and other locally available materials were used to produce some communicating writing; in particular, the date 1659 appeared on a wooden panel. Other images and words appeared using the fertiliser, perhaps most astonishing being a skull-like face that formed on the counter.

The investigators witnessed several phenomena. On their first arrival they were showered by bonemeal from 'an indeterminate point of origin'. During the following two hours they were subject to several experiences, though as Manfred cautiously put it: 'It was not always possible to determine with only two observers the precise order or sequence of the incidents or the exact position of everyone present at any given moment.'

The incident which he suggests must finally rest the doubts of the sceptics arose on a second visit a year later. Many events occurred during that second visit, but 'the beaker incident' was the one Manfred was most impressed by. Given the possible hazards of drink inside the shop being contaminated by fertiliser (as had happened on one occasion), Manfred, his colleague Pauline Runnalls and two others were to have their cup of tea outside. Four beakers were placed on a car bonnet. A beaker moved by itself and lightly touched Pauline on the head (all present, including Manfred, were adamant that they were standing in a group some way from the car). Pauline, brilliantly, took the initiative and requested the return of Elms' holiday money – and was immediately hit on the head by a penny and 5p piece.

The victims in this case were older than many expect to see in poltergeist cases – Tony Elms was fifty and Alf Taylor older than him. Indeed, according to Manfred Cassirer, Elms viewed Taylor as something of a father figure.

In examining the differences in poltergeist cases we have found that the foci can be grouped broadly. Young adolescents are classically associated with poltergeists, and many of these endure the more common 'short-duration' of manifestations. The poltergeist appears to be related to emergence at puberty. For example, Zugun's poltergeistery stopped when her periods arrived; Janet at Enfield had significant activity on the first day of her periods; at Sauchie it was noted that Virginia's poltergeistery 'peaked' every twenty-eight days – corresponding with the menstrual cycle – an observation exactly mirrored in the Amherst case. Even though the poltergeist was clearly related to those individuals, it was specifically related to them *at a certain time in their life*. When that time ended, and there was change, the poltergeist changed too – in most cases stopping. We suggest that whatever brings about the poltergeist is specific, and when the conditions change it cannot maintain itself. Later we shall be looking at frustration as a driving force; certainly adolescence represents a literally frustrating time – the teenager is neither childish enough to ask for help nor adult enough to deal with problems on his or her own. In some people, perhaps, that frustration exteriorises. Then, perhaps as the hormones change, the alteration is sufficient to 'dis-enable' the poltergeist; or perhaps the person 'finds themselves', and the resultant emotional and attitudinal changes stop the exteriorisation.

We contrast this situation to cases (including the Bromley case and the Hertfordshire case) where there are older people involved – and a notable absence of children. In these cases the victims often

258

suffer longer-duration poltergeists. The Hertfordshire case lasted over three years and showed no signs of ending until the death of Elizabeth. The Bromley case lasted at least fifteen months and, due to the 'negative attitude' of one of the men involved, the case was never carried to whatever conclusion might have been possible. We suggest that, because there are no hormonal or other changes involved in these cases, or because there is no natural way for people to 'grow', the cases last longer. Once the poltergeist has 'got underway' there is no change to break the existing dynamic. Perhaps such poltergeists arise at a time when a person is 'rethinking' their place in the world – during a mid-life crisis perhaps, or at retirement (the Bromley pair were running the business as a part-time 'hedge' against retirement) – and changes at that age are more difficult, more risky, to deal with. Hence, it takes longer to get through whatever adjustments are needed to rid the house of the poltergeist.

One other change in foci over the years lies in the proportion of females to males. At one time it was quoted that ninety-five per cent of poltergeist foci were female. We have no way of knowing if this figure is true or not – perhaps males simply did not feel comfortable reporting such experiences. Perhaps investigators, armed with the knowledge that females were likeliest to be the focus, even attributed some cases wrongly. But a high number of cases seem genuinely to have centred around females.

However, it seems from our general observations that more and more cases are now involving males. Some studies indeed indicate that there may now be more male foci than female. Perhaps this reflects the fact that these days males are encouraged by schools and society to 'get in touch' with what is often called the 'feminine' side – i.e. the intuitive, empathetic, creative side – of their personality. Perhaps it is some element of this so-called 'feminine' quality that triggers or responds to the poltergeist, and more males are now susceptible.

Living alone

We have noticed that there is a lack of reports of poltergeists from people who live alone. This is, at first glance, surprising – as these are the very people who should be most certain of objects being moved. (In some houses with children it is something of a miracle to find anything in its right place!) The majority of cases occur in families, or situations where there is someone to share the problem with the focus. Perhaps this is a factor. If the poltergeist is an exteriorisation, then perhaps its purpose is to make others relate to the 'generating person' – a cry for help.

We have located two cases where poltergeists affected people living alone.

One case, investigated by Rosamund Gage of the Sheffield Paranormal Research Group, involved a thirty-year-old man living alone. He reported noises, breakages, and furniture moving. He had had no other experiences, but had tried a little spoon bending so had some awareness of the paranormal. Movements always seemed to happen when he was present, never when he was away (contrasting to, say, the Hertfordshire case). It was noted by the investigator that 'the course of this energy we put down to Mr —'s interest in spoon bending and his state of mind. He had been suffering from depression for many years as a result of being abused as a child.' They pointed out that he was unemployed at the time, and that the phenomena stopped after he got a job. Unemployment is certainly one of the most frustrating of situations.

Another case was investigated by psychic and medium Jenny Bright, and her partner Dr David Cross. They reported that a man living alone was experiencing very loud banging noises and some movement of objects. Jenny, as a medium, might have been expected to believe that the source of this disturbance was 'spirits', and it commands respect that she investigated open-mindedly enough to locate a possible other cause in this case. The investigators learned that the man had recently ended a long-term sexual relationship, which was characterised by a great deal of 'passion'.

They determined that the manifestations were probably repressed sexual energy in its most obvious form, and advised the man that his poltergeist would go away when he was in another relationship. In the meantime, they suggested that he take up a sport that would use up his physical energy. This he did and the poltergeist disappeared.

To some extent these cases 'break the mould', but the circumstances do not necessarily preclude them as being cries for help – after all, they got the attention of the researchers.

The family unit

A further observation that arises from our researches is that poltergeist cases often start when one of the senior members of the household is absent. There appears to be a higher number when the father of the family is away – but this might only reflect the general point that fathers are out of the house more than mothers in many cases, and for longer periods. For example, in the Ramos case the mother had left the family. In the Enfield case the father had left. In Runcorn, John Glyn lived with his grandfather though we know his mother lived in another house nearby.

The activities at Tedworth started when Mr Mompesson was absent, though they continued after he had returned. The focus in that case was thought to be a maid, but it is possible she regarded Mompesson as a father figure. After all, she was away from her own family unit.

Since there are manifestations that start when the family is together as a group, we cannot regard this absence as a core factor, but it is worthy of note. Perhaps the upset of the family dynamic creates a change that triggers the poltergeist, or maybe the absence of a parent is simply one form of stress – and other cases (when the family group is together) have their other forms.

Medical issues

A number of medical and psychiatric conditions have been suggested as playing a part in the poltergeist phenomenon. However, we have found little evidence to support the connections.

Maurice Grosse and Guy Lyon Playfair tentatively considered that Janet (of Enfield) might have been displaying symptoms of Tourette's syndrome. (Maurice told us later they rejected the idea quite quickly.) This usually begins in childhood and is characterised by a tic – an involuntary repetitive muscle movement. Sounds are produced; these are usually inarticulate and meaningless, such as repeated throat clearing, grunts, barks, screams or sniffing, but sometimes comprehensible words. Common in around one third of cases is coprolalia, the compulsive repetition of obscene words. These children are often hyperactive and prone to sleepwalking. Some severely affected individuals may also have self-mutilating symptoms. Clearly there are some poltergeist cases where the focus displays some of these characteristics. However, although there may be similarities in outward manifestation, we see little reason to attribute the poltergeist to this condition. Tourette's syndrome can be diagnosed, and we are not aware of any confirmed diagnoses in poltergeist foci; furthermore, we are not aware of any sufferers of the syndrome who have reported poltergeist activity. Many poltergeist foci clearly do not fall into this category. Therefore, even if there are rare cases of overlap, Tourette's as an explanation for the poltergeist can be discounted.

The second condition that has been associated with poltergeists is Multiple Personality Disorder (MPD), or Dissociation of the personality. This is described in *The Filthy Lie* by Hellmut Karle: 'Two or more separate personalities seem to inhabit the same body; the person seems to have periods of time, which may last minutes, hours, days, or even weeks, for which they later have no memory at all, and during which time they behave in ways that are totally different from their normal ways. During these episodes, they call themselves by a different name, live quite a different life, and altogether appear to be a different person. In these cases the major (or primary) personality will have no knowledge of the other personality or personalities. The secondary personality will know of the primary but may or may not know of other secondary personalities. Only one personality at a time can be dominant. Presumably MPD could account for what are thought to be apports, disapports and the finding of objects out of their usual place. If a sub-personality within one individual in a household was taking or bringing things into the household without the knowledge of the main personality, then their appearances and disappearances would seem mysterious. In the Newark case (see Chapter Fifteen), Ernie threw things without apparently knowing it. We could suggest some dissociation is shown here.

This condition does not, however, explain the range of manifestations of the poltergeist. Therefore we conclude again that, though there may be overlap, this is not an explanation for the poltergeist.

Some physiological observations

If the poltergeist is being generated in some way by a person, then it would be remarkable if there were not some other kinds of more 'normal' signs that something is happening. In the Pontefract case, the poltergeistery was worse whenever the children had a particular stomach pain. This was interpreted as the poltergeist drawing energy from the children. In the Enfield case, Mrs Harper frequently got 'frontal' headaches just before a poltergeist event (four such events are specifically mentioned in *This House is Haunted*), and Janet, Mrs Harper's daughter, claimed she got a pain in the back of the head when something was about to happen. Matthew Manning confirmed that he also received similar 'warning' signs. And we note that Jung felt a pain in his diaphragm when he was arguing with Freud, just before there was a loud bang from a bookcase.

Quite what such signs mean is debatable – be it psychic warning, the poltergeist taking energy, or the body getting ready to 'do' something. But the suggestion is that there may be physical or physiological activities involved; and future researchers might take care to be on the look-out for such signs.

CONSIDERATIONS

There are a number of possibilities that arise from the poltergeist reports.

Repressed sexual energies

One suggestion made popular by Freudian psychology is that the source energy for poltergeist PK comes from repressed sexuality. (Nandor Fodor was the first to suggest this connection.) This at least offers a potential reconciliation between young people at puberty (represented by many cases: Enfield, Amherst, Sauchie, Zugun) and nuns and monks (as in the case of, say, St Pierre de Lyon) – both relatively common claimants of poltergeist activity. Both, presumably, have to deal with their sexual urges in some way. There is a similarity between repressed sexual urges and celibacy. There are those who believe there is great potential power in celibacy. Gandhi pronounced on this, suggesting that the energy of sex, if channelled correctly, can be a powerful spiritual force. Perhaps the poltergeist is the result of such unchannelled energy.

Hereward Carrington (in *The Story of Psychic Science*) comments: 'An energy seems to be radiated from the body . . . which induces the phenomena, when the sexual energies are blossoming into maturity within the body. It would almost seem as though these energies, instead of taking their normal course, were somehow turned into another channel, at such times, and were externalised beyond the limits of the body – producing the manifestations in question. The spontaneous outburst of these phenomena seems to be associated with the awakening of the sex-energies at that time which finds this curious method of externalisation . . .' It is also worth noting that some witches in the West use sex in their rituals but hold back from orgasm, believing that this makes them more powerful.

Within Eastern mysticism there is belief in a force known as kundalini, the pent-up sexual energy that lies dormant at the base of the astral equivalent of the spine – at the point of the lowest chakra. if awakened it is said to be a powerful force. Some analysts of Spontaneous Human Combustion believe that this may be the energy behind that extraordinary phenomenon. Meditation and yoga designed to clear the chakra pathways work towards releasing kundalini. All of this may be some aspect of the force behind poltergeist PK.

Trauma

Canon Carl Garner has pointed out that when he visits poltergeist victims he looks for signs of trauma in the past and trauma in the present. The following cases include aspects of possible trauma.

Northern Brazil

There is one case (reported in the journal of the SPR, Volume 58, No. 828, by Andre Percia de Carvalho) which suggests contributory factors of child abuse. The case concerns a family of nine people living together with a domineering father who beat his children. Debora Menezes, a psychology student, related how she, as a child, and her family were attacked in 1971 by a poltergeist.

The family lived in a village in Northern Brazil. Mrs Menezes first saw flowerpots on the veranda fall over. Later, stone throwing and object movements occurred in the house. One Sunday there was a storm of stones. A broom that was leaning on the door where everybody could see it flew, spun and fell on the floor. Everything was falling over inside the house, but without breaking. An armchair turned itself over.

The children were all beaten by the poltergeist. Debora remembered: 'We were all on the hammocks and suddenly felt a strong punch in our backs. We stayed together crying for an hour.' Mrs Menezes claimed the children had red marks on their bodies.

It was noted that the poltergeist was most active on Sundays, the only day of the week that Mr Menezes, a military man who showed 'strong aggression towards the family', was home all day. Yet

Debora also stated that during and after these happenings her parents gave more attention to the children. To this extent the poltergeist was actually helpful, a point we shall return to later in the chapter.

In considering trauma it is necessary to study those cases where the manifestations seemed to reflect specific concerns (for example, we have mentioned one woman's mastectomy and another's fears of a forthcoming marriage). There are other cases that suggest the poltergeist can result from sudden shock. Esther Cox at Amherst, for example, had been subjected to a sexual attack. In the case that arose in Ramos, a suburb of Rio de Janeiro (Journal of the SPR, Vol 58, No. 828), spontaneous fires were reported in the local papers. The focus was identified as thirteen-year-old Sara, one of several children in the house. Sara's grandmother admitted that the first fire had broken out on the day after she had severely beaten Sara, for failing to go to church as she had been told to do. The girl was thought to have responded with guilt, shouting, 'Yes, I am wrong. Kill me!' She had had a nightmare in which the Devil had threatened to burn her.

Eleonora Zugun's first poltergeist incident (when she was twelve years old) followed her move to her grandmother's house, and an incident the previous day when she had found some money with which she bought sweets and her grandmother had warned her that she would be possessed by the Devil, who had left the money to entice her. In this case, the driving energy could have been repressed anger – a grandmother is probably one authority figure you cannot hit out against. This would cause inner frustration, a factor we examine below.

TENTATIVE CONCLUSIONS
Given the data to hand there are a few possibilities on offer.

Frustration
It is widely accepted that stress seems to be present in virtually all cases of poltergeist manifestation. It would be difficult to argue

with certainty that it is present without exception, as the dynamics of family life in early claims were not studied or reported on. One or two analysts have suggested reasons for stress in some early cases – for example, that John Bell had a sexual involvement with his daughter, Betsy – but often there is no supporting evidence, the assumption having been made in light of more recent theories. But if those analysts have failed to spot the correct causes of stress, there may well still have been stresses at the heart of the family.

We can assume that all families, at times, are subject to stress – some families more or less all the time. There is no doubt that all modern cases where poltergeists have been studied and reported carefully show signs of potential stress. In Enfield, for example, the events commenced after a break-up of marriage – a strain that clearly continued into the poltergeist case. In Cardiff things started happening during a period of concern over the success of the business. Significantly, Enfield happened in the home, Cardiff in the workplace. The question that arises then is to identify the nature of the stress.

With this in mind, many questions arise; notably, why are there not *more* poltergeists? Most of us know people who live 'on edge' virtually all the time. Yet they do not seem to have any problems with poltergeists. There is probably a personality type that refuses to report poltergeists from fear of ridicule etc., and perhaps 'uptight' people fall into this category. If this was the case, though, we all would have heard about some manifestation, even if from a friend of a friend, yet there is no concentration of such reports. We are led to the possibility then that it is not the quantity of stress, but perhaps its nature that is important.

Perhaps one reason why poltergeists are rare, even though stress is common, is that it takes a particular level of stress (not necessarily an extreme pitch) to induce manifestation. Poltergeists develop as that level is being reached, and disappear when the stresses either fall away or get worse. This leads to the question of whether the stresses involved are long-term or short-term; it appears that poltergeists are associated more with the longer-term stresses that build up over time.

Perhaps only a certain type of stress causes poltergeists. If this were not the case, then we would have many reports of students manifesting poltergeists in examination rooms, or in their studies. But we do not often receive such reports. It would be foolish to speculate for too long on why this should be; perhaps the examinations provide a target for the energy and something to concentrate on. Perhaps poltergeists only arise when there is no way to reduce tension, no target to vent one's anger at. For example, just as Zugun could not hit her grandmother, so in work a person cannot hit their boss for perceived 'unfairness', and they are forced to 'bottle it up'.

Fodor looked closely at the psychological aspects of poltergeists. Rogo commented that Fodor, 'more than any other investigator before him, realised that the poltergeist was a vehicle of expression, that it was actually a projection of hostility and repression'. Other studies have indicated that repressed aggression and tension are the most common themes in foci and their families.

We mention a case above that involves a father abusing his children, speculating that it could result in 'targeting'. But the inner tensions that such abuse caused would probably be frustrating – how does a child hit back against an adult? – and the dynamic may be one of repressed anger in this case.

This leads us to suggest that perhaps the operative word for poltergeists is not stress but *frustration*. Perhaps it is pent-up anger without expression, leading to frustration where there is no simple release, that results in the apparently illogical poltergeist as a means of exteriorising mood. It creates something so extraordinary that the person has something else to be amazed at – even to be worried about – and perhaps therefore it serves a purpose in refocusing the person away from their problems. One case reported in *Deliverance* relates to a workplace where the focus was identified as one of the business partners. The partner had no way to escape his pressures. But when he faced up to his problems and confided them to his partner – who was then able to offer support and help – the poltergeist activity subsided.

In the Sauchie case, Dr Owen was told by Virginia's teacher after the poltergeist had gone that 'Virginia was much more outgoing than before and that the tension seemed to have left her'. Whatever the cause, the poltergeist seemed to have left one victim with an enhanced way of dealing with life.

In the chapter on PK we discussed two situations where poltergeists do not appear when they might have been expected to do so: children with their toys, and moving religious statues. Possibly the lack of frustration associated with these circumstances is the governing factor: no frustration of the right sort.

We spoke to Dr Andrew Bathie, a stress management consultant and psychotherapist, on his views of dealing with poltergeists. He suggested that: 'Mainstream psychology fails to deal effectively with many real-life situations people experience. The question of the reality of a poltergeist is secondary to the effect it has on people. I would first ask the person how it is affecting their life, and I would try to help them change their perception of it. There are always different ways of viewing situations, for the good or bad, and my job is to help them change their perception to the more positive. Whether that will get rid of the poltergeist is debatable, but if it is an exteriorisation of their inner energy then it probably will diminish because they will have changed their inner dynamic.'

There may be cases of poltergeists where no frustration is involved. If so, then we might learn something from a study of such cases. Although we have tried to find examples, we have never been satisfied that a particular case fits the criteria. One episode that seems to come close is the 'second stage' of the Cardiff case. After the activity stopped at the work premises – and stopped permanently for John and Pat, the original 'victims' – the poltergeist seems to have shifted to the home of a related couple, Fred and Gerry. Fred, now apparently the focus, had not been present when the disturbances started at the workplace so cannot have been part of the original case. We noted from talking to Fred and Gerry that they both seemed to enjoy the poltergeist, which manifests itself mostly by giving them money – sometimes around £5 per week. Fred, in fact, said that his feeling about being a poltergeist 'victim' was one of privilege – not the usual response from someone undergoing poltergeist activity (although some people come to that conclusion after it has gone away). However, when we asked them if they would like it to stay they both said no, they would prefer it to go away. So perhaps there is some frustration built into the case.

So in summary, we suggest that the driving force behind the poltergeist is not just stress, but frustration – the inner pain that comes from not being able to do anything about a situation that is found unbearable. Adolescents of course have great frustrations, adrift in that difficult time when they are too old to want to depend on help from adults and too young to take control of their own lives. But other people find themselves in frustrating positions throughout their lives where they are powerless to act: realisation that future promotion is unlikely; retirement when wanting to be active; not being appreciated by people at work, at home or at school; being in love but not having it reciprocated, and so on. We know of one case where a woman surrounded by poltergeistery is desperate to get pregnant and undertaking fertility treatment. Different people will have different inner translations of these situations – what can lead to suicidal tendencies for one person can be laughed off by another – but for some, perhaps, this extraordinary form of exteriorisation is the release valve.

The hunter or the hunted?

'All happy families resemble each other, while each unhappy family is unhappy in its own way.'

Tolstoy, *Anna Karenina.*

Just because it is clear that one individual is the focus of the poltergeist, it does not necessarily mean that only one individual is responsible. We have noted that there are a very few poltergeists reported by people living alone. Perhaps the reason is that it takes a group dynamic to create a poltergeist. One person in a family may well be central to the poltergeist, but it may take the family's inter-relationship to bring it about. The fact that poltergeists are still relatively rare may be because it takes a curious combination of factors, not just in one person but in a whole group, to make one happen.

Such an idea has not been ignored by other researchers (though we notice an increasing tendency to examine one individual alone), and it leads to another, more radical, theory relating to the focus: is it possible that the focus is disliked, or at least in some way viewed negatively, and is the *target* of PK generated by others? This would fit in neatly with the suggestion that poltergeist energy is from a group, rather than an individual, dynamic.

Poltergeists centre around one person either in their workplace or their home, but rarely at both. Does this suggest that a person is disliked in one of the locations by someone, or a group of people? Popularity at work is, at best, a fickle thing. In the case of Debora Menezes, mentioned above, the fact that the poltergeist was more active on the days when her father – who had abused all the children – was present opens the possibility of the manifestations being a subconscious targeting of her father. We might be looking at a 'group' dynamic, and perhaps that is a signpost to be looked for in other cases. In the case of Sara from Rio de Janeiro, we note that, in the words of the investigator Andre Percia de Carvalho, 'The neighbours described Sara as a very unstable person and did not like her . . .' We know that children going through puberty are prime candidates for poltergeist activity, and their internal changes are cited as a reason, but if such adolescents are difficult for all the family and others, perhaps they are receiving resentment for the upheaval they cause.

Consider the case of Annemarie Schneider, the identified focus in the Rosenheim poltergeist case. One facet of the case was that the speaking clock was called on the telephone many times – often so quickly that normal dialling was not humanly possible – suggesting some PK effect. One interpretation put on this is that Annemarie was desperate to know when she could go home (though she denied this when the suggestion was put to her). But it could just as easily have been that she was unpopular, and others wanted her to go home. She does not have to have been an inherently unpopular person; if one incident set off the happenings and she was then identified as the cause, that could have been reason enough for resentment.

On the other hand 'victim syndrome' has been identified and recognised by schools and police forces, amongst others. This maintains that some people are 'natural' victims, sending out subliminal signals. Such people are often the target of hostility wherever they go, which might explain why one focus could be subject to poltergeistery in several different locations if the manifestations are the result of a group dynamic.

We have noted in the Daly City case that phenomena surrounded a baby. The tensions of a mixed-religion marriage, brought to the fore at the time of the birth, could well have been the driving frustration and the reason for the 'targeting'.

Of course we know that the poltergeist usually performs only when the focus is present, but this makes sense in the 'group dynamic' context also; the group targets the focus when present, but 'out of sight is out of mind'. And it could explain the situation when the activity persists even when the focus is not present – bad feeling might still be there. The absence of the focus necessitates at least some modification of the theory that they directly generate the poltergeist.

There are many objections to this suggestion. In Annemarie's case it was reported that she had caused poltergeist effects in other workplaces, and on dates with her fiancé. It seems unlikely that different groups would all target one person in the same extraordinary way. And activity rarely continues when the identified focus is not present.

SPECULATIONS

Some theories cannot be justified by the evidence, but they deserve setting out here for future consideration by ourselves and others in this field of study.

Why do animals not have poltergeists?

Posing questions from 'the other end of the spectrum' sometimes leads us to some answers. We have concentrated a good deal, as do all poltergeist books, on the known and reported manifestations, and we note that they are always regarded as people-centred. Whether it is regarded as PK, the result of a non-human entity, a spirit of a dead person, or whatever – there is a marked absence of reports of animals affected by poltergeists.

We know of no reports of poltergeist activity in zoos, and these are the places we might expect it to happen, given that some animals are thought to suffer the very sort of frustration and unreleasable stress in some zoos that we have suggested might be the cause of the poltergeist in humans. Certainly several zoologists have noted that animals in captivity masturbate more, have a greater tendency to self-mutilation and sometimes acquire what look like compulsive disorders. In short, they seem frustrated.

But it seems unlikely from the wealth of evidence that animals are taking part in this poltergeist happening, and we are probably safe in assuming that the poltergeist – whatever it is – is a part of the human experience.

If that is so, then it is safe to examine the poltergeist from the perspective of what makes us different to the animals. Dr Owen, in *Can We Explain the Poltergeist?*, considers this question. Studying poltergeists, it is important to consider the inner, emotional driving forces of the victim. Animal consciousness is as great a mystery as the poltergeist, so the point can only be examined speculatively. We know that humans have psychoses, but there is some evidence that animals can acquire such conditions too.

Emotion alone may be the difference; perhaps animals lack emotions. But if they have some, do they have the wide range that we have? One major difference, impossible to state with certainty but argued by many, is that people have guilt and animals do not. Perhaps guilt is a part of the emotional content that makes up the energy for the poltergeist. In one sense guilt is an extreme frustration, a feeling that cannot be easily shed or ignored, and one that runs deep in people even when they have consciously put it aside.

Development

We note that poltergeists develop. They start with little scratching noises, and get 'bigger' and more complex in a variety of ways. We should be asking ourselves the negative question again – in how many homes have strange noises been ignored and nothing more has happened? Is it by concentrating on the noises – and by believing 'something' about their origin – a person is made vulnerable to a poltergeist? Certainly we believe that some cases which developed into possession did so because they were investigated by priests who believed in possession. Perhaps the poltergeist victim is influenced by someone – a friend, neighbour or investigator – into furthering the manifestations.

We should consider also the radical possibility that, if a person has no way to release their frustration, then perhaps the distraction offered by a poltergeist might be subconsciously welcomed.

Alternatively, if a person, even one that hears a few scratching noises, is too focused in some other way – a goal to achieve perhaps, or they are dealing directly with their frustrations – then perhaps what might have developed simply dies away. Such a negative is hard to prove, but it offers an interesting area for further research.

The 'bungee jumping' theory of poltergeist control
Most people, at some time, come up against a problem that they cannot deal with. Certain situations are common – house move, divorce, and so on. But there is also an endless range of some-times trivial matters which individuals become frustrated by; these of course vary from individual to individual. When assisted by friends or counsellors, most people can see an alternative to the viewpoint they are taking; often this 'unlocks' the frustration and makes it bearable, putting it in better context. Sometimes a way forward is possible. It is this sort of frustration that we think lies behind poltergeists – usually the more serious and deep-seated problems, of course. But even they are still just a matter of priority; making them the biggest and most insur-mountable difficulty to be overcome. In dealing with the fears and frustrations of changes in business environments (which is part of John Spencer's everyday work), there is considerable benefit in reassessing one's frustrations by accepting very tough challenges; the new problem becomes greater than the old. Similar techniques are used to deal with redundancy, and a range of other work-related issues.

This gave us the idea (with tongue somewhat in cheek, we admit) for the 'bungee jumping' theory of poltergeist control. By making the commitment, publicly to friends and relatives, that you are going to undertake something that is for you very scary – say, bungee jumping – you might spend so much time worrying about it that the problem causing your frustration is somewhat diminished. Perhaps, then, the poltergeist will diminish if the nature of your new fears is not of the type that can create poltergeists. Of course, it could also come back again after the bungee jump – this is not a foolproof plan, by any means – but 'repeater' poltergeists are extremely rare.

We can say little more about this, since it is an unexplored idea in this context; but we would be grateful to hear of the results of anyone attempting it!

Poltergeists can be good for you

Dr Owen and others have suggested that the poltergeist is not a curse but a cure. At one level, perhaps, it gets attention for those subconsciously seeking or needing attention. With regard to frustration, the cure might be to channel the force building up inside the person.

Psychologist Dr John Layard suggested: 'Poltergeists are not chance phenomena, but have a definite purpose, and this purpose, like all psychological phenomena ... is a curative one, having for its object the resolution of a psychological conflict.' He believes that all true poltergeist phenomena 'are also purposeful and probably occasioned by similar conditions of unresolved tension in the psyche of those involuntarily producing them'.

We might speculate that were it not outwardly discharged the build-up could be detrimental, causing cancer, heart or digestion problems perhaps. There is some evidence to link these illnesses, even stigmata and spontaneous human combustion, to self-generated 'mind over matter'; perhaps the poltergeist is an outward version of these inward energies, and it simply depends on the person's make-up whether or not they manifest something outward or inwardly. To this degree the poltergeist may be working for the focus, and if it creates certain tensions – fear, awe, and so on – perhaps it also relieves other tensions. In group situations, people who may have been angry at each other find themselves with something else to worry about; and there is nothing like a common enemy to unite antagonists. In individual situations we might consider the case of Julio in Miami: he did not like his new boss, and Roll even believed that he might sometimes have exhibited suicidal tendencies. Perhaps the poltergeist allowed him to work through that. In the Lynwood stone-throwing case the focus was Anthony Angelo; his mother stated, 'He resents washing cars and working his arms to the bone and gets no money.'

We observe that people living alone seem to be the most common victims of Spontaneous Human Combustion. Perhaps the energy that leaks from a person in frustration to cause a poltergeist, if not dispelled, can become a violent *inner* force. If there is no one to display frustration to, even in so seemingly absurd a manner as a poltergeist phenomenon, perhaps the force turns inward and is self-destructive. We admit this is intended only as food for thought; we have found no way to make a concrete connection between these two phenomena.

Chapter 15

Understanding Phoneygeists

In their book *The Story of the Poltergeist Down the Centuries*, Hereward Carrington and Nandor Fodor examine the possibility of likely fraud. In the conclusion to the chapter entitled 'The March of the Poltergeist', Carrington states: 'In the above collection of 375 typical poltergeist cases, we find on analysis that 26 of them were undoubtedly fraudulent, while 19 of them were doubtful. Assuming that *all* the doubtful cases were fraudulent, and adding this number to the "proved" cases (making 45 in all), we still find that the proportion of such cases is surprisingly small, since the number of "unexplained" cases equals 330. The proportion of "explained" cases is thus only about 7 per cent – i.e. less than one case in ten has ever been reduced to normal agency.

'This is certainly very different from the current assumption that practically *all* such cases have been proved to be fraudulent; and, as I have said, the evidence in many of them is exceedingly striking – as given in the original, detailed accounts.' We believe that the same assumptions and probably the same statistics are valid today. The poltergeist is too well witnessed, in too many situations, over too long a period of time, for it not to be a true phenomenon.

That said, some reports have probably been fraudulent,

including a few that have made the grade as 'classic' cases, and we would be naive not to accept this fact. In a subject as exploratory as the paranormal, researchers have to 'take their best shot', and inevitably they are going to make mistakes that will not, with certainty, be identified until the parameters are better understood.

To regard fraud as some sort of explanation would be reckless in this examination of a potentially rich understanding of the world and the human mind. So we must examine fraud, rather than be dismissive of it. Our starting point must be to examine why fraud should be committed.

There is a joke about two spirit guides discussing how to punish a sinning golfer. One suggests placing a curse on him so that he will never, ever have a hole-in-one. The other is more creative, and suggests giving the golfer eighteen holes-in-one – but ensuring that there is no one to witness it!

In short, there is a great pain in not being able to prove to others something you know to be true. For this reason we might expect there to be fraudulent happenings manufactured in circumstances of otherwise genuine poltergeist reports – fraud created only to show someone else what has genuinely happened, in a bid to get them to believe it. If a person has experienced a fascinating and astonishing event, it is a natural instinct to want not just to share that experience, but to be believed. Bear in mind that many poltergeists are short-lived, and by the time someone has been asked to investigate it is all over. And unfortunately the paranormal rarely produces proof that matches the demands of a materialistic society. So some people attempt to re-create the activity they have witnessed, and get caught. The result is often that the whole case is dismissed, understandably perhaps, but maybe also missing an important truth. Understanding fraud and getting behind it is important.

A similar aspect of fraud in poltergeist cases arises when children seek to copy the manifestations they have seen. Maurice Grosse was convinced that, while the Enfield case was a genuine case, he knew that some of the activities resulted from the children in the family faking certain events. This should not reduce the reliability of the case itself, or many other cases where this has arisen. The reason for such copying may not just be mischief – envy might come into it. A child who is the focus of the poltergeist is obviously going to get the attention not only of the family, but of researchers and perhaps reporters and the like. Other children in the household may want to capture some of that attention and duplicate events in order that people pay attention to them.

We should not ignore the possibility of someone deliberately constructing a case as an attempt to make money or gain fame. We are not aware of it ever happening, and think anyone trying it might be in for a disappointment anyway; having a poltergeist offers no gravitas. And the package that such a person would need to put together to attract large sums from the media would have to be so spectacular that fraud would eventually be either located, or confessed to someone 'breaking ranks'. Even the most spectacular cases have not made money for their claimants.

Perhaps more commonly there will be people who feel a need to gain some local notoriety, or who seek to control others (in this case the researchers). The fire service is forced to deal with a number of false call-outs during the year, which, it recognises, come from a desire to control others or seek attention. However, the nature of poltergeist research is such that this cannot be a major problem, irritating though any such call would be.

What can create a problem is when deliberate acts get confused with genuine poltergeistery.

Lynwood, California

In September 1960, at Lynwood in California, a stone-throwing poltergeist was bombarding a used car lot. Shortly after Anthony Angelo began working at the lot, some 200 missiles, stones, rocks, nuts and bolts were seen flying into the area, often with abnormal trajectory. The manager, Claude Mock, asked the police to help, and up to thirty officers were put on the case. The police saw Angelo hold a rock in his hand and smash it against the side of the car. However, even the police were quite satisfied that there was no question of Angelo being the person who was throwing the missiles into the car lot, as many stones still fell while he was in custody. When the police were put on the spot in court and asked whether they had seen any rocks thrown, they admitted that they had not. The defence offered that, 'due to the strange nature of the case, there must have been a supernatural cause, a cosmic disturbance, responsible'. Angelo was found not guilty.

The psychological motivation driving Angelo may well have been revealed in a telephone conversation between Angelo's mother and researcher Attila von Slazay, where the mother stated, 'He resents washing cars and working his arms to the bone and gets no money.' We might speculate that he was a genuinely angry young man and that this was the energy that caused the poltergeist, but the same anger also made him commit a consciously vandalistic act. It would have been easy to dismiss the case as fraudulent because of the conscious incident, were it not for the quality of the rest of the evidence in the report.

UNCONSCIOUS FRAUD

Automatism is a medical/psychiatric disorder where a person is unaware of, and has no conscious memory of, the actions that he or she does. However, some complex part of the brain must be at work, as these actions can be complicated, such as driving a car.

In the case in Newark, USA, there was a thirteen-year-old boy called Ernie who lived with his grandmother, Mrs Clark. (His father, a violent man, had died two years before and the grandmother was worried that he – in spirit – was causing the disturbances.) Many items fell or moved when Ernie was in the house, but not when he was absent. It was believed that some of the disturbances could not have been faked by the boy, but for the majority of events this seemed a logical supposition. Roll brought

Ernie and his grandmother to Duke Parapsychology Laboratory for testing, where he led them to a suite and excused himself. The suite was fitted with a two-way mirror, with Roll's colleague J. Gaither Pratt watching from the other side. Pratt watched Ernie – while his grandmother was out of the room – pick up and hide in his shirt two tapes from a table. Later these tapes were thrown at the lady. Mrs Clark reported the incident without appearing to be suspicious, and Ernie reported he did not know how the tapes had moved. The boy was then hypnotised and interviewed; he still denied any knowledge of how the tapes had moved. Soon after the hypnosis Ernie was subjected to a lie detector test where he again denied knowledge of the event. He passed the test.

The implication was that he really did not know what he was doing and had been witnessed doing. But some of the earliest events in Ernie's case do not suggest trickery and are thought to be genuinely paranormal. The boy's unconscious may then have driven him to produce some effects because he liked the result of what was happening. Perhaps he enjoyed the fear it gave his grandmother, or perhaps he was unhappy at home. Ernie was eventually moved to a foster home where he settled well.

HARDSHIP AND FRAUD

It has been suggested that poltergeists happen more in cases of hardship than in 'well-heeled' families. One survey suggested that 86% of poltergeists happened in council houses – given the numbers of cases in the workplace, that would leave very little room for privately owned houses! However, we are not convinced by the claim, and in our own examination have found little to substantiate it. We note that the 'survey' was conducted by the Chief Rehousing Officer of a metropolitan authority, and feel it is unlikely that the survey would have encompassed all private research, and perhaps not all church work. Several of the famous cases of years ago happened in large, obviously well-heeled households – though we acknowledge that they often centred around servants for whom the house was a workplace.

There have certainly been several cases arising in circumstances of what appears to be hardship. Enfield, Runcorn, Norwood, and Newark Street all involved families from the lower earning bands; but these were also families under circumstances of stress, partly brought on by their financial positions perhaps, and in some cases by more specific factors. We recently examined one case in North London in an obviously well-to-do family, above the average income for the country, who were seemingly happy. But they confirmed that the disturbances had first arisen during times of extreme stress.

One of the infamous claims made against poltergeist victims, based on the belief that poltergeists happen in council houses, is that people fake their claims in order to get rehoused. Obviously this must happen occasionally, but in our studies we have found this to be no explanation for poltergeists.

In *Deliverance* there is one report of a counsellor called in by a local authority, through the parish priest, to examine a poltergeist in a council house. Reports included noises, cold spots, blood-stains, voices, and movement of objects. But examination of the case produced inconsistent testimony, particularly when unexpected questions were posed, and an 'absence of real dread'. The examiners believed that the stories were based on the popular fiction of poltergeists. Looking into the background of the case showed that the family had been trying to get rehoused for some time. The council was advised on that basis, but the report notes that, when the family were later rehoused, there were no subsequent outbreaks in the original location. This may well be the correct explanation for this case, though we would point out that poltergeists are usually 'person-centred', so the absence of reports from the next tenants may mean very little. Furthermore the change of home for the 'victims' could well have caused a sufficient reduction of stress and frustration to stop the poltergeist if it were genuine.

Whatever the reality of that incident, we were also made aware of another case (through Canon Dominic Walker of the Anglican Church) where the tenants of a council house were complaining of poltergeist activity, and exhibiting real dread. They accepted a move from a semi-detached house to a smaller flat with fewer bedrooms in a high-rise block, which would not -- to most people at least – seem to be a positive move. But they were happy to take the move if it would get them out of a house they had come to fear. In this case there seems to be evidence of something very genuine behind their demand for relocation, rather than using it as part of a scam. In the event the poltergeist went with them, restarting two weeks after they moved into their new home. They were later moved back to their original house. The poltergeist activity stopped after the local vicar had spent some time helping a boy in the family. Clearly this poltergeist was not a device just to get rehoused. Indeed, Canon Walker witnessed some of the poltergeist events himself.

In the West Norwood case (which is referred to in Chapter Four), the investigator, Philip Paul, dealt with the possibility that the family were faking the claims in order to be rehoused. The case had acquired local notoriety, and the family concerned were becoming almost as agitated with the crowds outside their house as they were the poltergeist inside. Paul offered them a way out, saying, 'Of course, if your ghost isn't real, you could stop all this discomfort very quickly. Simply give an interview to the press and say you invented it as a joke. Then you will only have to suffer for a day or two longer, after which it will all die away and soon be forgotten.' Dennis, for the family, replied, 'These happenings and the crowds every night are turning us into nervous wrecks. But suppose we said we had invented the ghost and the noises get worse or something else happens so we have to call the police in again? Nobody will believe us at all next time.' The poltergeist was apparently real enough to not make the easy way out attractive! We admit that sometimes admitting a lie is a difficult thing to do, but it seems this family was honestly reporting. And we note the comments of Police Inspector Candler, who had dealt with the case: 'Nobody could persuade me that adult people would be as terrified as the Greenfields obviously were without having good reason for it. I am satisfied they were not playing tricks. Nobody could go to work all day and then sit up all night playing pranks over a long period like that. What it was I just don't know. It baffled me then and it baffles me still.'

Chapter 16

The Challenge of the Poltergeist

After many years of investigating poltergeists, we initiated ground-breaking informal meetings between various researchers and poltergeist foci. All parties have commented that these have proven most useful, educating and enlightening. One of the aspects that have come from these talks is the identification of a number of problems associated with investigation that serve as signposts for future investigators.

RESEARCH OR ERADICATION

We have mentioned that there is a basic dilemma between an affected person (or family) and the investigators. The former usually wants rid of their poltergeist, while the latter want to study it. In its extreme form, such study could result in 'holding on to' the poltergeist. In fact, the ability to hold or dispel a poltergeist is debatable – but the moral question is still an important one.

The approach must be tailored to the situation. Some people are desperately frightened or suffering from some other very negative viewpoint; in such cases every effort should be made to relieve that fear. Eradication of the poltergeist should then be the primary priority. Since there are no guaranteed methods and all situations are different, additional approaches may be necessary. Support for the family is needed, and it is important to recognise that the whole family should be involved, that it is not a one-person problem. The investigators may have to recognise that they are not the best people for these tasks, and that they may have to call in help from other agencies – the Church, psychotherapists, and so on.

Sometimes the family or person is as fascinated as the investigator. We know a case where a low level of activity continued over years; the family were more interested in knowing what was happening than in eradicating it. We see no reason why that should not be acceptable, and have found it very useful. This is unusual though. Ultimately a request for eradication usually comes about – most people tire of the disruption, even if they are not afraid of it – and then it is right and proper to respect that request and assist.

We should point out that the Church views poltergeists negatively and probably would not encourage this attitude, but theirs is only one viewpoint. However, if it is a viewpoint shared by the focus then it should be respected. There is the alternative argument that the poltergeist is doing something positive for the focus, and that it should be allowed to 'run its course' – or, at least, that the focus or family should dictate the agenda, as their intuition may be right and based on sound instinct.

WHO IS THE INVESTIGATOR?

When invited to investigate a poltergeist the researcher has to know what role the focus sees them having. They may think of him or her as a 'paranormal researcher', or a 'ghost researcher'. In that case they will expect them to discuss their poltergeist, or deal with it, in those terms. They may expect them to take the view that it is a 'spirit of the dead', or an entity – both very popular viewpoints within the general public. Should the researchers take the view that it is RSPK at work, they may find some surprise on the part of the family concerned. If they explain to them that the poltergeist possibly comes from within a member of their family – rather than that they are being 'attacked' by 'something' – they may not take kindly to the suggestion. In one case the affected family regarded such a viewpoint as 'blaming the victim'. The problem may be that researchers do not have the skills of psychotherapists. If those suggestions are to be raised where there may be resistance, perhaps such a person should be introduced (and even the introduction takes tact!). A psychotherapist who happens to be involved in paranormal research (we know of several) still has to understand what role is expected of him or her at the time.

IS OPEN-MINDEDNESS APPROPRIATE?

As researchers we believe it is right to be open-minded. The fact of poltergeists is proven, but their source is not. Frankly, no one knows for certain what causes one. To approach research on the basis of a biased viewpoint could improperly 'weight' certain evidence, leading to the rejection of good material, or overly supporting dubious events.

One investigator indicated that he thought a particular poltergeist was active because of the victim's psychological make-up, and that the case should therefore be dismissed. He was possibly of the view that 'real' poltergeists are, say, spirits of the dead, and that psychological problems are 'false poltergeists'. But such a viewpoint may be overlooking the very essence of the poltergeist. As we said earlier, no one really knows, and we believe that this investigator prematurely dropped the case.

However, assuming that at some point the poltergeist is to be eradicated, we believe that taking a strong line is the right approach. The Church, for example, has a strong line in believing that acceptance of Christ and pastoral care eradicates poltergeists. And it often does – though perhaps just for those who believe in Christ in the first place, we admit. Canon Carl Garner's very direct approach is very successful, and we have had several conversations with Canon Dominic Walker who takes slightly different views but has equal success. We know of several non-religious approaches that have the total commitment of their advocates, and they have worked in some cases. Perhaps one of these approaches is 'objectively' right; perhaps it is the placebo effect -- any approach will have the same effect if the person supports it. What seems not to work is open-mindedness. In one case a family was offered all the possibilities to get rid of a poltergeist, and it only confused them. Every type of eradication was tried, and nothing worked. We can never know for certain of course, but it is possible that, had one view been strongly backed, it might have had a more positive outcome.

Unfortunately this question has no certain answers; it is one of many things we simply do not understand about poltergeists.

THE MEDIA

The 'unexplained' is very fashionable at the time of writing, and there is considerable pressure from the media for researchers and witnesses to take part in programmes about the paranormal, including poltergeists.

Working with the media can have its advantages; the more that people are aware that their experiences are not unique, and that others have undergone them, the better most people seem to feel. We have seen that in our gatherings, which sometimes take on the air of 'support group' in a very informal way. Also, the media brings cases to researchers and research groups, without which research cannot be undertaken.

However, there are a number of cautions to consider. The media is primarily in the business of entertainment, not research. They like to wrap up a story for their viewers or readers, and to do this they sometimes reach simplistic or premature conclusions. Poltergeist cases do not stop or go away simply to make convenient copy. Similarly, the media likes drama. Sometimes less responsible programmes expect researchers or affected families to be 'economical with the truth', to make outrageous claims and generally 'beef up' their stories. Apart from any moral questions involved, this can lead to embarrassment and ridicule for the witnesses.

When an ongoing case reaches the public eye it can have extraordinary effects. The West Norwood case came to the attention of the media, and is one of few cases that seems to have attracted public attention similar to the historical reports such as Hydesville and Amherst. Investigator Philip Paul's description of the public's reaction is a cautionary tale: 'As the publicity spread, the Greenfields' lives became even more nightmarish. Their home was besieged by cranks and sensation seekers. Crowds gathered outside as dusk fell each evening. Arriving by every form of transport, the unwanted spectators spent the hours of darkness gazing up at the windows and hammering at the door with requests to be allowed in. Cars and motorcycles arrived and departed throughout the night, jostling for parking space among the groups of people in the tiny street. Some of the visitors even chipped at the brickwork in their determination to carry away some souvenir. Several times the police had to be summoned to prevent the sightseers gaining entry by force. Apart from the night-long noises of engines, the slamming of car doors and the racket of banter shouted among the onlookers, people also brought portable radios, ate and drank refreshments in their vehicles and threw their empty bottles and other litter into the road.'

In Sauchie, we discussed the media attention with one of Virginia's schoolmates. (She looked a lot like Virginia, and had agreed to 'decoy' for her at the request of the teacher.) She recalled: 'The school gates were closed of a morning from about ten to nine. They were padlocked and chained once everybody was in. That was to keep us in the school and keep the press out. The press climbed on the walls but staff kept them at a distance. One particular night there were a lot of press there when we were due to come out of school, so I was sent out as a decoy. I went out of the other gate so that the press followed me home, then they could get Virginia home without a lot of hassle. They followed me quite a long way up the road before it dawned on them that they were following the wrong person.' The press in that case were referred to by a church minister as having 'descended like one of the plagues of Egypt'.

DO WE KNOW WHAT FACTORS SHOULD BE INCLUDED/LOOKED FOR?

Research approaches throughout the history of the poltergeist have been wide and varied. Currently there is a good deal of research into the psychological possibilities. All this seems very valid, even making some headway, but the one thing the poltergeist lacks is what would make it acceptable to science – predictability and replication. The fact is that we cannot yet predict when or to whom one will happen, we cannot identify with certainty a type of person most prone to one, and we cannot produce the events in laboratory conditions. We may be overlooking the obvious – and the not so obvious – and this section is merely a note for researchers to consider as wide a study as possible. Who knows – one day we may realise that poltergeists happen where there is a predominance of the colour blue, where there are certain houseplants, certain pets, certain humidity, etc. Maybe it is RSPK, but generated by a cat, or a geranium, or a spider . . .

All silly ideas of course, but then . . .

If the conditions are indeed that complex, then it may be impossible to work them all out. Probably the conditions will become more obvious when someone spots them. But for the moment, keeping alert to possibilities is the only approach.

POLTERGEISTS DO NOT LIKE BEING INVESTIGATED

There is much evidence to suggest that poltergeists avoid being caught on film or other recording equipment, though they are happy to act in front of researchers and others. Something in the 'mechanism' seems resistant to 'final' proof. Such an admission gives glee to sceptics, who have their own viewpoint about these things; however, we believe there is sufficient evidence that it is a part of the way the phenomenon responds, and perhaps indicates that it is a 'human-controlled' experience. (We have, in books such as our *Encyclopedia of the World's Greatest Unsolved Mysteries*, set out examples of spontaneous equipment failure.)

Guy Lyon Playfair raises an interesting debate on the reluctance of poltergeists to be 'pinned down'. When respected researchers turned up to examine what he and Maurice Grosse had been witnessing, the poltergeist 'played it down'. Playfair speculates: 'It almost seemed that the poltergeist was out to incriminate [Janet], by producing third-rate phenomena in the presence of a first-rate observer.' He goes on to say: 'Perhaps . . . poltergeists are only allowed to give us so much evidence, preferably inconclusive . . . they prefer to keep us in doubt . . .'

A MORAL PROBLEM – DOES INVESTIGATION CREATE POLTERGEISTERY OR INTRODUCE IT?

We were part of a team that investigated a large public building in London. There had been many reports of haunting phenomena, and indeed during the setting up of equipment in the building one of the investigators was shocked to see an apparition. He was setting up computer equipment attached to the video monitors when he saw a woman in front of him; thinking she was a part of the team he introduced himself – and she disappeared. He was shaken and disturbed throughout the rest of the night, and unfortunately vowed never to join a ghostwatching team again. During the vigils held, there were several outbreaks of poltergeist activity. Several stones fell around investigators (on an earlier vigil a book had similarly arrived). We also found writing on a mirror in the toilets. The point is that none of these phenomena had occurred before the researchers started the investigation.

It may be that it was always going to happen, and our being there to see it was just lucky – but it may also be that it happened *because* we were there. This could be the case for a number of reasons. First, some inhabiting spirit may have decided a ghostwatch team was a good audience to 'play' for and perked up its activities. If this is so then we have to ask ourselves whether it is fair that we might encourage such activity. The second possibility is that poltergeists are the result of PK generated from the mind. And it may be that it was being generated from one of the ghostwatch team members. We may have had a potential 'focus' with us, perhaps one that needed a haunted location to 'trigger' him or her, if that is part of the mechanism. There is evidence that this happened in one of our teams. In three locations we found activity was happening when we were on site, and in every case it centred around one investigator. We believe that this person was the 'focus' of the activity. The phenomena, of course, can be real – i.e. paranormal – but *introduced* by us.

Veteran American researcher John Keel noted that, during his various paranormal investigations: 'Poltergeist manifestations seemed to break out wherever I went. It was difficult to judge whether I was unwittingly creating these situations, or whether they were entirely independent of my mind.' And we have suggested in earlier chapters that cases are sometimes moulded by the experiences and beliefs of the researchers. Clearly this is a question that must be approached by researchers and research groups around the world, if morally correct approaches to this subject are to be made.

Conclusion

This book should have demonstrated to you the reality of the poltergeist – a reality that has confronted and puzzled many people, continues to do so to the present day, and will no doubt continue to do so in the future.

We know a lot about the poltergeist. But what we do not know and have yet to discover is the greater task ahead. Our knowledge is so incomplete that, frankly, we do not even know if the term 'poltergeist' should be a noun or a verb. Is it a thing, or a collection of actions and happenings? Is it one thing or a syndrome? Can we truthfully say of any report that one is a poltergeist and another is not? Or should we say of all reports, this one is an 80% poltergeist, but this one is only 20%?

We have yet to discover how it does the things it is so clearly doing. What mechanisms and powers enable it to operate? In examining these we may discover as yet unclassified – even unsuspected – natural laws that will extend our understanding of science, and of the human mind.

While psychologists and scientists may find it easy to dismiss ghosts and other encounters as delusion or illusions (rightly or wrongly), the poltergeist offers quite a different problem, as the happenings are obvious, lasting, and often visible to several witnesses in extremely good conditions of observation. We must give credence either to the ability of psychokinesis as a much stronger force than that ever tested in the laboratory, or to something much stranger – the existence of surviving human spirits, devils or other entities (of one kind or another), capable of interaction with the physical world.

But if a poltergeist is a reflection of powers within the human mind, then perhaps this power is within us all. This leads to an interesting, even exciting, speculation. It is widely assumed that the poltergeist is a 'bad' thing; certainly those affected by them have little affection for them! But perhaps the energy that creates the poltergeist is neutral – simply a force of nature inherent in the mind. And just as wind and wave power can be harnessed, so might the energy of the poltergeist. And if so, then it might be harnessed for good; for human development and evolution. Just because the wind blows a wall down and kills a person, or a person drowns in the sea, we do not assume intent. The poltergeist may be an energy that presently only surfaces at times of frustration and repressed anger; hence it manifests in 'bad' ways. But if the energy could be understood, controlled, released at will, then it could be a quantum leap for humanity. If the range of manifestations it usually produces are the result of repression, anger and frustration, consider the extraordinary range it might produce as a result of positive, caring emotions.

And then we might see the Positive Poltergeist, less of a problem and more of an opportunity – a solution waiting for someone to come up with the right question.

Bibliography and Recommended Reading

Allen, Thomas, *Possessed*, Doubleday, 1993.

Bayless, Raymond, *The Enigma of the Poltergeist*, Parker Publishing, 1967.

Burks, Eddie & Cribbs, Gillian, *Ghosthunter*, Headline, 1995.

Carrington, Hereward & Fodor, Nandor, *The Story of the Poltergeist down the Centuries*, Rider & Co, 1953.

Cassirer, Manfred, *The Persecution of Mr Tony Elms*, Privately published, 1993.

Editors of Time-Life, *Hauntings*, Time-Life, 1989.

Fairley, John & Welfare, Simon, *Arthur C. Clarke's World of Strange Powers*, Collins, 1989.

Fodor, Nandor, *On the Trail of the Poltergeist*, Arco, 1958.

Gauld, Alan & Cornell, A. D., *Poltergeists*, Routledge & Kegan Paul, 1979.

Gregory, Richard L. (ed.), *The Oxford Companion to the Mind*, Oxford University Press, 1987.

Guiley, Rosemary Ellen, *The Guinness Encyclopedia of Ghosts and Spirits*, Guinness, 1992.

Hole, Christina, *Haunted England*, Fitzhouse, 1990 (orig. 1940).

Holzer, Hans, *True Ghost Stories*, Bristol Park Books, 1992.

Manning, Matthew, *The Link*, Colin Smythe, 1974.

McConnell, Brian, *The Possessed*, Headline, 1995.

Owen, A. R. G., *Can We Explain the Poltergeist?*, Helix, 1964.

Pearsall, Ronald, *The Table-Rappers*, Michael Joseph, 1972.

Perry, Michael (ed.), *Deliverance*, SPCK, 1987.

Playfair, Guy Lyon, *If This Be Magic*, Jonathan Cape, 1985.

Playfair, Guy Lyon, *The Indefinite Boundary*, Souvenir Press, 1976.

Playfair, Guy Lyon, *This House is Haunted*, Souvenir Press, 1980.

Playfair, Guy Lyon, *The Flying Cow*, Souvenir Press, 1975.

Price, Harry & Lambert R. S., *The Haunting of Cashen's Gap*, Methuen & Co, 1936.

Price, Harry, *Poltergeist*, Bracken Books, 1993 (orig. 1945).

Richards, John Thomas, *SORRAT: A History of the Neihardt Psychokinesis Experiments 1961–1981*, Scarecrow, 1982.

Rogo, D. Scott, *The Poltergeist Experience*, Aquarian Press, 1990.

Roll, William G., *The Poltergeist*, Scarecrow Press, 1976.

Sitwell, Sacheverell, *Poltergeists*, Faber and Faber, 1940.

Smith, Suzy, *Prominent American Ghosts*, World Publishing, 1967.

Spencer, John & Anne, *Spirit Within Her*, Boxtree, 1994.

Spencer, John & Anne, *The Encyclopedia of Ghosts and Spirits*, Headline, 1992.

Spencer, John & Anne, *The Encyclopedia of the World's Greatest Unsolved Mysteries*, Headline, 1995.

Spencer, John & Wells, Tony, *Ghostwatching*, Virgin, 1994.

Summers, Montague, *The History of Witchcraft*, Senate, 1994.

Thurston S J, Herbert (Crehan S J, J H. [ed.]), *Ghosts and Poltergeists*, Burns Oates, 1953.

Warren, Melanie & Wells, Tony, *Ghosts of the North*, Broadcast Books, 1995.

White, Terry, *The Sceptical Occultist*, Century, 1994.

Wilson, Colin, *Afterlife*, Harrap, 1985.

Wilson, Colin, *Poltergeist*, Putnam, 1981.

Journal of the Society for Psychical Research; and specifically Vol. 57, No. 823; Vol. 58, Nos. 827, 828, 829.

Anomaly (the journal of ASSAP); and specifically Issue 8, May 1991; Issue 10, May 1992.

Contacts and Organisations

The Authors can be contacted at:
The Leys, 2c Leyton Road, Harpenden, Herts, AL5 2TL
Telephone 01582 763218
Fax 01582 461979
e-mail jandaspencer @ dial.pipex.com

The Society for Psychical Research (SPR)
49 Marloes Road, Kensington, London, W8 6LA
Telephone/Fax 0171 937 8984
Contact: Eleanor O'Keefe (Secretary)

Association for the Scientific Study of Anomalous Phenomena
   (ASSAP)
Saint Aldhelm, 20 Paul Street, Frome, Somerset, BA11 1DX
Contact: Hugh Pincott
e-mail assap @ dial.pipex.com

Index of Names

301

Index of Cases

Major cases are indicated in **boldface**.

INDEX OF CASES

A selection of non-fiction from Headline

THE NEXT 500 YEARS	Adrian Berry	£7.99 ☐
FIGHT FOR THE TIGER	Michael Day	£7.99 ☐
LEFT FOOT FORWARD	Garry Nelson	£5.99 ☐
THE NATWEST PLAYFAIR CRICKET ANNUAL	Bill Frindall	£4.99 ☐
THE JACK THE RIPPER A–Z	Paul Begg, Martin Fido & Keith Skinner	£8.99 ☐
VEGETARIAN GRUB ON A GRANT	Cas Clarke	£5.99 ☐
PURE FRED	Rupert Fawcett	£6.99 ☐
THE SUPERNATURAL A–Z	James Randi	£6.99 ☐
ERIC CANTONA: MY STORY	Eric Cantona	£6.99 ☐
THE TRUTH IN THE LIGHT	Peter and Elizabeth Fenwick	£6.99 ☐
GOODBYE BAFANA	James Gregory	£6.99 ☐
MY OLD MAN AND THE SEA	Daniel Hayes and David Hayes	£5.99 ☐

All Headline books are available at your local bookshop or newsagent, or can be ordered direct from the publisher. Just tick the titles you want and fill in the form below. Prices and availability subject to change without notice.

Headline Book Publishing, Cash Sales Department, Bookpoint, 39 Milton Park, Abingdon, OXON, OX14 4TD, UK. If you have a credit card you may order by telephone – 01235 400400.

Please enclose a cheque or postal order made payable to Bookpoint Ltd to the value of the cover price and allow the following for postage and packing:

UK & BFPO: £1.00 for the first book, 50p for the second book and 30p for each additional book ordered up to a maximum charge of £3.00.
OVERSEAS & EIRE: £2.00 for the first book, £1.00 for the second book and 50p for each additional book.

Name ....

Address ....

....

....

If you would prefer to pay by credit card, please complete:
Please debit my Visa/Access/Diner's Card/American Express (delete as applicable) card no:

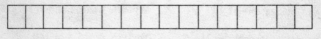

Signature .... Expiry Date ....